David Blundy was the Middle East correspondent for the *Sunday Times* from 1981 to 1986. He is now the Washington correspondent for the *Sunday Telegraph*. He made three trips to Libya while writing this book, and was in Tripoli during the American raid in April 1986. He is also the co-author of *With Geldof in Africa* (1985).

As a freelance journalist, Andrew Lycett is a regular contributor to *The Times*, the *Sunday Times* and many other publications. Over the past decade he has specialised largely in Africa and the Middle East.

Qaddafi
and the Libyan Revolution

New Revised Edition

David Blundy and Andrew Lycett

CORGI BOOKS

QADDAFI AND THE LIBYAN REVOLUTION

A CORGI BOOK 0 552 99307 7

Originally published in Great Britain by George Weidenfeld &
Nicolson Ltd.

PRINTING HISTORY
Weidenfeld & Nicolson edition published 1987
Corgi revised edition published 1988

This book is set in 10/11 pt Plantin
by Colset Private Limited, Singapore.

Corgi Books are published by Transworld Publishers Ltd.,
61–63 Uxbridge Road, Ealing, London W5 5SA, in Australia
by Transworld Publishers (Australia) Pty. Ltd., 15–23 Helles
Avenue, Moorebank, NSW 2170, and in New Zealand by
Transworld Publishers (N.Z.) Ltd., Cnr. Moselle and
Waipareira Avenues, Henderson, Auckland.

Made and printed in Great Britain by
The Guernsey Press Co. Ltd., Guernsey, Channel Islands.

Contents

Illustrations

Wearing traditional Arab robes in London, 1966

Qaddafi makes his first public appearance after the coup, September 1969

With Presidents Sadat and Assad in Damascus, August 1971 (*Remoivile/Sygma*)

Praying in the Sirtic desert, 1973 (*G. Chauvel/Sygma*)

Qaddafi's parents and members of his family in their tent in the Sirtic desert, 1976 (*London Express News Service*)

With his mother (*Kirtlev/Sygma*)

Explaining a fine political point to members of a people's congress in Sebha (*Pierre Boulat/Sipa Press*)

Qaddafi, the statesman – Tunisia, 1983 (*Hammi/M'Sadek/Sipa Press*)

The photograph that tricked Qaddafi into believing that the assassination attempt on former Prime Minister Abdul Hamid Bakoush had succeeded, November 1984 (*Associated Press*)

Qaddafi's right-hand man, Major Abdul Salam Jalloud – Tripoli, 1986 (*Associated Press*)

At prayer in his private plane (*Kirtlev/Sygma*)

During talks with Mikhail Gorbachov, October 1985 (*Popperfoto*)

The flamboyant dresser: in Italianate suit (*UPI/Bettmann Newsphotos*) . . . and flowing cloak (*Morvan/Sipa Press*)

Qaddafi's wife Safiya declaiming against US aggression following the raid on Tripoli, April 1986 (*Keystone Press*)

Making his international political comeback after the US raid at the meeting of the Nonaligned Movement in Harare, September 1986 (*Popperfoto; Patrick Durand/Sygma*)

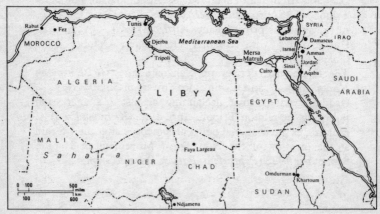

Acknowledgements

We would like to thank a number of people who, in various ways, have helped us with this book: Linda Osband, our editor at Weidenfeld, and her assistant, Maria Leach; Cathi Stallings, our research assistant in Washington; Marie Colvin, former UPI bureau chief in Paris and now *Sunday Times* Middle East correspondent; Mark Hosenball, James Adams, Peter Wilsher and Stephen Milligan from the *Sunday Times*; Alistair Brett, senior legal assistant at Times Newspapers; Lewis Chester, author and former *Sunday Times* feature writer; Patrick Seale of the *Observer*; Judith Miller and Edward Schumacher of the *New York Times*; David McKittrick of the *Independent*; Hirsh Goodman and Roy Isaacowitz of the *Jerusalem Post*; Hugh Dunnachie, British consul in Tripoli; Lisa Anderson, of Harvard University; Charles Glass of ABC; Mohammed Heikal, Egyptian author and journalist; Bruno Kreisky, former Austrian Chancellor; US ambassadors Herman Eilts and David Newsom; Colonel Ted Lough, who trained Qaddafi as a young cadet, and members of the British military mission in Libya; senior British diplomats who served in Libya; Bona Malwal, Sudanese journalist and academic; Henry Schuler of the Centre for Strategic and International Studies at Georgetown University; Sir Peter Wakefield, Lillian Harris and Terence Mirabelli.

In addition there are many others in Libya, the Middle East, North Africa, Europe, Britain and the United States, who helped us with their time and insights but who cannot be named.

The literature on Libya is not particularly huge. We found

the following books, which might serve as a further reading list on the Qaddafi years, useful:

Patrick Seale and Maureen McConville, *The Hilton Assignment* (Temple Smith, London, 1973)

Ruth First, *Libya: The Elusive Revolution* (Penguin, London, 1974)

Mirella Bianco, *Gadafi: Voice from the Desert* (Longman, London, 1975)

Mohammed Heikal, *The Road to Ramadan* (Collins, London, 1975)

Omar el Fathaly and Monte Palmer, *Political Development and Social Change in Libya* (Toronto and Lexington, Lexington Books, D.C. Heath and Co., 1980)

Frank Waddams, *The Libyan Oil Industry* (Croom Helm, London, 1980)

John Wright, *Libya: A Modern History* (Croom Helm, London, 1981)

John Cooley, *Libyan Sandstorm: The Complete Account of Qaddafi's Revolution* (Sidgwick and Jackson, London, 1982)

Marius K. Deeb and Mary Jane Deeb, *Libya since the Revolution* (Praeger, New York, 1982)

Joseph Goulden, *The Death Merchant* (Simon and Schuster, New York, 1984)

A particular note of thanks to Professor John Davis of the University of Kent, who lent us the manuscript of his book *Libyan Politics: Tribe and Revolution* (published by I.B. Tauris in Britain in 1987) and who gave us permission to cite from it freely. Our debt to him is clear.

David Blundy and Andrew Lycett
November 1986

1 The American Raid

Deep below the ground in a bunker designed by West German engineers to withstand anything short of a nuclear attack, on Monday, 14 April 1986, Colonel Qaddafi dined late and alone.

Qaddafi's bunker, which serves as his home and office, is in the Aziziya barracks two miles from the centre of Tripoli. They are shaped like a huge tear-drop about six miles long. From the outside it is a forbidding place, surrounded by a high wall fitted with sensors, alarms and remote-control infra-red cameras which constantly scan the access roads. The pictures are fed back to the bank of television screens in the main security room. Most of the external defence is less discreet. A battery of French-made Crotale anti-aircraft missiles are perched outside the barracks on a raised piece of land to defend against aerial attack. There is a chicane of concrete blocks at the main entrance to deter suicide bombers. A large Russian tank squats behind a concrete revetment to ward off attack from the ground. Tanks and armoured personnel carriers are parked inside the gate. Soldiers armed with automatic rifles, machine-guns and anti-tank weapons man the entrances and the walls. The compound is dominated by the 100-foot metal skeleton of a communications mast which keeps Qaddafi in touch with his senior army officers in Sirte, Benghazi and the main military control centre at the oasis town of Jufrah, 125 miles due south of Sirte in the middle of the desert.

Inside it is quite a pleasant place to live, with the security of a prison but the facilities of a country club. There are two tennis-courts, a football-pitch, gardens and lawns. Qaddafi's wife and family occupy a large, two-storey building, their opulent living-room decorated with glass screens and paintings and furnished with ranks of sofas. Qaddafi is not formally estranged from his wife, but he lives separately. He has a Bedouin tent where he entertains his official guests. It is pitched near the tennis-courts in the shade of a line of trees, about 200 yards from the family house. It is drab, olive green on the outside but brightly coloured like a patchwork quilt on the inside.

11

Qaddafi's thoughts, culled from his Green Book, are embroidered into the fabric. There are simple mats on the floor, cushions for his guests, a coffee table and a single camp-bed tucked away at the back. Guests are sometimes distracted by the bellowing and belching of two camels tethered outside to add the authentic sound and smell of the Sirtic desert. It is an odd combination of Bedouin tradition and high tech. A power cable snakes under a flap in the tent and ends in a jumble of sockets for the colour television, video recorder and music system. There are bookshelves with copies of his own Green Book and tomes on Arab history, a green telephone, tapes of Egyptian popular music and a tiny, gold globe of the world, the kind a tourist shop might sell, marking the important cities in coloured jewels: Mecca, London, Washington, Paris.

At midnight Qaddafi entertained in his tent George Howe, the leader of the Lebanese Communist Party. He wanted to discuss the intricacies of Lebanon, where Libyan subventions to political parties and militias had given him a vested interest. Just before 1 a.m. he made the short walk to his v-shaped administration building, which has outside it an arch topped by a huge sculpture of an eagle, past the guards who seem to spend their time watching Libyan educational television and down two flights of stairs to his bunker.

This is a large suite with a lecture room and an office decorated in the odd, impersonal style of a dentist's waiting-room with a painting of a palm tree against a setting sun and a bowl of artificial flowers crudely made of fabric. A bathroom leads off the bedroom, divided from the office by a curtain where Qaddafi's Pierre Cardin pyjamas hang from a hook. The rooms are permeated by the sweet smell of Givenchy, his favourite gentleman's cologne.

If Qaddafi was worried that evening he did not show it. One of his East European aides said that he had been, over the past few days, in better spirits than usual. He had taken to walking, each morning, across the compound to his family house to have breakfast with his wife and to play with his children. He had been to his gymnasium regularly each day to work out and he had kicked a football around on the pitch.

But his back ached, and he had been treated daily by his Yugoslav masseuse. He complained of a discomfort in his throat which had made his voice husky, sometimes barely above a whisper. His doctors had examined him and found nothing physically wrong. They were treating it as a psychosomatic problem, but not a serious one. Qaddafi had taken recently to a strange form of relaxation and meditation: he would lie flat on the floor of his office and cover his body and face with a sheet. He would stay there for as long as two hours and his bodyguards were ordered to allow no one to disturb him.

As Qaddafi tried to relax early on that Tuesday morning, Operation Eldorado Canyon, as the United States Pentagon code-named it, had already been launched from airfields in the English countryside. Twenty-four F1-11 fighter bombers from the US 48th Tactical Fighter Wing at Lakenheath in England, five EF-111 flying radar stations, twenty-eight flying petrol stations and a high-flying SR-71 Blackbird reconnaissance aircraft had taken off at 6.30 p.m. on Monday evening, 5.30 Libyan time. They flew towards Libya, skirting France and Spain, whose governments had not given the Americans permission to fly over their territory, making two huge loops as the fighters refuelled. They were, at that moment, streaking at supersonic speed across the Mediterranean.

A hundred miles or so off the Libyan coast, east of Tripoli, due north of the second biggest city, Benghazi, Vice-Admiral Frank Kelso, commander of the US Sixth Fleet, stood on the bridge of the USS *Coronado*. He had under his control two aircraft carriers, the *Coral Sea* and the *America*, with their complement of cruisers and destroyers, nuclear-powered hunter-killer submarines, a helicopter carrier, approximately 1,800 marines in the amphibious Task Force 62 and eleven squadrons of attack aircraft, guided and protected by four Hawkeye radar planes.

The US planes faced, in theory, a formidable Libyan defence. For a small Third World nation Libya is remarkably, almost ridiculously, well armed. It has more tanks per head of population than any other country. It has 535 combat aircraft, including the French-built Mirage and Russian Mig 21, 23 and 25; three brigades of surface-to-air missiles; thirty French Crotale systems, seventy-two Russian Sam 2 and 3 batteries, and additional long-range Sam 5 missiles bought after Qaddafi's talks in Moscow six months before, along with 1,500 Soviet advisers to run, fire and maintain them. According to a British radar engineer who worked on the Libyan system, parts of these air defences are more sophisticated than Britain's. He said that much of the equipment is Western European and American, despite the United States ban on exporting such military hardware to Libya. Crates of US equipment shipped through foreign subsidiaries of US companies used to arrive in Libya regularly and there were large imports just before the raid. The words 'Made in the USA' were stripped off the crates and the computers.

Libya's military power is more daunting on paper than in reality. Many of the planes are still in the crates they arrived in. Libyan pilots have been trained by Pakistan, India, the Soviet Union and members of the Eastern bloc. Until the middle of 1986 Libyans still regularly went to British schools for training as civilian pilots. They remain poor combat pilots and find it difficult to fly at night, although many of their fighters are equipped with night-flying computers. The Libyans were so unsure of their air power that, at the first sign that the US fleet was returning into the Mediterranean, most of the operational aircraft were pulled back from the front line into the sanctuary of desert airfields.

Qaddafi's army is ill trained and unreliable. Uncertain of its loyalty, after a number army-inspired coup attempts, he fed into its ranks members of the revolutionary committees, whose fanatical loyalty was not matched by their military ability. This caused bad feeling with the regular army officers, which in turn created the very coup attempts and unrest it was meant to suppress. The navy was unhappy at the prospect of being put in the front line against the US fleet without the benefit of air support.

The weakest link in the air defence system proved to be the Russian Sam 5. These systems are old-fashioned. The guidance systems in the missiles and the radar that homes in on the target worked sporadically, if at all. The Russians technicians had been unable or unwilling to fix them. The Libyans were forced to call on the services of British and European technicians to service the Russian equipment. Just before the raid, a Sam 5 battery had gone down. Despite urgent pleas to the Russians, nothing had been done.

When Qaddafi spoke boldly about challenging the might of the United States alone, he did not perhaps realize quite how alone he was. His major ally and arms supplier is the Soviet Union, which pledged support for Libya in public, but in private, through its ambassador to Tripoli, Oleg Peresidkin, urged restraint. Russia would not be dragged into a confrontation with the United States. Its fleet had been sent to a far corner of the Mediterranean and would not even provide Libya with a basic monitoring service, giving a warning of the US attack. Soviet nuclear submarines were lurking far away from the Gulf of Sirte. Russian technicians in the Sam 5 missile batteries were ordered to stay away from their stations, taking cover deep underground. Qaddafi's Arab allies were to send fulsome telegrams of support and condolence, but not a single plane, missile or soldier to help their brother in Libya.

The immediate cause of the arrival of the US armada off the shores of Libya was, by the standards of modern terrorism, a small incident ten days before and 2,000 miles away in a discotheque in West Berlin.

A bomb had exploded, killing two people, one of them an American serviceman, and injuring 230 others, including twenty-three Americans. The US State Department said it had 'irrefutable evidence' that Libyans working for the people's bureau (the Libyan term for an embassy) in East Berlin had planned the attack. This evidence was based on intercepted telephone calls from Tripoli to the people's bureau in East Berlin. According to a US intelligence analyst, these messages were intercepted by the British, decoded and sent to the Americans.

The first was on 25 March from the Bureau of External Security in Tripoli to the German bureau. United States officials maintain that it provided a 'clear indication' of a terrorist operation to be carried out in West Berlin and British intelligence experts, who saw the message first, agree with them. One phrase read, 'carry out the plan'. The United States was so convinced by the evidence that it decided to inform the Russians. The Soviet counsellor in Washington, Oleg M. Sokolov, was summoned to the State Department and told that the Libyans from East Berlin, the Russian sector, would be mounting an attack on the Western sector. Could he do something about it? The Russians, according to the United States, did not act.

The second key intercept was on 4 April when the people's bureau in East Berlin alerted Tripoli that the attack would be carried out the following morning. This message said: 'It will happen soon, the bomb will blow, American soldiers must be hit.' Hours later, after the attack, the bureau reported that the plan had been carried out. The message said: 'Action carried out, no trail left.' On 6 April there was a final message congratulating the bureau on its success and exhorting it to carry out further 'heroic acts'.

The Berlin bombing was the incident that the United States administration had been waiting for. An American had been killed and there was a Libyan fingerprint on the bomb. The administration had been out to get Qaddafi, and had publicly stated it, since 1981. The State Department had built up a dossier of evidence against him which we will examine in detail later in this book. There had been other recent incidents: two attacks in December 1985 at Rome and Vienna airports killing twenty civilians, five of them American including an eleven-year-old girl. The Americans blamed the Libyans for providing money, training and passports for the two attacks. According to investigators in Rome and Vienna, the terrorists were members of the Abu Nidal group, rebel Palestinians supported by Libya, and its main Arab ally, Syria. The Rome investigators interrogated a surviving terrorist and discovered that he had been trained in a Syrian-controlled area of the Bekaa Valley by a Syrian intelligence officer. There is evidence, however, that this may have been an attack spawned by the recent co-operation of the Libyan and Syrian governments.

Anyway, it did not really matter. Washington made the decision to go after Qaddafi against the advice of the CIA. According to an analyst who prepared 'dozens of reports' on Libyan terrorism and saw hundreds of classified documents on the subject, the agency argued that Libya was not the prime source of terror. It also argued that a military attack by the United States would be counter-productive. 'What happened on the night of the raid flew in the face of the analysis and intelligence that we had gathered', said the analyst. The CIA argued that force would not topple Qaddafi and would run the risk of making him a hero in the Arab world. It might also benefit Qaddafi internally. The main threat came from discontented officers in his army, and the use of force by the United States might rally these officers behind him. The CIA also argued against the imposition of economic sanctions against Libya. 'Reagan was consistently told that economic sanctions would not work,' said the analyst. 'First, because nobody else, the Europeans in particular, would join us. Second, because even if they did, Qaddafi would not be persuaded to change his policy by a lack of funds. This ignored the kind of society that he ruled.'

The CIA also argued that military action might lead to further terrorism, if not by Qaddafi, then by the radical Arab groups. In a secret report to the White House, the CIA pointed out that 'Qaddafi has consistently avoided targeting the United States because he is afraid of retaliation. This pushes him towards more open targeting.'

However, Admiral Bobby Ray Inman, the former head of the top-secret National Security Agency and the deputy directly of the CIA from 1981 to 1982, says that during his tenure at the CIA there was increasing evidence that Libya intended to hit US targets. The alleged Libyan plot to send a hit team to assassinate President Reagan, which was much decried in the United States, was based, Inman says, on 'hard and convincing evidence. Qaddafi told the Ethiopian President, Haile Mariam Mengistu, that he planned to kill Reagan. We had information about the planning of the attempt. The Libyans intended to hit a presidential convoy in the United States.' Inman reveals that it was a detailed plan similar to an earlier Libyan plot to kill US ambassador, Herman Eilts, which is described in this book. He says that the plot was hatched and then, for reasons which he does not know, aborted.

The White House chose to ignore its official intelligence experts.

The reasons had more perhaps to do with internal American policy than the threat from Libya. The administration had been made to look impotent by terrorism since the bombing of the marine base and embassy in Beirut in 1983. It needed a successful show of force. Although Syria appeared from intelligence reports to be a more vigorous supporter of international terrorism than Libya, an attack on Syria carried dangers of a confrontation with the Soviet Union, and the chances of a strike without major casualties were slim. Libya was a soft target and the administration rightly predicted that no one, not even the Arab countries, would really care about Qaddafi's fate.

The marines who stood on the deck of the USS *Coronado* may not have been aware that the history of United States/Libyan relations had come full circle. For the popular US marines' ballad, 'From the halls of Montezuma to the shores of Tripoli', refers to the shore towards which they were then steaming and to the first naval engagement by the fledgling independent republic of America more than 180 years before. If Admiral Kelso had studied this history, he would have seen that the parallels were uncanny. For that earlier adventure not only saw a US naval task force going to war against a Libyan government, but it too was a response to state-supported terrorism and was carried out despite the perfidy of the European governments. In 1801 pirates, manning corsairs under the direction of the ruler of Tripoli, the Bashaw, were harassing US merchant ships in the Mediterranean. The American consul's opinion of the Bashaw was hardly less scathing than the present US government's view of the modern ruler of Libya: 'There is no stability in our tyrant,' the consul wrote. 'There is no confidence to be placed in him; he would sacrifice his mother if she interfered with his interest.'

The Americans appealed for help from the British and French. They declined, for they paid huge bribes to the Bashaw not to molest their own shipping and were glad to see the pirates prey on US shipping and mop up the competition. As Lord Sheffield put it shamelessly in a House of Commons debate: 'The Americans cannot pretend a navy and therefore the great nations should suffer the Barbary pirates as a check on the activities of the smaller Italian states and America.' In 1803 the United States sent the contemporary equivalent of the Sixth Fleet to blockade Tripoli harbour, but the warship *Philadelphia* ran aground on an uncharted reef and, under attack from the Bashaw's cannon, the 308 officers and crew surrendered. This US defeat is still celebrated by the Libyans, who have issued a postage stamp showing the shipwrecked *Philadelphia*. The Bashaw held the Americans hostage for nineteen months and three days until the

US consul from Tunis, Captain William Eaton, led a small force of US marines against Tripoli. The Bashaw capitulated and the Americans were released.

The Americans began to apply their latest round of military pressure on Libya in March 1986. Kelso brought the Sixth Fleet for manoeuvres in the Gulf of Sirte and ordered it to cross what Qaddafi called 'the line of death', an imaginary line along the 32.3 parallel stretching between Benghazi and Misurata. It was drawn by Qaddafi in 1973 when he claimed the Gulf of Sirte as his territorial waters, ignoring the internationally observed twelve-mile limit. American jets had flown regularly into the airspace above the Gulf over the years and had enjoyed a brief skirmish in August 1981 when Libyan SU22 fighters took on two US F14 Tomcats and were blasted out of the skies. On Monday 24 March American warships passed into the Gulf for the first time.

At 1.52 that Monday afternoon Libyan radar saw the blips of two F14 Tomcats about seventy miles off the Libyan coast, and the order was given for two SA5 Gammon missiles to be fired from a battery near the town of Sirte. It was relatively easy for the *Yorktown*, a ship in the Sixth Fleet with advanced electronic warfare equipment, to jam the missiles' guidance systems and turn them harmlessly off course.

This gave the Americans the excuse they needed, and there is little doubt that over the previous few days Kelso had deliberately attempted to rouse Qaddafi into a military response. Not only had the fleet and planes flown within his 'line of death' but, according to a British radar engineer who worked for the Libyans, the Tomcats had also crossed the twelve-mile limit and flown missions over Libyan land, breaking international law. 'I watched the planes fly approximately eight miles into Libyan air space,' he said. 'I don't think the Libyans had any choice but to hit back.' The engineer said that the US warplanes made their approach using a normal civil airline traffic route and following in the wake of a Libyan aeroplane so that they would be masked by its radar blips.

After Libya's futile attempt to shoot down the US fighters, Kelso gave the order for an air and missile attack on Libyan missile and radar bases in Sirte and on Libyan missile boats. The US military strikes were a muted success. The Pentagon claimed that EA6B Grumman prowler aircraft, which are packed with electronic equipment, jammed the Libyan radar scopes and scrambled their communications. The engineer says that the US effort failed because the Libyan radar transmissions jumped randomly from one frequency to another. There was a brief delay before the American computers in the Grummans could catch up. He watched the screens in a bunker in Tripoli for two days and says that at no point was the radar jammed.

When Kelso ordered the fleet to steam away from the Libyan shore, Libyan intelligence had no doubt that it would return. It claimed, at the time, to have intercepted radio traffic from the Sixth Fleet which indicated that it would return in the second week of April. It did, but this time for more than an exercise.

As Qaddafi walked at 1.30 a.m. on 15 April from his living quarters along an underground passage to his military command centre he did not need intelligence from the Soviet fleet to warn him of the attack. It was perhaps the least secret air strike in history. It has been heralded by the world's press for the past three days. At 7 p.m. on Monday evening an American television correspondent was told by his Washington office that 'something would happen that night or the next morning'. At 1 a.m. an American reporter staying at the El Khebir Hotel in Tripoli was told by the foreign desk of his newspaper that a raid would take place that night.

The previous evening the British consul, Hugh Dunnachie, the only official British representative in Libya after diplomatic relations were broken off in 1984, had entertained two reporters, one of the authors and Marie Colvin from United Press International, at his villa on the corniche. Just after 1.30 a.m. one of the more bizarre incidents surrounding the raid occurred. Marie Colvin was telephoned at the consul's residence by a member of the Libyan Ministry of Information (strictly, the Secretariat of the General People's Congress for Information) who said that US planes were bombing Benghazi and that a raid on Tripoli was imminent. She tried to call Qaddafi's office at the Aziziya barracks but there was no reply.

It is almost incredible, but it seems that no one told Qaddafi. A few weeks after the raid, during an interview, Qaddafi asked Colvin why, if she knew the raid was going to happen, she had not told him. Colvin pointed out that it was not the role of a news agency reporter to give this kind of information to a head of state. Also, if she and most of the international press corps knew about the raid, why didn't he? Nobody told me,' said Qaddafi. Colvin said that she had tried to call his office. Qaddafi was impressed and grateful. In a televised speech he said that, although the US administration had tried to kill him, the American people loved him. As an example of their love he cited an American woman who, he said, had called to warn him just before the raid. 'I did not use your name because Reagan would have you killed if he knew,' Qaddafi told Colvin later.

A few minutes before 2 a.m. even Qaddafi noticed something was happening. The windows and doors rattled in the British consul's residence, chandeliers shook and the building itself trembled as thirteen F1-11 fighter bombers and three radar-jamming planes swooped in low over the sea and then, as they prepared for their bombing runs, rose to 500 feet and, at a speed of more than 500 m.p.h., roared over the city. The first bombs and missiles hit the airport and another wave of bombers swooped down on the Aziziya barracks.

Carrier-based planes from the Sixth Fleet – Hornet and Tomcat fighters, Corsair light attack jets, Hawkeye command planes and anti-radar prowlers – had already hit targets in Benghazi.

Tripoli was tragically unprepared. The city lights were on as the planes screamed in over the harbour. There were no sirens to give the alert. Ten minutes later, on the corniche in Tripoli, anti-aircraft and missile fire were heard as the sky lit up with red tracer and the white cones of small Sam missiles. It was too late. The US raids on Tripoli took eleven minutes. By the time most of the air defences started up, the planes were reporting the words 'feet wet', which meant they were safely over the Mediterranean. Only one plane failed to call in. The Americans had successfully jammed, and made useless, the bulk of Libya's air defence radar, but a gunner at the Aziziya barracks, quicker off the mark than most of his colleagues, had opened up with an old-fashioned ZSU23 four-barrelled gun. He put up a sheet of fire and an F1-11, flown by Captain Fernando Ribas-Dominicci, was hit. It exploded in flames and crashed into the Mediterranean ten miles off the coast.

A few members of the revolutionary committees, Qaddafi's hard-core political elite, were on the streets carrying Kalashnikov rifles, but seemed unsure about what to do with them. Cars careered along the corniche, their tyres screaming and their headlights full on, breaking every rule of civil defence. It was not until three days after the raid that leaflets, giving instructions on what to do during a raid, were handed out on the street. Some people that night were fleeing the city in panic, others were driving to their military units. Others, according to a Libyan newspaper report, were running away from their units.

Qaddafi claimed later that he had been in his house with his family when the attack began. He said that his wife, who suffered from back pain, had been strapped into her bed to avoid movements which might damage her back and that he had rushed to her bedside and started undoing the straps. However, a number of sources say that Qaddafi was well below ground in his command centre. His wife and children were asleep on the ground floor of their house in the barracks. They had not sought shelter nor taken the slightest precaution to guard against attack.

Everything went wrong. Qaddafi's defences fell apart. Even the radar did not work that night. A Ministry of Information official said that the F1-11s from the British airfields had flown in low from the west, just off the Tunisian coast, and taken the Libyan air defences by surprise. They had expected an attack from the east or the north, from the Gulf of Sirte.

The rules of engagement for Operation Eldorado Canyon had been strictly formulated, or so it was claimed in the official US explanation to the British Cabinet: the planes should strike only targets that could be precisely defined and shown to be related to terrorist and military activity. The weapons officer in each plane had to have a 'double lock-on' before he could release his bombs, which meant that he had to fix the target, not only with his forward-looking infra-red night sight, but also with his Pave Track radar. Any plane which failed to achieve this was under orders to leave the target area and jettison its bombs over the sea.

Such reassurances meant little to the residents of Bin Ashur, a suburb of Tripoli. At dawn that morning the Ministry of Information gathered the journalists at the El Khebir Hotel and loaded them on to buses. They were taken about two miles to an area of villas and smart apartments where the city's bourgeoisie lived. In the dawn light it was a surreal scene. The revolutionary committees manned checkpoints as bulldozers moved rubble through the murk and dust. Around them stood the dazed residents. One man, a playwright who had studied in America and spoke fluent English, said that he was asleep when he heard a roaring sound, presumably the first wave of bombers flying over. He went to the balcony of his apartment and, he said, 'A circle of fire seemed to be falling directly on my head. There was a terrible explosion.'

At least a dozen bombs and missiles fell in the area, making craters ten feet deep, knocking out the front of an apartment building and scoring direct hits on private villas. The house next to the French embassy was destroyed and the embassy itself severely damaged. One bomb or missile landed in the centre of a park and children's playground. A child's foot was sticking out of the rubble of one building. The body of an old man was fixed in a crouch as if he had been getting out of bed when the bombs hit. Another old man lay on a stretcher outside his villa, killed by falling rubble. It was a gruesome sight. The back wall of one house had been blown in, killing one member of the family. Pieces of flesh lay on the floor.

The Americans at first denied that the damage and casualties had been caused by US bombs and missiles. Later the Pentagon changed its story. One official theory was that the US pilot Ribas-Dominicci, hit by ground fire over the Aziziya barracks, had wrenched his F1-11, loaded with four 2,000-pound bombs, into a 70-degree turn towards the sea. The bombs might have been snapped off the wing by centrifugal force, to fall on Bin Ashur.

If that is true, it is a remarkable coincidence. For in the middle of Bin Ashur, a hundred yards from the French embassy, is an innocuous-looking two-storey office building topped by a huge radio mast. One resident described it as the 'Libyan CIA'. Its official title is the Bureau of External Security, and it is from there that Libyan terrorist campaigns are planned and directed.

The Libyans were so keen to show the world the horror of civilian deaths and injuries that Libyan officials interrupted operations and ushered journalists and television teams into the central hospital to view patients on the operating table. Wounded people were wheeled out into the hospital corridors and fresh wounds were exposed. At the city mortuary the press were shown eleven bodies – six men, three women and two children. There was a bucket in the room containing the skin of two people. The press was then herded into another bus by information officials and driven for an hour into the country to see an American plane shot down during the raid. It proved elusive and was almost certainly non-existent. The bus drove down tracks in the country and into empty fields. There was no trace of the plane.

Libyan officials were not willing to show or even discuss damage to military targets. There is no doubt that the raid had some military success. Soviet-built Ilyushin transport jets were wrecked at Tripoli military airport, a severe blow to Qaddafi's ability to move troops and equipment. Benghazi airport, which like Tripoli is both civilian and military, was severely damaged and a new Sam 5 missile site destroyed. The Jamahiriya military barracks in Benghazi received direct hits and so did a naval academy, a frogmen's training school and a camp for training Palestinian guerrillas, just west of Tripoli.

The attack on Qaddafi's Aziziya compound was a military failure. Qaddafi himself was deep underground. The administration building, where he lives, was missed by two bombs which fell thirty yards away, knocking out the windows but doing no structural damage. The tennis-courts received two direct hits and a bomb fell outside the front door of the building where Qaddafi's family lives. Blasts tore through the small bedrooms to the right of the living-room, injuring two of Qaddafi's sons and killing his fifteen-month-old adopted daughter, Hanna. Hanna was publicly acknowledged only in death. During interviews only a month before Qaddafi had said, sadly, that he had only one daughter, eight-year-old Aisha, and wished that he had more. He did not say that his wife, Safiya, had adopted a baby girl ten months before.

The Americans had thought that Qaddafi lived in his Bedouin tent. He does not, but if he had he would have escaped. The bombs missed the tent and hit the tennis-court near by. The blast knocked over a lamppost which fell on the tent, denting the fabric. A glass of roses had been knocked to the floor, but the glass was unbroken.

US forces could not accurately observe the damage because cloud obscured the targets from the cameras of satellites and Blackbird surveillance aircraft (which flew over Tripoli provoking energetic but futile bursts of anti-aircraft fire). In Tripoli there was only confusion and misinformation. Rumours circulated that the American bombing had triggered an internal revolt and there were unexplained bursts of small-arms fire in the city. A West German engineer working on a project at the Wheelus air force base just to the east of Tripoli phoned his embassy in panic to say that planes were attacking the airbase and that fires were burning inside it. This was eight hours after the American planes had left Tripoli, three hours after they had landed back at their bases in Britain or on board the Sixth Fleet carriers. The West German told his embassy that he did not believe the planes he saw were American. A Dutch expatriate also saw an air attack on Wheelus at about the same time. He said he saw rockets fired from planes.

The Libyan authorities say the Americans attacked again, although there is no evidence to support this. Diplomats and analysts in Tripoli believe that the US bombing sparked a spontaneous coup attempt by disaffected, middle-ranking army officers. The only sortie flown by the Libyan air force, some of them say, was against a rebel convoy of the Libyan army which was moving on Wheelus to take control. There were reports of revolts in the navy, the air force, the army and the revolutionary committees.

It seems, and there can be no certainty, that there was no organized coup attempt in the immediate aftermath of the raid. However, in the confusion, groups of officers, furious that Qaddafi had brought the wrath of the United States upon them, took to the streets firing randomly in the air in protest. Members of the revolutionary committees, who have their own jeeps and caches of light arms, mobilized to put down what they believed was an American-inspired coup attempt. Army units, loyal to Qaddafi, believed that the revolutionary committees were part of the US coup attempt and opened fire. These sporadic battles took place for two days after the raid and although the death toll was relatively low, perhaps only eight or nine, they caused more panic and confusion.

Officials of the Libyan Ministry of Information, harassed men with stubble on their chins who lack or are unwilling to give even the most basic snippets of information, were not much help. Their efforts to show that not a single military target had been hit by the Americans became absurd. A warehouse in Benghazi, surrounded by barbed wire, with soldiers and a military helicopter inside it, which had indeed been hit, possibly by an American missile, was described as a 'powdered-milk factory' by an official. Eventually the official relented under questioning. 'All right, all right, it is something military, maybe,' he said.

In the same city a day after the raid, officials took journalists to a house where, they claimed, a 500-pound US bomb had fallen outside, failed to explode, bounced through a wall, landed on a bed and crushed an old man to death. The small hole in the bedroom wall seemed more likely to have been created by a Libyan anti-aircraft shell. This was certainly the opinion of a group of Libyan boys playing in the rubble. They pointed at the hole in the wall and said, 'Libyan shell, Libyan.' Ministry of Information officials picked up pieces of rubble and began to stone the boys.

The Minister of Information, Mohammed Sharif al din Fayturi, claimed, two days after the raid, that a total of twenty-eight American planes had been shot down by the Libyan air defence units, four of them that very day. The US Pentagon said it had lost one plane. 'Where are the planes and the pilots?' the journalists asked Fayturi. 'The pilots are dead. They were killed by local people,' he said. 'Where are their bodies?' said the journalists. Fayturi talked in a whisper to an aide. 'They are not dead,' he said. 'The four pilots ejected from their planes, landed by parachute and changed into civilian clothes to look like Libyans. They ran away and they are being pursued by dogs.' The next day he was asked whether the dogs had found the pilots. He looked confused. 'What dogs?' he asked.

This drizzle of lies was too much even for the *Jamahiriya*, the weekly newspaper of the revolutionary committees. It is known as the mouthpiece of Qaddafi and his deputy, Major Abdul Salam Jalloud. In a rare piece of self-criticism, it attacked the government-controlled radio and television coverage of the raid: 'We do not need war broadcasts that describe planes falling like the brown leaves in autumn,' it said.

After the raid on Tripoli Qaddafi failed to appear in public and rumours began that he had been killed or deposed or had run away.

The city was tense. The press was banned from leaving the hotel without an official escort. Each evening anti-aircraft fire would start up. There was no official explanation and people wondered if the American planes had returned or, more ominously, if a *coup d'état* was in progress.

Two days later Qaddafi flickered on to the Libyan television screens wearing the uniform of a naval officer with three rows of medals on his chest. He announced that Libya had won a great victory; henceforth his country would be known officially not just as the Libyan Jamahiriya but as the Great Jamahiriya. 'Turn on your lights, dance in the streets, we are not afraid of America,' he said. Half an hour later, the Tripoli electricity board, which had plunged the city into darkness after the US planes were already on their way back to Britain and the Sixth Fleet, obliged. The lights along the corniche came on, and a small group of demonstrators, mostly revolutionary committee members and Ministry of Information officials, threw their arms around each other's shoulders and did little jigs in Green Square.

It was not a convincing performance. Qaddafi had received a blow which few Western leaders could have survived. He had been caught pathetically unprepared; his defences had failed abysmally. His armed forces had performed badly in a crisis. There was little to show for the billions of dollars he had spent on his armoury. A canyon emerged between Qaddafi's rhetoric and reality. He had threatened terrible consequences if the Americans attacked. Suicide squads were supposed to be on the alert to hit US targets in Europe and even on the American mainland. A Libyan pilot had talked to reporters before the raid about how he and his crew were standing by on a desert airfield with a plane packed with explosives for a suicide attack on the US fleet. In the event, nothing happened.

Qaddafi's allies, so generous with their telegrams of solidarity, did not lift a finger when the US planes attacked. The Soviet fleet arrived in Tripoli harbour two weeks after the raid. Colonel Alexander Kvalchok, commander of the naval brigade, laid wreaths at the graves of Libyans killed by the US bombs and stood for one minute in silence. It represented the sum total of Soviet support.

After the raid Qaddafi and Major Abdul Salam Jalloud spoke with a restraint unknown in the recent history of Libya. They attacked the 'savage, barbaric aggression' of President Reagan and his ally, the 'child murderer' Margaret Thatcher. Britain was duly marked in black on the weather map on Libyan television, joining the United States, South Africa and Egypt. Israel is not marked at all. Qaddafi called the Americans and British 'a species which are between pigs and human beings and have not developed yet to become ordinary human beings'. But there was no talk of retaliation or suicide attacks, and the only acts of reprisal were the murders of two British teachers in Beirut the previous month, on the orders of Libyan intelligence.

The raid would have meant the end for any elected leader. It had shown the vulnerability of Libya, the failure of its military, its internal instability and its isolation in the world. There were reports from the CIA that Qaddafi was suffering from acute depression and was no longer in control of Libya, and press reports that he had been ousted in an internal coup and that he was taking 'mood control' drugs. He appeared in a televised speech in May looking ill (his face strangely swollen) and sounding incoherent.

But once again Qaddafi defied his critics and bounced back on to the world stage. A week later he was giving interviews and looking well. 'Why are they saying that my face looks puffy?' he asked an inter-viewer. He explained that he had been fasting during the holy month of Ramadan and had felt tired when he appeared on television. He claimed that Libya had won a great victory over the Americans. In military terms this was, of course, nonsense but it had a grain of truth. Once again he had put Libya, which throughout its history had been a pawn in the hands of foreign invaders, back on the international map. He had challenged one of the world's superpowers and survived. America had run into diplomatic problems with its NATO allies over the raid and had been condemned roundly at the United Nations. Libyan television carried long reports about British opposition to Mrs Thatcher's decision to allow the United States to use British bases. The Arab world, which had done nothing to help him, was, after the attack, full of praise and admiration for his brave stand.

Through the miasma of rhetoric, propaganda, rumour and allega-tion it is difficult to gain more than a shadowy outline of Qaddafi or the country he rules. The West's ignorance of Libya is paralleled only by Qaddafi's ignorance of the West. Is he the vicious dictator of an oppressed people – the image which the Western governments and press most often project – or is he a charismatic leader of what he himself describes as a 'Utopia' by the Mediterranean, appointed by popular assent and beloved by the radical Arab world?

2 Qaddafi Superstar

A huge crowd stretched from the main doors of the General People's Congress hall in Tripoli, through the dust and gloom of early evening, across the dual carriageway to a line of coaches. The crowd was mostly young; boys and girls shouted, giggled and chanted. The girls pushed, shoved and screamed as they tried to squeeze through the narrow door into the auditorium. Bouncers stood outside, using their shoulders, and sometimes their fists, to keep the youngsters in line. From inside the hall came the rhythmic shouts of another 3,000 teenagers. In the West it would take a rock and roll superstar, Mick Jagger perhaps, to pull such an audience.

This, however, was the Socialist People's Libyan Arab Jamahiriya in February 1986 and the crowd was queuing to get into the Libyan equivalent of the Conservative Party conference. Topping the bill was the Libyan leader, the guide of the Libyan revolution, author of the three-part Green Book, the inspiration of Arab unity and world revolution: Colonel Muammar Qaddafi.

Nobody had bought tickets for this performance of course, but neither was attendance voluntary. Libyan officials like to call such gatherings 'spontaneous demonstrations'. They are, in fact, carefully planned. At one 'spontaneous demonstration' by foreign workers in Tripoli, the Pakistanis who attended were paid a generous bonus, about £50 each, to shout slogans supporting Qaddafi and the revolution in Arabic. Not speaking Arabic they had not the faintest idea what they were shouting.

The youngsters at the conference that night had been bused in from schools and army training centres all over the city and issued with the standard revolutionary green scarves. Some of the girls had been at the Women's Military Academy in Tripoli the day before, where they had learned to fire an anti-aircraft gun and strip an automatic rifle. They had performed a sort of military ballet as, delicately, they thrust bayonets into an imaginary US marine. After each exercise, they smiled and blushed at the foreign reporters, most of them

27

Americans, who surrounded them. They all said, perhaps a little too eagerly to be convincing, that they had volunteered for suicide squads to fight the US Sixth Fleet and the American military wherever they were, even in the Black House (which is what the revolutionaries call the White House in a rare attempt at a joke) in Washington DC.

They squeezed into the auditorium. Six television cameras were positioned through the hall, feeding the proceedings live to the people of Libya. Five men in army uniform sat on the podium and took turns to shout slogans into the microphone. They were echoed by the audience who jumped up in their seats to wave their fists and scream with revolutionary zeal: 'We will die for Qaddafi', 'Death, death, death to the USA', 'Shit, shit and shit on the US Sixth Fleet'. Foreign reporters were herded by ministry officials to the front of the hall, under a spotlight, directly beneath the podium, where they stood with trepidation. Despite the rhetoric the crowd was good-humoured.

One young man who chanted and waved his fist in the front row, standing on his seat, accidentally bumped the head of an American reporter, a living example of the Great Satan. 'I am terribly sorry,' he said. 'It was an accident. Please, I will stand a little higher up.' He resumed his chant: 'Death, death, death to Reagan.'

Excitement mounted as they waited for the leader's arrival. He is always late, and quite often he does not arrive at all. Libyan officials refuse to discuss it, but this is for security reasons. His appearances are never announced beforehand and officials, dignitaries and crowds of supporters have often waited for hours for him to turn up and then gone home disappointed.

After an hour he slipped on to the stage from the wings surrounded by bodyguards in the manner of an American presidential candidate. But this was revolutionary theatre. As Qaddafi raised his fist, there was an explosion of chanting. He milked the crowd, his head tilted back, the trace of a smile on his face, swaying slightly on his feet. His face appeared in monstrous proportions on a huge screen at the front of the hall. Every few minutes he glanced down at two television monitors which, on his insistence, are placed directly in front of him. He adjusted his collar and fluffed up his hair. His smile only slipped once. As he moved to the front of the stage to touch the hands of his supporters, which he does in the manner of a religious leader holding their hands between his own, one of his guards stepped between him and a supporter. Qaddafi's eyes narrowed, he shouted and shoved the guard roughly out of the way. His smile flashed back.

Qaddafi spoke for two and a half hours from a single page of notes about Nasser, Arab unity, the Palestinian problem and Libya's confrontation with the United States. He condemned the Zionist State of Israel and the arrogant United States, and threatened suicide attacks against US targets. In any other country such a threat would be extraordinary. In Libya it is unremarkable. Diplomats here find Qaddafi's speeches so predictable that one has a checklist of topics – anti-Zionist, anti-Egyptian, anti-American, Arab unity – which he ticks as they crop up in almost every public statement. At the bottom of the form is a small box for any new subject that Qaddafi might mention. The box is usually empty.

It was dull material for his young audience, nor is Qaddafi a very good orator. His gestures are stiff, his gaze fixes on a point twenty feet above his audience and his voice tends to drone. After half an hour of Arab nationalism a boy in the second row from the stage fell asleep and his head rolled on to the shoulder of his friend. A security man leaned across and gently woke him. It was no good. Within a few minutes the leader's voice had lulled him into another dream. The tedium became infectious. Rows of heads lolled, snapped erect and lolled again. Some of the young people used the time for more important purposes. Although Libya is liberated compared to some Muslim countries – women go to school and university, have jobs and enter the army – it is still conservative. The sexes seldom mix and for the youngsters that night it was a rare opportunity. They were divided in the auditorium by the aisles, but those sitting at the end of the row could talk to the person of the opposite sex on the end of the next row and hold hands. The boys and girls shouted at each other and threw notes.

Although many of the young Libyans paid scant attention to the speech, what Qaddafi said that night touched on many of the motives that drive him and shape the policies of modern Libya. He spoke at length about the late President Gamal Abdul Nasser of Egypt, who died a year after Qaddafi took power. Nasser remains his hero and he is still guided by his thoughts, although, according to one of Nasser's closest confidants, the Egyptian author Mohammed Heikal, Nasser would have deeply disapproved of the direction his young protégé has taken. Nasser thought of Qaddafi as 'a nice boy, but terribly naive', said Heikal. As a boy in the Sirtic desert, Qaddafi listened to his speeches crackling over the transistor radio from Cairo, and learned them by heart. Heikal remembers chiding Qaddafi just after the coup by telling him that he had learned a lot, but absorbed too little. Nasser's thoughts are still the pillars of his foreign policy. Nasser had spoken of the circles of influence which had Egypt as the centre: the circles of Arab, Islamic and African unity. Arab unity, roughly defined as the link between people who share the Arabic language, remains Qaddafi's goal. He believes that if Arab countries stopped feuding and pooled their money, knowledge and military might, they would create a power bloc that could rival the super-powers and destroy the State of Israel.

Qaddafi is the ultimate rejectionist of the Egypt/Israel peace treaty. His views are simple, passionate and brutal: Israel should not exist and any compromise, such as the Camp David treaty, is a betrayal; Israel should be Palestine; any Jews who were in Palestine before the State of Israel was created in 1948 could stay, the rest would have to go. The only way to achieve this end, he says, is 'continuous war'. This is not a solution that appeals, or seems practical, to the West or to moderate Arab states, but it went down well with four members of the audience that night: senior representatives of the extremist Palestinian groups, the Popular Front for the Liberation of Palestine, General Command and the Democratic Front for the Liberation of Palestine. Qaddafi funds them, gives them arms and trains their members.

As usual he lambasted the United States, calling it 'arrogant', 'savage', 'barbaric' and 'imperialist'. His hatred for the United States, which he shares with other radical Arab states and move-ments, is based partly on what he sees as its imperialist influence in the Third World but mostly on its support for Israel, which, Qaddafi often points out, would not be a regional super-power without Ameri-can aid. He chronicles the crimes carried out by Israel against the Arabs and the Palestinians, and argues that, if the United States really wants to stop terrorism, it should use its power to give the Palestinians a homeland and not support a state which has carried out a long, bloody and unjustified invasion of an Arab country, Lebanon. He consistently draws a line between 'terrorism' and 'wars of libera-tion', although he seems to approve of terrorism when it is carried out for what he believes is a just cause. He says often: 'I am against terrorism, but I support the just causes of liberation. I am ready to fight. I do not support terrorism but I am revolutionary man. If you say I am a terrorist that means George Washington was a terrorist.'

Qaddafi has done as much as any other Arab leader in recent history to strive for Arab and Islamic unity. He has tried, though failed, to forge treaties between Libya and other Arab and African countries. He has provided money and training for far-flung Muslim minorities in Thailand and the Philippines. He has supported and funded the groups who fight against Israel. He has fuelled an eclectic group of what the West calls terrorists and he calls revolutionaries, from the IRA to the Baader-Meinhof gang in Germany, the Japanese Red Army, the Italian Red Brigades, insurgents in El Salvador and Nicaragua, and dissidents in Iran, Sudan and Spain. Few areas of the world are immune from his interference. He has struck blows against Western imperialism which, from Tripoli's point of view, have been so successful that they have drawn the wrath of the Sixth Fleet.

At home he can point to a number of successes, as his audience that night demonstrated. The young people were well dressed, well fed and well educated. Libyans now earn more per capita than the British. The disparity in annual incomes, from about £6,000 for manual workers to £30,000 for the captains of industry, is smaller than in most countries. Libya's wealth has been fairly spread throughout society. Every Libyan has a job and a decent salary. He gets free, and often excellent, education, medical and health services. New colleges and hospitals are impressive by any international standard. All Libyans have a house or a flat, a car and most have televisions, video recorders and telephones. Compared with most citizens of Third World countries, and with many in the first world, Libyans have it very good indeed.

This audience represented Qaddafi's real constituency, the people who have grown up in Libya knowing no alternative to his revolution, their minds awash with its rhetoric. The barrage of propaganda is impossible to avoid. It fills the radio and television, the streets and even the lifts and public rooms of the hotels in Tripoli where political meetings are piped through loudspeakers. Qaddafi's thoughts are plastered across walls in the airport arrival and departure lounges, across buildings and streets, on postage stamps and ballpoint pens which have inscribed on their side cryptic slogans from his Green Book, such as 'In need freedom is latent.' Libyan television broadcasts pop music videos in which the leader's thoughts have been put to a disco rhythm and performed by young, usually Maltese, pop musicians. One of them is called 'The Third Universal Theory' and the lyrics, backed by drums and electric guitar, go:

> The universal theory has seen the light,
> Bringing to Mankind peace and delight,
> The tree, oh, of justice, people's rule and socialism,
> Completely different from laissez-faire and capitalism,
> Based on religion and nationalism.

Qaddafi's picture is everywhere, hanging in the streets, stuck on walls, on the exterior and interior of all public buildings and offices.

31

A one-room tailor's shop near Green Square has fourteen pictures of the Colonel in the window and on the walls.

Qaddafi says that he dislikes the personality cult and has exhorted people to stop it. 'What can I do? They insist,' he said. But Qaddafi still beams from official government stamps, watch faces and satchels of children going to school. A foreign visitor who had tea with him remembers the shock as she looked down and saw his smiling face shimmering up from the bottom of the cup.

Few Libyans have actually met him. Although a populist at heart he is now more remote from the people than most Western leaders. When he first took power he would drive around town in a battered Volkswagen; he and his wife did their shopping in the local supermarket. Several assassination attempts – he has a scar on his shoulder after one of his own army officers shot him – and botched coups later, his security is elaborate. When he leaves the Aziziya barracks two convoys of armoured cars set off in opposite directions. He is in one of them, the other is a decoy. When he flies, two planes take off. The jet he intends to use flies for up to two hours before he boards it in case a bomb, triggered by altitude, has been secreted on board. To the irritation of other world leaders he will often not announce his arrival until his plane is in their air space. He once told the Tunisian government that he was coming by car and the cabinet turned out to meet him at the border. They waited in vain. For security reasons he flew into Tunis airport. His plane was codenamed 'Eagle' but the pilot would not, again for security reasons, give Qaddafi's name: when he asked for permission to land, he just said, 'We have a VIP on board.'

Western ambassadors and diplomats have only the most perfunctory access to him. He considers them all to be spies, and shuns them. The Western intelligence agencies work hard at gathering information, but one analyst who used to work at the US State Department said most of these reports are 'rubbish': 'The problem is that we do not have good intelligence. We know very little about Qaddafi.' This extends even to the simple matter of spelling his name. When the word Qaddafi is spoken by his countrymen it is a short, incomprehensible explosion of guttural sounds which do not transliterate easily into the Latin alphabet. There are reportedly over 600 ways of spelling it; they vary from the simple Gadafy, through the more correct Qaddafi to the ornate Qhaddhafi and the exotic Kazafuy.

The Reagan administration is unambiguous about Qaddafi. He is 'the most dangerous man in the world', a 'mad dog'. According to some CIA reports he is indeed mad. One said that during a trip to Majorca in 1985 he wore make-up and carried a teddy bear, and that he refused to sleep on bed sheets provided by the hotel for security reasons. A 1982 report said that 'he is judged to suffer from a severe personality disorder . . . under severe stress he is subject to episodes of bizarre behaviour when his judgement may be faulty'. Other CIA material has suggested that during the past several years he has taken excessive amounts of sleeping pills, followed by other pills to wake him up in the morning. His depressions became so severe, according to another report, that he wandered the corridors of the Aziziya barracks 'muttering incoherently' and 'talking gibberish'. The Israelis have said that he suffers from severe haemorrhoids and epileptic fits. The late President Sadat was so concerned about Qaddafi's mental state that, during an official visit to Cairo, when Qaddafi complained of pain in his eyes, he tried to persuade him to have a brain scan. Qaddafi refused.

There are many stories about Qaddafi's physical disabilities. At one function in Tripoli Qaddafi had to walk up some steps to the podium. He did so with difficulty and appeared to be limping. 'Look at his leg,' said one diplomat. 'He's had a stroke.' 'Look at his shoes,' replied an Italian colleague. Qaddafi was teetering, like a young girl at her first dance, on huge Cuban heels.

Qaddafi has taken pains to persuade the West that he is not 'a mad dog' but a family man who loves his children. To prove this point, in January 1986, a time of great tension with the United States, he invited five women from the international press corps to meet him, his wife and some of their children at home. The ladies were received in his tent at the Aziziya barracks and introduced to Safiya, his second wife and mother of six of his seven children. He talked about how he had been misunderstood by the West: 'Reagan should come and see that I don't live in the trenches wearing hand grenades in my belt. The lies that I don't smile and have no family or that I am full of hate would be proved false.' He described how he met his wife when he was in hospital with appendicitis soon after he came to power in 1969. Safiya, who is a striking, rather formidable woman with long black hair and intense eyes, was a nurse in the hospital and said that as she stood at the leader's bedside it was 'love at first sight'. (Qaddafi married his first wife, Fatiha, a year earlier. But by all accounts, it was a formal, rather cursory liaison with a middle-class family from the old regime. Fatiha's father was General Khalid, a senior officer in King Idris's army.) Qaddafi has a well-rehearsed speech for Western audiences. He lists his favourite books: *Uncle Tom's Cabin*, *Roots* and

The Outsider by Colin Wilson. He says that he likes Beethoven and enjoys playing football. As he stroked the hair of his daughter Aisha, he said he wanted another daughter. He thought his daughter might have political potential and he wanted his six sons to be doctors helping poor people in Africa.

His image as a family man was marred, somewhat, when he made passes at three of the five women reporters. His reason for inviting the women, not the men, was ideological, he said. He wanted to promote women's rights and, indeed, in Libya he has done so. There was a more basic reason: Qaddafi likes women, despite long-standing speculation about his homosexual leanings.

He has a group of regular female partners, called in Tripoli 'the three'. Two of them are Yugoslav, his masseuse and a nurse, and one is said to be East German. He is not averse to expanding the team. He has propositioned many Western women who have interviewed him. One of them, an American, who felt the Colonel's hand on her thigh and protested too sharply, was bundled out of the barracks in the middle of the night and left to find her own way back to her hotel.

He had what can only be described as a crush on another woman journalist. After the first interview, which involved some artless fumbling by Qaddafi, he asked if he could see her again. 'Why don't you call me?' she replied. 'It is difficult for me to call your hotel,' he said. Eventually he plucked up the courage and told one of his aides to call the woman's hotel room, then he picked up the phone. She was summoned to the barracks late at night and taken to his apartment underground where, in what seemed to be a regular ceremony at the Aziziya barracks, a white dress and a pair of green shoes stood on a chair. A woman attendant told her that the leader wanted her to put the dress and shoes on. When she refused, the woman looked surprised. When Qaddafi came into the room he asked her why she had not changed into the clothes provided. 'Don't you like them?' he said. 'Are they the wrong colour?' He is not subtle. 'You have brave eyes,' he said. 'Can you make me forget my troubles for a day. Or at least for an hour?' He does have a certain chivalry. He asked another woman journalist to sleep with him and, when she also refused and said that she did not know him well enough and would feel 'like a whore', he was impressed. 'I respect you,' he said.

He is not always so unsuccessful. An Austrian journalist, Renate Possamig, went to Tripoli to interview him in the mid-1980s and says that he 'begged her' to become his third wife. She says that he showered her with jewellery and clothes and she admits that she was so fascinated by him that she became a Muslim:

He took me into his library. While the door was closed he kissed me passionately. We lay on the carpet and I felt excited and secure. His arms and shoulders were strong. I was swept away by his romantic brown eyes. I forgot he was Qaddafi. But suddenly I couldn't bear being in his arms any longer. I could see heartaches ahead. He had two other wives anyway. Suddenly I saw a tired man; beneath that dark handsome exterior, there's a sad, lonely man.

Possamig was luckier than other women swept away by those romantic brown eyes. An American reporter, who described Qaddafi as 'kind of cute' and wrestled with him in his underground boudoir, was also given a present. Qaddafi, after saying how much he admired her, took off the watch he wore on his wrist and gave it to her. It was a cheap Taiwanese replica of a Rolex with Qaddafi's face imprinted on the dial. It was seven minutes slow when he gave it to her and later that evening at the El Khebir Hotel it stopped completely.

Qaddafi also appears to have charmed Imelda Marcos, wife of the former President of the Philippines. She was sent to Tripoli as a glamorous envoy to negotiate with Qaddafi over his support for the Muslim Moro insurgents in the southern Philippines. The chemistry between them evidently worked, because Qaddafi stopped funding the Moros after Imelda's second visit. In the summer of 1985 she told the former editor of the *Daily Telegraph*, William Deedes, that Qaddafi had sent her a romantic telegram and a signed copy of the Koran, and had asked her to become a Muslim. She said she found Qaddafi 'macho'. The CIA was interested enough in her visits to Libya to send the head of the CIA, William Casey, to debrief her. A guest at the dinner party where Deedes met Mrs Marcos asked the critical question: 'Did you actually sleep with Colonel Qaddafi?' 'What a question to ask a girl!' she replied coquettishly.

Working on the principle that Qaddafi has an eye for the ladies and that the quickest route to an exclusive interview is through a pretty woman, some Western newspapers and television networks shamelessly recruit their youngest and prettiest correspondents for the Tripoli assignment. One American magazine dispatched an enticing twenty-two-year-old who decided to increase her allure by dressing entirely in green, the colour of the revolution. In a green skirt, green blouse and green scarf she cruised the lobby of the El Khebir Hotel in her green high-heeled shoes in what turned out to be the futile hope of catching the eye of a senior Qaddafi aide and being escorted to the inner sanctum of the Aziziya barracks.

Qaddafi may have resented the sartorial competition, for he is extraordinarily vain. He dresses flamboyantly and sometimes changes his outfit three times in a day, from his naval uniform with the gold braid and medals to his Arab headdress or to his powder-blue jumpsuit with a complex array of zips and buttons. A visitor to the Aziziya barracks during a crisis found him adorned in a red silk shirt, a gold cape and lizard-skin slippers, like a young man about to go to a fashionable discotheque. He enjoys being a leader of fashion. 'Whatever I wear becomes a fad,' he said one evening in Tripoli. 'I wear a certain shirt and suddenly everyone is wearing it.' He said that he gets many letters from American women telling him that he is handsome: 'They often say they like my hair.'

The main impression that Qaddafi gives in his interviews to the Western press is not of insanity, but of a profound naivety. His ideas of the West are perhaps no more simple that the average American's view of Libya, but they are disturbing in a head of state. On America: 'I hear it is a complex society inside. Many Americans do not know about the outside world, they have no information about the people in Africa. I hear there are many people without houses there who commit suicide. The money that Reagan will spend on Star Wars, why should he not spend it on the American people?' On England, where he spent six months training with the army: 'It is a racist country and in London the people look very unhappy, they are always rushing underground [on the tube]. The people are too busy, always busy. There is a lot of smoke. When you wear white clothes they are black when you go home. The small villages are better. The people there have strong family ties.'

During one interview with an American reporter in the Aziziya barracks Qaddafi had a small Sony radio tuned to the BBC Arabic service. It is one of his few sources of unbiased information. Libya's radio and television, newspapers and official press agency provide an almost exclusive diet of flattery for the Libyan leadership. They list telegrams of support from friendly countries and organizations and any opposition, however small, to Libya's enemies. The news agency, Jana, reported that day, for example,

a host of telegrams of support received by 'the Leader'. These telegrams were from the workers of plastics and combustion in Lebanon, the Arab revolution youth in Holland, the Moroccan colony in Australia, the Islamic cultural centre in Holland, Muslim masses in Manila, the Islamic studies institute students in Maldive, society students in South Togo, the administrative body of the Islamic centre in Caracas and a telegram from the Kurdish Islamic Army. It began: 'O great Leader, we, the Kurdish Islamic Army, stress to you now that we are ready to immediately join in the frontline against the armies of the prejudiced crusades. We are waiting for your signal to go from our positions to any position you deem appropriate for our moves.'

In reality, the Kurdish Islamic Army is prepared to do no such thing, but in the welter of daily telegrams it would take a more cynical man than Qaddafi to believe that Tripoli is not the centre of the world and that it does not command almost universal respect. Such reports, which many in Libya take literally, show that Libya's enemies are plagued by troubles and incipient revolt.

Qaddafi's foreign service, which is now dominated by zealots from his revolutionary committees, ought to provide a more realistic view of the world but it does not. A former Libyan ambassador to Romania and Jordan, Aziz Shenib, described the cables he would send back to Libya. 'I relied heavily on the *Economist*'s Foreign Report newsletter', he said. 'I found many small items which I translated and sent back to Tripoli. To my astonishment Qaddafi was pleased to read about them. Most of them were absolute rubbish.' Shenib's job was to spy on Libya's allies. 'We had excellent relations with Algeria but Qaddafi wanted to know every damn thing about them. Was there a possibility to buy people, to persuade Algerians to work for Libyan intelligence, and Syrians to work for the Libyans? It was ridiculous. His main object seemed to be to recruit people from Arab countries.'

The person in the West who is closest to Qaddafi, who has won his confidence and to a certain extent his friendship, is Bruno Kreisky, the former Chancellor of Austria. Kreisky is a Jew, which might have been an insurmountable problem because Qaddafi's hatred of Israel, Zionists and Jews in general is almost Hitlerian. The two men are, none the less, friends and have met nine times. Kreisky describes Qaddafi as a 'revolutionary' who does not think about the consequences of his actions and who will never ignore terror as a means to achieve his ends.

Kreisky does not share his views, but believes that Qaddafi can be talked to and negotiated with. They first met in Libya in the early 1970s when Kreisky was leading a Socialist International Middle East peace mission. He landed in a Libyan Mystère jet, piloted by a Pakistani, on a motorway in the desert. Qaddafi had pitched his tent nearby and kept Kreisky waiting for an hour in the desert sun before he received him. 'I told him that it was not very polite to keep people waiting for an hour,' said Kreisky. 'He seemed surprised that I said that, then he apologized.' Their talks got nowhere, over a meal which Kreisky describes as 'terrible'. Qaddafi said he wanted an Arab revolution, that there was nothing to discuss about Israel and that the social democratic parties of Europe were 'traitors' to the Arab cause.

Kreisky persevered and invited Qaddafi on a semi-official visit to Austria. Qaddafi asked for his views on Libya's foreign policy, and Kreisky told him bluntly that it was not very good. He said that the war Qaddafi was waging in Chad might lead to tensions in the Mediterranean and disturb his relations with Europe. Qaddafi asked, 'What do I do?' Kreisky told him that he should speak to the socialist governments in Spain, Portugal, France, Italy, Malta and Greece. 'Okay. Yes I will see them all,' answered Qaddafi. Kreisky pointed out that nobody would see him unless he made his peace with President Mitterrand over Chad, where French and Libyan troops were fighting, and Qaddafi said, 'Okay, I'll try it.' A series of secret meetings followed with Kreisky as the intermediary. They ended in a treaty between France and Libya for the simultaneous withdrawal of troops from Chad.

Kreisky believes this shows that it is possible to negotiate with Qaddafi, although the French think it reveals the opposite because Qaddafi reneged on the deal. The French duly withdrew their troops; the Libyans made a token withdrawal and then not only redeployed but reinforced their troops in northern Chad.

The Israelis, Qaddafi's greatest enemies, take him seriously and do not dismiss him as a madman. Analysts from the Mossad, Israel's intelligence service, admire his brinkmanship, his ability to provoke and destabilize, then withdraw or strike a bargain. They study his military intervention in Chad as an example of crisis management. They believe that his support and funding of revolutionary movements is not a blank cheque for any terrorist group. He picks and chooses, supports then rejects according to the thrust of his foreign policy.

As Qaddafi relaxes at night in his bunker in the Aziziya barracks listening to Egyptian music on his tape cassette, he has a strangely inflated view of Libya's role in the world. The Foreign Ministry telex will have chattered out its usual diet of praise from leaders and organizations in the Third World and his envoys will have reported on the problems and disasters that plague his enemies. His view of Libya's domestic situation is even rosier. 'I have created a Utopia here in Libya,' he said. 'Not an imaginary one that people write about in books, but a concrete Utopia.'

Qaddafi's Green Book, the blueprint of the revolution, leans heavily on Marx and the Prophet Mohammed. There also seems, to the visitor to Libya, to be a dose of George Orwell's *1984* and a touch of Lewis Carroll. Sir Thomas More would not recognize his 'imaginary island . . . enjoying a perfect social, legal and political system' in modern Libya.

It is not the Utopian society but the prospect of hard cash which lures thousands of foreign workers to Libya. The regular British Caledonian flights from Gatwick airport near London to Tripoli in the spring of 1986 had the ambience of a football club outing. They were full of British workers, mostly from the North of England, going to their lucrative jobs in the Libyan oilfields. Libya is a Muslim country and drink is, officially, forbidden. Some of the British workers would finish their duty-free whisky while they waited in the departure lounge at Gatwick airport. On board the drinks trolley would fly up and down the aisles. When the plane touched down at Tripoli airport there would be shouts of: 'Here we go, here we go', and another planeload of expatriate workers would stagger through Libyan immigration, empty miniature bottles of Glenfiddich whisky spilling on to the tarmac.

In sober moments these workers agree that Libya is not so bad. 'You keep your head down. You don't talk about politics,' said a Geordie who worked in a desert oilfield. 'If you do that, Libyans aren't bad blokes. They'd do anything to help you out, like.' The foreigners live separately in modern housing estates near the major towns and keep to themselves. There is no public entertainment, no plays, cinemas, restaurants or clubs, so they watch video films, play darts and go to parties at each other's houses.

And they drink. Alcoholism is perhaps the biggest danger for the expatriate worker. They brew home-made beer and pure alcohol, called flash, which is cut usually with orange juice. The Libyan authorities take a lenient view of this illegal activity and allow foreigners to drink themselves to death without official harassment. Flash is deadly stuff which even experienced drinkers find hard to handle.

A Texan who worked for a company that provided spare parts for the oil industry said that he had dropped out of the Tripoli cocktail circuit. 'I didn't want to get flash burned,' he said. He is typical of many Americans, perhaps a thousand, who defied the US President's January 1986 ban on working in Libya. He lives a quiet life in an office near the Beach Hotel in Tripoli and is defiantly Texan. He wears a large hat and embossed leather cowboy boots; in his office he has a stuffed stoat with a bullet hole in its forehead. 'That there stoat attacked a friend of mine while he was sleeping. Shot it dead, straight between the eyes.' There are no such dangers lurking in Tripoli. 'I've had no trouble from the Libyans,' he said. 'Fine people and I earn a hell of a better living than I would back in the States.'

On the surface Libya is a placid place. For a country that has hosted most of the world's terrorist groups, there is remarkably little overt security. Armed men are rarely seen on the streets or at the airport. Foreign embassies which in other capitals are designed like fortresses have no noticeable defences, and the British consul's residence on the corniche has less security than a suburban house in London. The windows are not bullet-proof, and some do not even close. The front gate is open and so, usually, is the front door. Visitors just wander in.

Under a different political system it has all the physical possibilities of a tourist rather than a terrorist haven. Tripoli is a pretty city, with Italian squares and houses, an old city with narrow winding streets and a huge Turkish fort, built in the shape of a ship, close to Green Square.

The city stands on the Mediterranean and enjoys a perfect climate with a daily average of 61 degrees Fahrenheit in winter and 86 in summer. There is virtually no rain between June and September and the only quirk in this perfect weather is the occasional *khamsin*, a hot wind that sweeps in from the Sahara, increasing in speed and heat as it crosses Libya's flat, arid countryside. Herodotus described how a *khamsin* destroyed the Libyan tribe of Psylli by drying up their water supplies.

Sadly, Tripoli in the mid-1980s is a dismal place. Jamahiriya Street, which used to be one of the busiest shopping areas, the Oxford Street or Fifth Avenue of Libya, is almost deserted. More than half the shops are closed and those that remain open have almost nothing to sell: a single, cheap digital watch in one, a few shoes in another, a Green Book and an empty carton of Kodak film in a third. They are closed or empty for a mixture of economic and revolutionary reasons. Qaddafi has ruled that people should be 'partners not wage slaves' and small businesses, no longer allowed to hire staff and unable to find partners, have closed down. The old city, where the bazaar merchants had their shops, is empty and decaying. Libyans buy what goods they can find in the state supermarkets – ugly concrete buildings called 'supermarket 103' and 'supermarket 101'. One Wednesday morning, a queue of 100 people was pushing to get into supermarket 103. On the ground floor, the food section, there were row after row of freezers, all of them empty except for a few broken bars of butter. There was no meat, fish or bread.

It is a police state, although no one is sure who the police are. Officially they do not exist. They were abolished by Qaddafi as a revolutionary gesture, along with the Ministry of Justice and the Ministry of Light Industry. In theory the people police themselves, although, after Qaddafi's ban, men wearing police uniforms, driving police cars and working in police stations could still be seen. But their role was uncertain, as an odd incident in Green Square revealed. A policeman was standing on the steps of the police station when a police car pulled up outside. Two other policemen got out, grabbed the first policeman, pushed him into the car and drove away. There was no official explanation for this. 'There are no policeman,' said a spokesman for the Ministry of Information.

As well as the officially non-existent policemen, there are secret police from the Bureau of External Security, other security services, the army and the revolutionary committees. They are trained by Eastern-bloc specialists: the Romanians train and advise the police, the East Germans control military intelligence, the Czechs and Poles control political intelligence. With this plethora of security services everyone is more than a little afraid.

With the possible exception of Albania, Libya is the most closed society in the world. Direct questions to Libyan officials bring convoluted answers or, often, none at all. Ordinary Libyans are forbidden to talk to foreigners. One young man was having coffee in a hotel in Tripoli, and chatted briefly to two British journalists. He spoke English fluently with a cockney accent and said that he had learned it, courtesy of Her Majesty's prison in Brixton, London, where he served a year for 'GBH' (grievous bodily harm). 'I clobbered some bloke in a bar,' he said. 'With a broken bottle, I was well loaded.' He has returned to be a loyal member of Qaddafi's revolution, said that he liked Libya and was trying to find a job. This innocent conversation was monitored by a member of one of the security services. The young man was arrested and interrogated shortly afterwards.

Libyan press and television are under tight government control. Telephones, telexes, houses and hotel rooms are bugged and monitored with the latest European technology. Revolutionary committee members, the young turks of Qaddafi's revolution, are everywhere in shops, factories and the streets sniffing out the ideologically impure.

In theory, the people rule Libya, according to Qaddafi's Green Book, through 187 people's assemblies which appoint members to an annual General People's Congress. Broadcast live on Libyan television, this has the emotional atmosphere of an evangelical prayer meeting. Every few minutes the members erupt in a chorus of chanting: 'We are Qaddafi', 'Death to America'. Debate is limited; some subjects such as defence are never discussed and crucial issues such as budgets are skirted over. The congress tends to be a rubber stamp for Qaddafi's own policies, although, occasionally, it deviates from the leader's ideological line. It exerted a certain power when Qaddafi wanted to ban formal schooling for young children and said they should be taught at home by their parents. The congress opposed him, and the schools stayed open. In 1985 the congress wanted to fire almost the entire Libyan cabinet, including Foreign Minister Ali Treiki. At the last minute Qaddafi appealed for it to desist because he did not have the experienced men to replace them. The congress acquiesced, albeit reluctantly.

That is not, however, how most decisions are taken in Libya. The head of the central bank, for example, found himself the recipient of two contradictory instructions. Major Jalloud sent him a note telling him to transfer several million dollars to foreign banks, while Qaddafi ordered him to keep the money in Libya. The head of the bank pondered the problem. He decided that the best course was to avoid contradicting either of these powerful men. He did not have to ponder long, for it is understood that he had a heart attack.

One day in June 1986 a member of the Ministry of Information was reading a local paper. 'Oh God,' he said. 'They have changed the names of the months.' June had been renamed The Month of Summer. He phoned the Ministry, which had not heard of the change; then he phoned the newspaper editor, who said that Qaddafi had indeed renamed the months, and gave him the list. He scribbled them down. August had been renamed 'The Question-mark Month'. The official asked the editor why. 'Because Qaddafi couldn't think of a name for August, so "Question-mark Month" will have to do for the time being,' said the editor. The official, a loyal supporter of Qaddafi's revolution, could not ignore the ludicrous nature of some of its commands. 'There is a very good reason for these changes,' he said. 'Unfortunately neither I nor anybody else can think what it is.' August eventually became the month of Al Gillah, meaning harvest.

The complexity and almost surreal air of Qaddafi's revolution can be glimpsed at Al Fatah University campus in Tripoli. It is forbidden for foreigners to speak to students and only members of the revolutionary committees, the proselytizers of the revolution, can act as spokesmen. One of the committee members, Mustafa Abukhder, who was twenty-four and in his final year of medical studies, agreed to talk to a group of journalist. Was he a student leader? 'No, there are no leaders,' said Mustafa. Was it permissible to talk to other students? 'No, you must talk to members of the revolutionary committee,' said Mustafa. How many people are members of the committee? 'Every student is a member,' said Mustafa. If all the other students are members of the revolutionary committee, could they be talked to? 'No,' said Mustafa. He had a broad and permanent smile. Why was he smiling? 'I am not smiling,' said Mustafa. 'I always look like this. It is good for the muscles of my face. If you frown, like you, you get lines on your face.'

Mustafa said that in January the workers at the university had all been sacked and moved to factories where they could be 'more productive'. Did they all want to go? 'Of course,' he replied. How is the university run, who cooks the food, cleans the buildings and weeds the lawns? 'We all do,' said Mustafa. 'We have rotas and all the students do the different jobs. It works very well.' But the students at Al Fatah are not nearly as revolutionary as those at Berkeley and the London School of Economics in the late 1960s, who wanted to do away with exams and appoint the academic staff. Mustafa was shocked at the suggestion: 'How could we pick the teachers? We are not qualified. The students could not decide on the academic courses or the exams. That is nonsense. It is the job of the teachers.'

Conversation even with intelligent, government-approved Libyans is difficult. Ahmed Ibrahim al Fagih is author of *The Gazelles*, perhaps the only Libyan play to be performed in London. Al Fagih has prospered under Qaddafi's revolution. His life-style would be envied by most Western authors. He earns about £15,000 a year from the state for writing books. He also gets royalties from his published work. He goes to the Canary Islands for his holidays and his house, which he built and owns, has all modern comforts. His son has an electric guitar, a symbol of Western culture which is frowned on by revolutionary zealots. Early in 1986 Western musical instruments were ceremonially burned in Green Square. Al Fagih said that his books and plays are not censored, but added that his writing was not political. Criticism of religion or the revolution might, he said, meet with official disapproval.

Al Fagih was not being candid. *The Gazelles* is less a play than an ideological tract which reflects, more or less exactly, Qaddafi's ideas. Had it deviated, even slightly, from the official view, it would never have been published and al Fagih, like many members of the former Libyan writers' union, would have found himself in a prison cell. He

43

asked, over lunch at the El Khebir, about the problems in Britain. A few were mentioned: unemployment, poverty, riots in the inner cities, the health service, education. And what, al Fagih was asked, are the problems in Libya? He looked blank. 'What problems?' he said.

Qaddafi has a lot of problems; perhaps the most critical is that from the beginning of 1986 he started to run out of money. The price of a barrel of oil slumped from US $30 to just over $10. As the cost of getting the oil out of the ground, selling and transporting it is about $5 a barrel, the Libyan profit declined from $25 to $5 in six months. Oil income fell from $22 billion a year to $10 billion, then slumped below $8 billion. Imports were cut from $10 billion to $7.5 billion in 1985 and there were further swingeing cuts in 1986. Libya still overspent by $2 billion, and this is Qaddafi's fault. He continued to spend billions on the most sophisticated military hardware from the Soviet Union and Eastern Europe, Argentina and Brazil and to launch grandiose schemes like the Great Man-made River to pump water from underground reservoirs to irrigate large tracts of desert. It is a splendid idea, but the cost could be as much as an astonishing $20 billion.

Qaddafi has brought in austerity measures tough enough to have caused riots in, and even toppled the governments of, Morocco or Egypt. It is a tribute to his popularity, or perhaps to his ruthless control, that the people have accepted their empty shops and shelves, albeit with considerable reluctance.

He does not, as politicians in the West usually do, sugar the pill of his policies. On the contrary, he has told Libyans that he is cutting some imports, not to save the national budget, but because it is good for them: the people should be more self-sufficient and learn to do without Western luxuries. His critics accuse him of being despotic, cruel, arrogant, vain and stupid, but not corrupt. His life-style is modest compared to all the other leaders of the Arab world. He does not have palaces, Rolls-Royces, bathrooms with gold-plated taps, fine paintings or crystal chandeliers like the oil-rich rulers of the Gulf. Nor is there any evidence that he has secreted his country's money away into numbered bank accounts in Switzerland. He is, even his critics agree, financially clean. There is a streak of asceticism running through his life and philosophy that leads back to the Bedouin traditions of the Libyan deserts.

3 Birth of a Leader

Qaddafi was born in a tent in the desert, about twenty miles due south of the seaside town of Sirte. It is not the Hollywood desert of golden sand and rolling dunes, but a flay grey expanse of rocks and bushes. It is burning hot in summer and freezing in winter from the winds that whip off the Mediterranean. Most Libyans live in the towns scattered along the thin coastal strip or at the oases inland. The vast bulk of Libya's 680,000 square miles lies within the Sahara, and Qaddafi spent his infancy and early childhood in a tiny segment of this bulk. It is a place that most people would consider uninhabitable. The climate is cruel and there are none of the basic comforts that the modern West takes for granted: no running water, sewerage or electricity. Qaddafi's family subsisted much as his ancestors had done over the centuries.

Qaddafi's father, Mohammed Abdul Salam bin Hamed bin Mohammed, also known as Abu Meniar (father of the knife), which Qaddafi took as his middle name, and his mother Aisha, were poor Bedouin. Both are now dead; his mother died in 1978 and his father, well over ninety years old, in 1985. Qaddafi remained close to them even when he came to power, although in a curious cultural anachronism he insisted for years that they continue to live in their tent.

His father, a herder of camels and goats, eked out an existence at the bottom of the pile in one of the poorest countries in the world. He belonged to the Qaddadfa, a small tribe with a strange and unpleasant connotation in Arabic: Qaddadfa means those who spit out, or vomit. (His cousin's name Qaddafadam means, literally, 'spitter or vomiter of blood'.) It is possible that this is just etymological bad luck. The tribe's name derives from a Berber word and was Arabized into its present form.

Like most tribes in Libya the Qaddadfa were basically Bedouin Arabs, but showed strains of some of the other peoples who had inhabited and conquered Libya over the years – Berbers, Circassians, Turks, even Jews, who had been important traders in Mediterranean littoral towns such as Misurata.

The Berbers were the original inhabitants of inland Libya. Herodotus describes how in the first millennium before Christ the principal Berber tribe, the Garamantes, from Germa, near modern-day Sebha in the Fezzan, modernized desert warfare with their chariots. The Garamantes controlled the desert caravan routes south–north from the Sahara to the Mediterranean and east–west from Egypt to Mauritania.

Berber hegemony was challenged from the seventh to the eleventh centuries AD by Arab invasions from the east. Arab penetration by two branches of the Arabian tribe, the Bani Sulaim, was most successful in Cyrenaica, where are based most of the present-day tribes which describe themselves as Sa'adi, denoting their relationship to their reputed ancestress, Sa'ada of the Bani Sulaim. Even today the nine main Sa'adi tribes – the large and powerful Abaidat, the Hassa, the Ailat Fayid, the Awlad Hamad (or Bara'asa), the Darsa, the Abid, the Arafa, the Awaqir and the Magharba, consider themselves to be free tribes, whose position in the country is by right of conquest. The lesser, more heterogeneous Marabtin tribes, such as the Zuwaya, are traditionally vassals who have access to their land and water by grace of the Sa'adi.

As the tribes have migrated across Libya, these distinctions have inevitably become more blurred, particularly in Tripolitania and the Fezzan, where there was more Turkish, Berber and (in the south) even Tebu, Hausa and Bornu influence.

The Qaddadfa are one of the more intermixed of the tribes. They are one of the Arab al Gharb, the Arabs of the West, who over the years had been driven out of the lush pastures of the Cyrenaican plateau to the more barren deserts around Sirte by an alliance of Sa'adi tribes led by the Bara'asa (later King Idris's most staunch supporters) and the Magharba.

A lowly tribe, the Qaddadfa nevertheless came under the aegis of the powerful reformist Sufi teachers, the Senussi, in the mid-nineteenth century. Because of the inhospitable nature of the Sirtic desert, the Qaddadfa used to migrate 150–300 miles with their herds to the oases of the Fezzan during winter. In the process, again over a long period of time, they became the vassals of two larger tribes, the numerous Wafala from south of Misurata and, to a lesser extent, the Awlad Suleiman, headed by the powerful Seif al Nasser family, from the Fezzan. As he migrated from the Sirtic desert to the Fezzan, Qaddafi's father herded camels and goats for the Awlad Suleiman – an act which young Muammar long resented.

At the start of the nineteenth century, under the piratical

Karamanli dynasty which nominally ruled Libya for the Ottoman Turks from 1711 to 1911, the Awlad Suleiman, led by Sheikh Abd al Jelil Seif al Nasser, combined with the Qaddadfa and the Warfala to overthrow the ageing Karamanli Bashaw Yussef and put his son Mohammed on the throne instead. Such alliances between the tribes were necessary to maintain power, and it was not long after Qaddafi himself took control in Libya that he was forgetting his grudge with the Awlad Suleiman and linking it to the Warfala and the Mega'ha, from south of Tripoli, to form the bedrock of his regime.

Qaddafi was the youngest child and the only boy. He had three sisters. (One is now dead of cancer, another married a local man from Sirte and the third married Messaoud Abdul Hafez, later Governor of the Fezzan.)

The exact date of his birth is unknown. Qaddafi maintains that it was the spring of 1942. As he would lop at least two years off his age to enter elementary school in Misurata, it is possible that he was born in 1940, or even before. He has said that he remembers the tank battles that raged across the desert during the Second World War, but if his officially recognized date of birth is correct, then he was a babe in arms when the Germans and Italians fought the British and Allied troops during the North Africa campaign, which ended in May 1943. The sound of the German Stukas, which carried out thousands of bombing raids on Libyan territory – 1,000 on Benghazi alone – and the rumble of tanks in the first major armoured battles in the history of warfare, may linger somewhere in his infant subconscious. The fighting was to the east of Qaddafi's home. His parents would not have followed the battles in detail but with their hatred of the Italians they must have watched as the fighting ebbed and flowed past their tents in the Sirtic desert. First the Italians were pushed west across the desert by the British. Next Rommel and his Fifth Light Armoured Division swept the British back across Libya, dislodged them from Benghazi and Tobruk and threatened the Allies in Egypt. Then in October 1942 General Montgomery, commander of the Eighth Army, routed the Germans at the battle of Alamein, one of the most decisive of the Second World War, and the Germans, in rapid retreat, passed back through Sirte *en route* for Tunis. Neither they, nor the Italians, would dominate Libyan soil again.

A common mistake by non-Libyans is to believe that there can be little left in Libya that does not bear the stamp of the foreign occupiers. The Libyans, on the contrary, maintained a fierce level of tribal pride and independence. During the nineteenth century, the Libyan tribes, under only nominal Turkish rule because they were on the outer rim of the Ottoman empire, controlled three ancient trade routes from the Mediterranean to Central Africa.

Although Qaddafi would later deny this stain on his heritage, the main commodity was slaves; despite pressure from Britain and other European powers to curb the slave trade, it continued in Libya, on these remote desert routes, through the nineteenth century. Half the northbound trade was in slaves and 5,000 a year survived the terrible journey across the Sahara.

Qaddafi's parents were illiterate but, in the tradition of the Bedouin, they told stories about their tribe and its history, of tribal heroes and foreign villains. The seeds of the anti-imperialism, the suspicion and dislike of foreigners which would overshadow the foreign policy of Qaddafi's Libya, were planted here at the family hearth. From his religious teacher, whom his father brought in to give his son weekly lessons on the Koran, he heard the story of the Grand Senussi, Mohammed bin Ali al Senussi, one of the great heroes of Libyan history and the man responsible for giving the disparate tribes of the three provinces. Tripolitania, Cyrenaica and the Fezzan, a sense of pride, religion and national identity.

The Grand Senussi was born at the end of the eighteenth century and traced his descent from Fatima, the daughter of the Prophet Mohammed. He studied religion at Fez, in Morocco, then in Cairo, where, like Qaddafi 150 years later, he was branded as unorthodox, even heretical by the Egyptian religious leaders. Al Senussi went to Mecca, then to a remote oasis in the Cyrenaican desert where he established his first Sufi-inspired *zawiya* (or religious lodge). In 1856 he moved his headquarters inland to Jaghbub, close to the Egyptian border. His ascetic, fundamentalist brand of Islam appealed to the warlike Bedouin, and al Senussi became the only figure who could bring law and order to the tribes.

Within three generations the Senussi order spread from Fez to Damascus and from Constantinople to India. It had lodges across north-east Africa, Sudan, Egypt and Arabia. Its success was an essay for the young Qaddafi in the power of Islam to unite not only disparate tribes but countries, and to have an international influence that he would strive for as leader of Libya.

'The Turkish administration may have been negligent and incompetent,' according to John Wright in *Libya: A Modern History*, 'but it was not needlessly harsh or overbearing.' Even such faint praise could not be used about the Italians, who began a cruel and oppressive colonization in 1911. They invaded in massive force armed with the latest war technology, including planes and airships. They met tough resistance from the tribes of Tripolitania, Cyrenaica and the Fezzan. The Italians suffered humiliating defeats and, like invaders before them, withdrew to the coastal strip. From there they set out not merely to rule but to colonize Libya. They saw Libya as their 'fourth shore' and by the end of their occupation more than 100,000 Italians had settled on Libyan land.

At the beginning of the First World War in 1914, the Senussi leader Sayyid Ahmed al Sharif decided to ally with the Turks, who fought with the Germans against the British and Italians. It was the wrong decision. In 1915 the Germans encouraged the Senussi to launch an attack on British positions in the Egyptian Western desert. The order was decisively defeated in battle at Mersa Matruh, whereupon Sayyid Ahmed al Sharif gave up control to his cousin Sayyid Mohammed Idris.

Preferring the quiet life, as he intended to do throughout his rule, Sayyid Mohammed Idris (later King Idris I) promptly made peace with Britain. Idris also treated with the Italians, arriving at a compromise which recognized his reduced sovereignty inland in return for *de facto* Italian control over the coastal towns.

After the war, with a liberal regime in Rome and a number of republics springing up in Europe, Tripolitania pronounced its independence from Italy as an Arab republic, al Jumhuriya al Trabulsiya. However, this political spring did not last long. For soon after his accession to power in 1922, the Italian Fascist dictator, Benito Mussolini, set about the reconquest of Libya, claiming: 'Civilization in fact is what Italy is creating on the fourth shore of our sea – Western civilization in general and Fascist civilization in particular.'

In April 1922 the Tripolitanians, in despair of being able to resolve their own inter-tribal differences, and on the defensive against the Italians, offered to recognize Idris as Amir of all Libya. Idris himself was not up to the challenge. He went into exile in Egypt shortly afterwards. Meanwhile the rump of the Senussi, led by the more militant Sayyid Ahmed al Sharif and by *zawiya* leaders such as Omar Mukhtar, waged a brave guerrilla campaign against Italian penetration of Libya.

In the late 1920s Mussolini sent his most respected general, Rudolfo Graziani, to mop up the resistance. Graziani did so with brutal efficiency. The chronicle of war crimes laid against the Italian general is lengthy. It is claimed that the Italians bombed civilians, killing large numbers of women, children and old people. They raped and disembowelled women, they trampled on copies of the Koran, and they forced men into aeroplanes and threw them out from a height of 400 metres.

Graziani was disturbed by what he called the 'clamour of unpopularity and slander and disparagement which was spread everywhere against me'. He wrote in his book, *The Agony of the Rebellion*, 'My conscience is tranquil and undaunted to see Cyrenaica saved, by pure Fascism, from that invading Levantism which sought to escape from the civilizing Latin force.'

It was 'saved' at a terrible cost. Under Graziani's civilizing force 12,000 Libyans were executed every year and nomads were moved to concentration camps, where they died in their tens of thousands. A 200-mile barbed-wire fence was built along the border with Egypt to stop Libyans escaping. Few Libyan families survived this period intact and Qaddafi lost a grandfather. Three hundred members of his tribe were forced by the Italians to flee into neighbouring Chad.

If Graziani was the arch villain in the Libyan demonology, Qaddafi's boyhood hero was the elderly schoolmaster turned guerrilla leader, Omar Mukhtar. He is one of Libya's modern martyrs and many of Qaddafi's major speeches refer to him. The film, *Lion of the Desert*, which stars Anthony Quinn as Mukhtar and Oliver Reed as Graziani, has been dubbed into Arabic and is shown, almost nightly, on Libyan television.

Mukhtar controlled a rebel band of between 2,000 and 6,000 men, who, as the Italians moved south from Benghazi and Tobruk, attacked their supply lines and harassed their forces. Mukhtar became an expert at the lightning strike against Italian forces, made mostly at night so that Mukhtar gained the reputation of being the 'nocturnal governor' of Cyrenaica, as he moved his men, collected supplies, taxes and recruits from the Bedouin. On 11 September 1931 Mukhtar was captured after he fell from his horse during a clash with Italian troops and was pinned beneath it. Graziani, who was on holiday in Italy, rushed back to preside over his summary trial and execution in front of 20,000 Bedouin. The Libyan resistance quickly crumbled.

After Tripoli finally fell to Montgomery's Eighth Army in January 1943, Libya was destitute. The Italians had done little to promote the country's development, illiteracy was over 90 per cent, and there was no industry and as yet no oil.

What is more, the future of the country was desperately uncertain. British Foreign Secretary Anthony Eden had promised in the House of Commons in January 1942 that, 'His Majesty's government is determined that at the end of the war the Senussi of Cyrenaica will under no circumstances again fall under Italian domination.'

Britain was happy to bring back the exiled Sayyid Idris, who was welcomed with open arms in Cyrenaica. But his writ did not run so easily in Tripolitania, which now looked back to its republican experiments from 1918 to 1922. And then there was the question of continued foreign presence in Libya. By 1943 a Free French brigade under General Leclerc was firmly established in the southern province of the Fezzan. France, anxious to protect its Central and West African interests, was keen to stay on there. The same year the United States air force took over Mellala (later Wheelus) airbase, east of Tripoli, and within the next two years had spent a reported $100 million developing it.

The reality was that the leading world powers, including the Soviet Union, quickly realized Libya's post-war strategic importance. The country that dominated Libya could control the sea routes of the Mediterranean. It would be well placed to influence events in sub-Saharan Africa and also, crucially in Sudan and Egypt, the cradle of Islamic civilization.

As the Council of Foreign Ministers of Britain, France, the United States and the Soviet Union began to discuss the future of Italy's former colonies in 1945, it became clear that all the participants coveted parts of the country in one way or another. Once it had found its feet Italy claimed a right to, or, failing that, at least trusteeship to, its territories acquired before the introduction of Fascism.

In May 1949 the new British Foreign Secretary, Ernest Bevin, and his Italian opposite number, Count Carlo Sforza, came up with a compromise that envisaged granting trusteeships to Britain in Cyrenaica, Italy in Tripolitania and France in the Fezzan, prior to Libya's independence ten years later.

The plan proved unpopular in Libya and, indeed, throughout the Arab world. Skilful lobbying by Libyan delegates prevented it being adopted by the UN General Assembly in 1949. (The reversal of an expected majority in favour of the so-called Bevin–Sforza plan is credited to the single vote of the Haitian, Emile Saint Lot, who now has a street named after him in Tripoli.)

Instead, the UN General Assembly decided Libya should become a sovereign state. UN Commissioner Dr Adrian Pelt of the Netherlands still had to wrestle with strong regional rivalries. The Tripolitanian political parties (linked together in the National Congress Party) objected to the proposal that Sayyid Idris al Senussi should be hereditary monarch, and no one could decide where the capital should be. Eventually it was agreed that Tripoli and Benghazi should be joint capitals, with the seat of government alternating each year.

Nevertheless, by October 1951, a 213-article constitution had been agreed by the National Assembly. On 24 December 1951 Libya became independent under a hereditary monarchy. The government was organized on federal lines, with a bicameral parliament made up of a senate and a house of representatives. As far as Abdul Hamid Bakoush, who was later to become Prime Minister, was concerned, 'Libya was just a tray of sand in 1951. It had an income of £3 million a year, and that came from Britain and the US in rent for the bases on Libyan territory.'

At the time his country was gaining its independence, Qaddafi enrolled at the primary school in Sirte and took the first tentative steps on the road that would lead to the overthrow of the new Libyan monarch, King Idris. He was the first member of his family to read, write and have a formal education. He attended the school during the day and slept on the floor of a mosque at night. He made the long trek home through the desert every Thursday, at the start of the Muslim weekend, and returned on Friday night. He was, according to his father, a serious, taciturn, pious child and had to overcome the double burden of being the oldest boy in class and a Bedouin (and thus treated with some contempt as a country bumpkin by city dwellers).

Qaddafi stayed at his Sirte primary school until he was fourteen, when his family moved to the town of Sebha in the Fezzan. His father became a caretaker on the property of the local tribal leader Seif al Nasser Mohammed and lived in a shack two miles outside the town. Qaddafi enrolled at the Sebha secondary school.

If the Libyan revolution has a starting-point, it is in the classroom of the Sebha school. The charismatic young Qaddafi attracted a number of friends who were to remain with him until he took over power in 1969. Among them was Abdul Salam Jalloud, a member of the Mega'ha tribe who quickly became, and remains to this day, his trusted right-hand man. The two were inseparable, according to a teacher, Abdul Wafi al Ghadi, who described Qaddafi as 'gifted, conscientious and solitary, with a sobriety bordering on asceticism'.

These were heady days in Libya. After centuries of occupation the young citizens of this newly independent country, under the weak King Idris, were flexing their political muscle for the first time. The young were being educated, had access to newspapers, magazines and books, and listened avidly to the radio and to the powerful rhetoric of the Egyptian leader Gamal Abdul Nasser on the Voice of Cairo on Egyptian radio. Qaddafi would also have read the Egyptian papers which circulated widely in Libya and have spoken to Egyptians, many of them fervent Nasserites, who taught in the schools and served in the bureaucracy.

Qaddafi listened to the radio. He memorized Nasser's speeches and could recite them, word for word, to his schoolmates. They thundered daily over the airwaves into Libya, attacking Western imperialism in general and the presence of foreign bases on Libyan soil in particular. They spoke of Arab pride, nationalism and unity.

Next to the Koran the most important book for the adolescent Qaddafi was Nasser's *Philosophy of the Revolution*, which describes how he formed the 'army officers' club' and overthrew the Egyptian monarchy in 1952. Despite its dry title, part of the narrative reads like a thriller and gripped the imagination of the boys at Sebha:

> Our life during that period [as they plotted the revolution] was like a thrilling detective story. We had dark secrets and passwords. We lurked in the shadows; we had caches of pistols and hand-grenades, and firing bullets was our cherished hopes. We made many attempts in this direction and I can still remember our emotions and feelings as we dashed along that melodramatic path.

Like Qaddafi, Nasser's first 'glimmer of Arab awareness began to steal into my consciousness when I was a student in secondary school. I used to go out on a general strike with my comrades every year on the second of December to protest the Balfour Declaration which Britain had made on behalf of the Jews.' Nasser outlines the three pillars of Arab strength:

> When I try to analyse the elements of our strength there are three main sources: the first is that we are a community of neighbouring peoples linked by all the material and moral ties possible.
>
> The second is our land itself and its position on the map. The third is oil, a sinew of material civilization without which all its machines would cease to function.

Nasser's short book contains the inspiration and the blueprint of Qaddafi's revolution.

Nasser's words were in stark contrast to the policies of King Idris, whose squeaky voice would describe a policy which trod a fine line between support for the Arab world and economic dependence on the West, flirting with the Soviet Union while maintaining strong Western alliances. The impoverished government may have had little alternative to this cautious foreign policy, but to the fervent young Nasserites it seemed bland, almost craven.

Idris, despite his honourable bloodline as a Senussi, was a weak man. He liked to think of himself more as a religious than a political leader. He preferred the company of his books to that of people. Power rested in the hands of his family and close associates. Corruption was rife. Libya had joined the Arab League in 1953 and then signed a twenty-year treaty of friendship and alliance with Britain. In return for military facilities, notably staging-posts at Idris airport near Tripoli and Al Adem near Tobruk, the British promised to give Libya £1 million a year in economic aid, more than £2 million in budgetary aid over five years and arms supplies. Under a September 1954 agreement which pledged $42 million in aid over ten years, the United States was allowed to keep its airbase at Wheelus outside Tripoli. Wheelus acted as a staging-post for the American army and air force, along with the Al Watiyah bombing range in Tripolitania, which was used to test bombs and missiles. These bases provided Libya's largest source of income.

The Western and Arab strands of Libya's policy began to unravel dangerously at the time of the Suez crisis in 1956. The Prime Minister, Mustafa bin Halim, ran the risk of alienating his Western allies by supporting Nasser's nationalization of the canal in July and forcing a guarantee from Britain and the United States that the Libyan bases would not be used against Egypt. When Israeli, British and French troops invaded the canal zone there were demands in Libya for full military support for Egypt and for the breaking off of diplomatic relations with Britain and France. Some nationalists went as far as calling for attacks on the British bases. On 31 October bin Halim issued a decree declaring the country in a state of siege, but the Egyptian military attaché in Tripoli, Ismail Sadiq, distributed arms to Libyans and encouraged attacks on British installations. Bin Halim defused the crisis. The Egyptian attaché was escorted to the Egyptian border and expelled. President Nasser sent a note of apology to King Idris.

There was no overt political opposition in Libya – this was banned by Idris shortly after his reign began – but the trade unions became a base for anti-monarchist sympathies and the government took steps to curb union membership, although it was not the total ban the Qaddafi would impose in the 1970s.

What opposition did develop in the late 1950s and 1960s was small and clandestine: there were Baathists, Muslim Brothers, and, by far the most popular, largely because of their pan-Arab, anti-Western message, the Nasserites.

Anti-government feeling was strong enough, however, for the United States to be concerned about the fragile state of Libya. A secret report from the deputy director of naval intelligence, Charles B. Martell, written in October 1957, described 'a gradual deterioration of US–Libyan relations under the weak and ineffectual Abdul Majid Kubar [Libyan Prime Minister who succeeded bin Halim]'. The report said:

> Criticism of the United States has been growing both in official circles and in the press. . . . Egyptian anti-Western propaganda efforts have increased, largely through press media and the large number of Egyptian school teachers employed in Libya. These efforts have had considerable success with the Libyan public because of their concentration on the theme of Arab nationalism and the ever-popular denunciations of 'imperialists'.

It was an accurate report and concisely summed up the mood of the schoolboy on the first steps of his revolutionary career at the secondary school in Sebha.

Qaddafi was the oldest student in his class, and the taciturn boy that his teacher remembers had turned into a rhetorical firebrand. One of his classmates remembers that Qaddafi would harangue his colleagues from a garden wall. His friends sometimes carried a small stool around with them so that he could stand on it and make a speech.

His ambition had already extended beyond the schoolroom. One of his teachers at Sebha was an Egyptian, Mahmoud Efay, who said that Qaddafi once came to see him after class and handed him a note which asked three questions: 'What is a pyramid organization and which is the best manner to organize such a structure? Does the possibility of organizing a revolution in Libya exist? If a revolution were to be carried out in Libya would Egypt come to the assistance of the Libyan people?' Efay says he was sympathetic to the young revolutionary and explained the principles of pyramid organization. He pointed out the necessity of keeping each of the organization's departments separate from one another and how difficult it was for the central leadership to achieve maximum efficiency and co-ordination. Efay also told him that every revolution needed the support of the army. Qaddafi had received his first lesson in revolutionary tactics.

Qaddafi soon came to the notice of the local authorities. In October 1961 he organized a demonstration to protest against Syria's decision to break its agreement of unity with Egypt. This was not an issue likely to inflame the blood of Libyans, most of whom disliked Egypt and Syria and could not have cared less whether they united or not. Only the tiny number of Baathists in Libya would have shown more than a passing interest in it. According to Frederick Muscat, who has written a flattering and officially approved biography of Qaddafi, Muammar spent a week planning the demonstration. It was, Muscat says, the first test of his secret organization of schoolfriends which Qaddafi had begun to form two years before.

Qaddafi had developed a reputation at school for political trouble-making and a group had formed around him, including Jalloud, Hussein Sharif, Ibrahim Ibjad and Mohammed Khalil. He had tapped a source of youthful rebellion in Sebha and, on the morning of 5 October, he led a crowd of demonstrators into the town centre. They held Egyptian flags and portraits of Nasser. Qaddafi stood on his little stool and gave a rousing speech railing against the presence of foreign bases in Libya. He then organized a whip-round of 5 piastres a head to send cables of support to the Egyptian President. There were scuffles with the local police and twenty students were arrested.

The next day he was hauled up before the head of the town's ruling family, Seif al Nasser Mohammed. Nasser had reasons other than the demonstration to dislike him. Qaddafi and five of his friends had also been involved in a protest that was religious rather than political. They had gone to the hotel in Sebha run by an Egyptian, Yani Enkaledad, and had broken the windows and bottles in protest against the alcohol which, they claimed, was being drunk on the premises. Yani's partner was Seif al Nasser Mohammed.

Nasser told Qaddafi that he would be expelled from the Sebha school and a month later the expulsion, signed by the Minister of Education, was sent to the school's headmaster:

> With reference to the report submitted by you the deputy principal of Sebha central school and the controller of the boarding section concerning the students who led the 5 October 1961 demonstration I convey to you the penalties which we deemed necessary to be applied against the following students who perpetrated acts contrary to their duties as students:
> 1) Muammar Abu Meniar al Qaddafi discharged from the school and prevented from studying at the schools of the state.

Qaddafi, and Muscat, have described his expulsion as 'oppressive' and 'cruel'. By the standards of modern Libya under Qaddafi it was distinctly mild. Students at Benghazi and Tripoli Universities have been hanged for similar offences. The reluctance of the monarchy to stamp down on its dissidents, and the inefficiency of its police and secret service, were weaknesses in the system that Qaddafi would exploit over the next eight years.

In fact the authorities showed compassion. Qaddafi's father appealed to Seif al Nasser Mohammed to find his son a place at another school in Misurata, which he did. There was one problem. Qaddafi was nineteen and too old to enrol at a secondary school. He went to a sympathetic official in the municipal department in Sebha who gave him a false birth certificate. At the secondary school his underground civilian movement, started in Sebha, began to grow. Qaddafi's claim that it already had 'thousands of supporters' cannot be checked, but it seems unlikely. According to his colleague and fellow revolutionary in Misurata, Omar Meheishi, who spoke nostalgically about the early days with Qaddafi and others who took part in the coup on Libyan television in 1970, Qaddafi won a certain local fame: 'He had become notorious for his frank speaking and his invective directed against the English-language inspector Mr Johnson. One day when Mr Johnson was questioning a pupil whom Qaddafi was trying to prompt with the answers, the inspector, reasonably enough, was angry and ordered him to be quiet. Then Muammar got up and coldly reminded him that he had no place among us, he was no more than an agent of imperialism. When I heard this I was so struck by his audacity that I wanted to meet him, to get to know him.' Meheishi said that the group had decided to follow Nasser 'and Nasser alone. Our line was to support Arab nationalism.'

Qaddafi's colleagues were still flirting with a number of revolutionary movements: the Baathists; the Arab Nationalist Movement, set up in Beirut by George Habash who would later start the radical Palestinian group the Popular Front for the Liberation of Palestine; and even Castro's revolution in Cuba. However, they had a cohesion and strict discipline unusual for revolutionary students. Qaddafi laid down the rules: no drinking, no card playing, no fooling around with women. Members of the group were told to pray regularly and study hard. 'We were careful on the other hand to let some of our members appear as card players in order to avoid attracting the attention of the authorities,' Qaddafi told Egyptian television in 1969 as he relived the years leading up to the coup. 'The rules of our meetings were very strict. All committee members were obliged to be present and the absence of only one of us meant that a meeting was invalid.'

He had soaked up the Arab revolutionary ideas which poured out of Egypt under Nasser and, although he seemed to have no clear ideology of his own, he had produced a potent cocktail of revolution and Islamic fundamentalism. He was disciplined and immensely hard-working, and he had tapped into the reservoirs of underground discontent that existed in Libya under King Idris. He was poised to plan the revolution and, taking the advice of his mentor, President Nasser, and his Egyptian schoolmaster in Sebha, he decided that the most fertile ground lay in the Libyan armed forces.

4   The Young Cadet

A British non-commissioned officer with a huge handlebar moustache, nick-named by his Libyan cadets Abu Shanip (father of moustaches), was giving a lecture at the Royal Libyan Military Academy in Benghazi. A member of the British Military Mission to Libya, he stood before a sand tray and, with the help of small models, showed the deployment of a battalion in the desert. He asked one of the officer cadets, Muammar Qaddafi, a question. 'He looked me straight in the eyes, turned his head and spat on the floor,' said the NCO.

Qaddafi was not a model soldier. He had enrolled in the academy, set up in 1957 as the Libyan equivalent of Sandhurst to produce the first generation of young officers in the fledgling Libyan army, in the seventh intake in 1963. It was one of the many lapses in Libyan security under King Idris that Qaddafi was allowed to join the army at all, especially the Cyrenaican Defence Force, the elite group designed to protect the King. He already had a record with both the police and the Libyan security services. Either they did not bother to check his files, or they thought that a sharp dose of military service would knock the rebellious ideas out of his head. They were wrong.

The regular Libyan army was small, about 5,000 men, and poorly armed. The officers were trained by the British Military Mission which had fifty-four warrant officers and senior NCOs deployed throughout Libya. It was headed by Colonel Ted Lough from 1960 to 1966. During the 1960s Lough and his men sensed a restlessness among the cadets and felt that trouble was brewing. 'I noticed a wind blowing from the East,' said Lough. 'A lot of the cadets were pro-Nasser, anti-Western and particularly anti-American.'

Although Colonel Lough had hundreds of Libyan cadets and officers under his command during his six years as commanding officers, Qaddafi stands out clearly and unpleasantly in his memory. 'He was our most backward cadet,' said Lough. 'He did twice as long as the others at the Benghazi academy; 98 per cent of the cadets passed their exams, 2 per cent failed, and he was one of them. He was probably not as stupid as I thought at the time. Part of his problem was that he wouldn't learn English. I didn't like him and he made life difficult for my officers and men because he went out of his way to be rude to them.'

The NCO, who has asked that his name should not be published because he fears reprisals, said that Qaddafi was protected by the Libyan commander in chief at Benghazi. Qaddafi was reported frequently for insubordination and rudeness but nothing was ever done. 'I treated him with kid gloves. There was nothing I could do. We were only there in an advisory capacity. We had no executive power, so we had to lump it.'

Lough and the NCO both accuse the young cadet of crimes more serious than rudeness. They both believe that Qaddafi was responsible for the murder of one of his fellow cadets and the mistreatment of many more. 'He was inherently cruel,' said Lough.

The NCO was at the rifle butts at the academy when the cadets were having target practice under a Libyan officer. Qaddafi, the senior cadet because he was the oldest and had been there the longest, was second in command. The NCO was about 50 yards away when he saw

> this bloke tied hands and feet being dragged towards the butts. He was loosely tied and they let him get free. He was fifty or sixty yards out from the firing point, and the officer gave the order and Qaddafi and a couple of the others started firing at him, or playing with him really. They fired to the right, then to the left. The bloke was running this way and that. Then they shot him. The officer went over, took out his revolver and gave him the *coup de grâce*. . . . They left the body lying there and then they kind of celebrated. They were all laughing.

The NCO made an official report to his senior officer, Lough, the next morning. He believed that the man had been accused of 'some sexual offence, possibly homosexuality', and that Qaddafi's fellow officers had carried out a summary execution. Lough, in turn, reported the killing to the Libyan chief of staff, but nothing, he says, was done.

Both Lough and his NCO say that this incident was extreme and isolated, but that discipline in general in the Libyan army was harsh. It depended largely on fear. Living conditions were also primitive, on the level, they say, of the British army in the 1930s. Punishment was common. If any of the cadets were found guilty of a sexual or religious offence, the whole of the academy would come on parade, the guilty cadet would have to stand in front and they would all come up and hit him across the face, starting with Qaddafi because he was the senior cadet.

Qaddafi did not always avoid punishment, according to Lough and his NCO. When the commander of the academy was away, a Major Jalal Dalgeli was in charge. He had 'no time for Qaddafi' and would punish him for insolence. They remember seeing the future leader of Libya crawling on his hands and knees in the gravel in the burning heat, his rucksack full of sand to weigh him down. He was forced to crawl until the skin came off his knees.

These unpleasant aspects of his military career have been left out of the official accounts. But if Qaddafi, as Lough maintains, was a rotten officer cadet, it is not surprising. His intention was not to become an upstanding officer in the army of King Idris, but to overthrow it. According to his fellow officer, Jalloud, who, according to Lough, was better military material, Qaddafi would have preferred a civilian career and did not enjoy his army service.

At school in Misurata he had decided to plan the revolution with two parallel organizations, civilian and military. His friend from primary school in Sirte, Mohammed Khalil, would recruit the civilians: traders, teachers, workers and civil servants. Qaddafi warned him specifically to be cautious about attempting to enlist anyone older than themselves. It was to be a youthful revolution. Qaddafi would join the army and subvert it. He realized that the officers were not 'intellectually' ready to follow the revolutionary path, but that nationalism, which had a strong emotional pull in the army, and personal friendship might seduce them.

He set about sedition in a meticulous way. In each barracks two officers were charged with assembling information: stocks of arms, lists of officers, their names and seniority. The first meeting of the central committee of the Free Officers' Movement, as Qaddafi called his incipient revolutionary group, was held on the beach at Talmisa in 1964. As Qaddafi explained on Egyptian television in 1969:

As these meetings became more and more frequent we were faced with many difficulties; we had to meet during vacations and often late at night. We also had to seek out places far from the town and sometimes we had to travel hundreds of miles and to put up with long sessions in atrocious weather. We would often sleep in the open. Of course all members of the committee had to buy private cars and put them at the disposal of the Movement. We decided that the entire pay of all free officers should constitute a fund upon which the Movement could draw at any time and up to any amount that might be necessary. Later it was decided that each member of the central committee should present a monthly report on officers not belonging to the Movement, especially on officers of a higher rank so as to avoid injustice when the moment came.

At Misurata and the academy Qaddafi quickly recruited the corps of his revolution. One of them, Captain Sulaiman Mahmoud, spoke to Mirella Bianco about Qaddafi's careful choice of co-conspirators; as she wrote in *Gadafi: Voice from the Desert*: 'He observed them one by one, gathering the greatest possible amount of information about each officer he selected, so that by the time an approach was made he would be sure that the new recruit was worthy of confidence and psychologically ready to follow him.'

Qaddafi operated a cell structure, with each member of the 'first cells' being called upon to set up a second cell. However, even he was not careful enough. Of his close colleagues in the growing Free Officers' Movement in Misurata, a number, including Omar Meheishi and Abdul Moneim al Houni, later members of his twelve-man Revolutionary Command Council, would betray him.

Although Qaddafi worked evenings, weekends and days off at his main job, subversion, it seems odd that he should have been so successful so quickly and that the army was made of such malleable stuff. Even the British military advisers, who existed on the fringe of the Libyan army establishment and the government, knew that something was up.

'Our relations with King Idris were very good,' said Lough, 'although I thought he was a silly old man. He sat in Tobruk drinking camel's milk and eating dates. He didn't know what was going on. He was afraid of his own army. We got him six Centurion tanks but he was so anxious about an army revolt that he locked them away.'

The role of the British advisers was not as straightforward as it appeared, officially. The NCO was clear about his role: 'We were there not really to train the army but to keep an eye on it, to find out what was going on. We made regular reports about it to the British embassy people. I felt for a long time that something pretty drastic was going to happen.' He also said that one of its functions was to see that the Libyan army was not armed too effectively. This was deemed to be in the interest of both the Foreign Office in London and of King Idris in Libya.

'We got them pudding basins but no weapons. Under pressure from me London did send them out some Bren guns but our policy was not to arm them too well,' said Lough, who thought most of the officers were more interested in politics than the army. 'There were obviously changes going on. The educated Libyans got commissions into the army, then they sat around in the coffee shops talking politics. They certainly didn't like going into the desert. They had two armoured divisions with Saladin armoured cars, but they did less travelling in a month than we did in a week.'

And if 'conditions were ripe for revolution', as Lough believed as early as 1965, his main suspect was Qaddafi. Lough made a series of reports on him to the representative of British intelligence in Libya, the commercial attaché at the British embassy in Tripoli. Lough is still angry that the British Foreign Office paid what he believes was such scant attention to his intelligence reports.

Lough suspected Qaddafi of being involved in the assassination of the commander of the Benghazi Military Academy in 1963. In fact he thought Qaddafi pulled the trigger:

> He was shot near the academy and rushed to the military hospital. I suspected that Qaddafi had been involved because we knew then that he was the head of a pretty suspicious group of young officers. I held the commander's hand at the hospital. He was critically wounded and I asked him who had shot him. He murmured a first name, Muammar, then he died.

Lough's second report was in 1964 when Qaddafi joined the army's signals unit in Benghazi: 'He ordered the most elaborate radio equipment, which was way beyond their needs. They had a radio transmitter which could cover the whole of Libya. My signals adviser told me what was going on, but I couldn't get access to the set. It was in a secure part of the compound in Benghazi. Qaddafi had got himself into a strong position with a weak commanding officer.'

Lough reported this to the intelligence officer at the British embassy. Five years before Qaddafi's coup took place he was already on file with the British government as a key suspect.

Lough's irritation that the Foreign Office and intelligence services did not take him seriously appears to be justified. Qaddafi in 1966 was trying to get abroad for further military training. His motives had less to do with revolution than with curiosity, since he had never left Libya before. He applied first to be sent on a four-month military training mission to the United States, and with five of his colleagues was interviewed by the deputy head of mission at the US embassy in Tripoli, Herman Eilts. Eilts was struck by Qaddafi's boyish naivety, but impressed with the deference that the others showed him: 'He was already showing signs of leadership.' It was an unremarkable meeting, but not in retrospect. Thirteen years later the naive young officer cadet would plan Eilts's assassination in Cairo. Qaddafi was not granted permission to go to the United States, but not because of any ban Eilts imposed: 'Maybe the Libyan authorities were on to Qaddafi at that time and they turned him down. I never heard any more about it.'

In 1966, despite Lough's reports that Qaddafi was a troublemaker, a murderer, a possible assassin and a revolutionary, he was granted permission to attend a four-month training course in Britain. 'I can't understand it. He must have slipped through the net,' said Lough.

Qaddafi went first to Beaconsfield, where he spent four weeks studying English, before going to a three-month 'troop leader' course at the Royal Armoured Corps headquarters in Bovington in Dorset to learn about driving maintenance, signals and gunnery on armoured vehicles – probably the Saladin armoured car that the Libyans used for desert patrols, and possibly the Centurion tank. He was trained to use the signals equipment on these vehicles, and to fire the 76 and 105 mm tank guns. His English teacher at Beaconsfield, who has asked not to be named, vaguely remembers him as an 'unremarkable and rather pleasant young man' who sent him a Christmas card the following year. 'Many of the students did that,' he said.

According to Frederick Muscat, Qaddafi hated Beaconsfield, London and the British in general: 'Beneath its artificial aura of prosperity the young revolutionary could see the darker side of this seemingly carefree city.' He was offended by the racial discrimination in London: 'Only the coloured people swept the streets of London, drove its buses, washed the dishes in the restaurants and pimped their lives away for meagre earnings which barely permitted them to subsist.' It is difficult to take Qaddafi seriously here since in revolutionary Libya only the immigrant workers from Tunisia, Morocco or Chad do the menial tasks of sweeping the streets or working in hotels and restaurants.

Muscat continues: 'He was determined that Libya had to go through a process of revolution but likewise he was determined that the revolution would not be allowed to lead Libya or to lower the Libyan people to what he considered the social and moral decay into which London had fallen.'

Qaddafi spent his time in a mood of high moral disgust: 'As he walked past Eros he tried to put his thoughts in order. Admittedly Britain had come a long way in terms of material progress but the people were still slaves, slaves to modern materialism.' He insisted on wearing his traditional Bedouin robes in London, although he rarely does so in Tripoli. Muscat concludes the London episode as dismally as he began it: 'The remaining few weeks in London dragged into days and finally the time came for Muammar to leave Britain and return home.'

At home the government of King Idris appeared to be crumbling even without the help of Qaddafi and his revolutionary movement. The United States was anxious about the weakness of the King and the threat this posed to its strategic and, increasingly, economic interests in Libya. An oil boom, one of the most spectacular in history, reminiscent in the greed and graft it aroused of the American gold rush, was under way.

The first big strikes had been made in 1959 under the Sirtic desert, where Qaddafi's father and his forefathers had eked out a living and herded their camels. Just below them lay oceans of the purest and most accessible oil in the world. No state developed and exploited its new-found oil faster than Libya in the 1960s. By the end of the decade it had overtaken Kuwait to become the fourth-largest oil producer in the world. The international oil companies, smelling not only the pure crude, but also its location in a then pro-Western country with US and British military bases in place to protect the oilfields, flapped like buzzards around the Libyan government in a rush to get oil concessions.

The Libyan government did not handle its new resources well. A secret US government memorandum to the President, John Kennedy, on 16 October 1962 describes 'sheer financial chaos in Libya. Despite prospects of huge oil revenues, Libyans have gone in for so much uncontrolled spending (and grafting) that a cash shortage has arisen. Naturally they want us to bail them out. A few words from you to the Crown Prince about fiscal responsibility could help save us several million bucks.'

If the few words were indeed uttered, nobody listened. Instead of pacifying discontent in Libya, the oil funds made things worse. Corruption among those close to the royal palace was rife. The young revolutionaries felt that money was pouring into the pockets of a privileged elite and that the international oil companies were exploiting the weak and gullible government of King Idris. Their suspicions were at least partly justified, although Idris's government was no more corrupt than those of many other oil-producing countries and less than some. Efforts were made to use the revenues to build schools, universities and hospitals, and money did trickle down to the ordinary Libyans. But the pace was not fast enough.

Frank Waddams, an expert on the Libyan oil industry, wrote in

The Libyan Oil Industry: 'The Libyan government had no experience of oil taxation. This knowledge was all on the side of the major internationals who advised the government and succeeded in obtaining an ideal contract from their own viewpoint. The favourable terms of the Libyan law were a foretaste of paradise for the oil companies.' Waddams pointed out that the companies 'controlled the posted prices for oil, had superior knowledge of operations and markets, an overwhelming possession of technical and financial resources and a built-in resistance to changes adverse to themselves'.

The US government, with its millions of dollars' worth of investments, watched the country carefully and did not like what it saw. In a secret report called 'US Policy Towards Libya' and dated 15 March 1960, the US National Security Council painted a bleak but accurate picture:

> There is little loyalty to him [the King] among the younger urban elements who do not now have significant political power but who will have such power in the future. Although there are no political parties in Libya there are a number of loose political factions and interest groups and pan-Arab nationalism has considerable appeal, particularly to the younger urban elements.

It recommended that the Libyan government should 'curb temptations to ostentation and graft inherent in large oil revenues'.

The United States appeared, from this secret document, to be looking to the British government to intervene if the Idris regime were toppled. The report says: 'Although the British would be reluctant to intervene with force in Libya to maintain a regime favourable to their interests, they would probably do so if it seemed the only way to preserve their position.'

The NSC laid down policy guidelines, which were approved by the President. Guidelines 34, 35 and 36 would have supported the worst fears of Qaddafi and his co-conspirators about the 'imperialist' designs on Libya:

> 34) identify and discreetly maintain contact through appropriate channels with those groups in Libya which are likely to play a significant role in the event of the King's death. 35) Develop contingency plans regarding action to be taken in the event of a violent upheaval in Libya and co-ordinate appropriate aspects of such planning with the UK. 36) Be prepared to respond to a Libyan request for armed assistance under the American doctrine for the Middle East and co-ordinate planning for such assistance

with the UK's plans for carrying out its obligations under the UK–Libyan treaty of alliance.

By June 1967, when Israel went to war against Egypt and the Arab states, there were few in Libya or outside it who believed Idris could survive. Although the Libyan government issued a statement pledging its support for the Arab nation and its hostility to Zionism, it simply did not have the military resources to enter the fray. Arab nationalist feelings were running so high that the people had no time for Idris's pragmatism. There were demonstrations in Tripoli, Jews were killed by mobs, and there were attacks on British and American property. The oil workers led by Dr Sulaiman Maghribi, later Qaddafi's first Prime Minister, imposed a total oil embargo for a month, costing Libya $71.5 million a day in lost revenue.

A secret report to the White House from the National Security Council on 17 June 1967 said:

> Herewith a fear that will mount: a Nasser takeover of Libya after US–UK bases are withdrawn. The takeover could be either from within or without, probably the former; it would put Nasser on easy street with oil and bring great pressure to bear on Tunisia. We shall try to buy time on the bases. A good deal depends on whether the King can sweat it out.

The King was certainly sweating. By the late 1960s different groups of plotters were circling the throne like aircraft waiting to land at an international airport.

Peter Wakefield, now Sir Peter, and then counsellor and consul-general at the British embassy in Benghazi, believes that the turmoil in Libya after the 1967 war was the real starting-point for Qaddafi's coup. According to Wakefield, Qaddafi was sent by the Libyan government with a contingent of soldiers to help Egypt at the time of the Six Day War, but it had only just reached the frontier when the war was over and the government saw no point in sending them on. 'Some of the young officers were so upset by this that there was dissension in the contingent,' said Wakefield. 'One or two of them insisted on going over to Egypt. Qaddafi, however, came back.'

Wakefield said that at the outbreak of the war Benghazi 'went out of control':

> This is not generally known because there were no correspondents there at the time. At 8 a.m. on the first day of the war the British embassy started phoning everyone up and telling them to evacuate or lie low. By 9 a.m. the mob was around the Benghazi embassy

building and tried to burn us down. It burned the consulate next door and we were very lucky to get the staff out over the top. Libyans burned up some British armoured cars which had come into town from the Royal Inniskilling Fusiliers' camp just outside Benghazi. They dumped some of the men on our doorstep; they were badly burned but luckily still alive. I ordered the Inniskillings into the embassy and they got in without bloodshed.

Then the mob moved off to have a go at the Americans. Just at the moment the phones came back on line the Americans were being very hard pressed. I asked them, 'Would they like to be evacuated?' They said, 'yes please.' I smashed up the machines [for sending ciphers] and took the Americans with us to the Inniskilling camp. That night we evacuated all the Brits including the Bluebell dancing girls [who were performing in a night-club] and we spent the night in the camp. The authorities gained control the next day.

In 1969 at least three and possibly four groups were jostling to unseat the King. One of the plots, by Abdul Aziz al Shehli, the chief of staff of the army, may have enjoyed the royal seal of approval. It is believed that the King wanted to make way for Abdul Aziz and his brother Omar, his favourites, but he knew that he was so unpopular among the Libyan people that to give any successor a seal of approval would be a political death warrant. So he would go on his holidays, allow the al Shehlis to depose him, then return and live happily ever after in his palace in Tobruk.

Another coup was being organized by a Libyan army colonel and is said to have had the backing of the Iraqi government. Yet another was plotted by the former Libyan Prime Minister Bakoush, who had resigned the year before. 'The country was up for grabs in 1969,' he said:

I knew of a group of intellectuals and army officers who were planning to take over. I was part of this group. I cannot give you the other names because most of them are still in Libya. We were delayed because of an internal argument. One faction wanted to assure continuity and not have a *coup d'état* that led to another coup. The argument was about whether, when we took power from the King by force, we would keep him as a symbol and allow him to remain as King in name only.

If everyone had been a little more patient the King would have resigned of his own accord. When Idris packed his 400 suitcases and went on his summer holiday to Greece and Turkey, he was old, ill and fed up. He had tried to abdicate once before but was persuaded by the royal court to stay because no suitable successor could be found. In Athens the old mood came over him again. He called the head of the parliament and the head of the upper house to Greece and handed them his abdication letter. He told them to call an emergency session of the parliament and announce his abdication.

According to Wakefield, the British government also knew about the King's intention to abdicate, but reports were 'vague':

> We were wondering who the hell would take over. Abdul Aziz al Shehli was in a position to do so but we never discovered a real plan. The older brother Omar was so discredited there was no possibility of his doing it. In the circumstances we simply encouraged the government to be on the look-out and to take precautions. One battalion of the Cyrenaican Defence Force was on the alert but Qaddafi actually managed to infiltrate it through a particularly good young officer. Because of my concern about the situation I was due for an appointment that Monday morning, 1 September, with the Prime Minister.

In July 1970 David Newsom, the US ambassador to Tripoli until shortly before the coup in 1969, told a congressional foreign relations committee:

> One thing that is not generally recognized is the fact that there are wide-spread reports, which many people are inclined to believe, that because of some attacks which, for the first time in Libyan history, were directed against the King himself in the period just prior to the coup, the King may either himself have abdicated or was arranging a coup of his own with some of the elements around him against the Crown Prince in whom he never had confidence. So that it is quite certain that the coup came at a time of considerable political uncertainty, including uncertainty as to what the King's own intentions were.

The King hesitated too long. Qaddafi's plans were already well laid and, Bakoush says, the Americans knew about his plot and assisted him. This is denied by the US State Department and by David Newsom, who says that he first heard about Qaddafi after the coup when the British gave him the statements by Colonel Lough and his NCO. He told the foreign relations committee:

> It is pretty hard for anyone outside of the country to spot the precise time or nature of a political upheaval when the Prime Minister and the King of the country are themselves caught by

surprise. However, the record will show that in my period before departing from Libya I expressed to Washington, and I expressed to most of the senior political leaders on whom I called, my concern at the growing detachment of the King from the responsibilities of power in Libya, the growing corruption and interference in governmental affairs which was becoming characteristic of a number of people around the King, and I left with an expressed personal concern that the situation politically in Libya was not healthy.

However, Bakoush says the Americans knew because he had told them:

I heard about Qaddafi's coup attempt two months before it took place. I knew the names of five or six of the men concerned. I was the Libyan ambassador in Paris and I went to the American embassy to have a chat about it. I talked in particular to the CIA station chief there. This was almost two months before the coup and I told them all about it. I also went to see Idris in Turkey and told him. He refused to go back to Libya.

Bakoush says he was not the only source of US information:

The Americans had contacts with Qaddafi through the embassy in Tripoli. They encouraged him to take over. There were dozens of CIA operatives in Libya at that time and they knew what was going on. The Americans were frightened of the senior officers and the intelligentsia in Libya because they thought that these people were independent and could not be run as puppets.

They thought there would be a link between these people and Nasser in Egypt and they were afraid that Libya would move out of their hands into a close alliance with Egypt. So they discovered this group of ignorant young officers, unknown to everyone, led by Qaddafi. They seemed weak, inspired largely by personal ambition and could, in the US opinion, be controlled.

There have been many conspiracy theories about the United States role in Qaddafi's coup, but for the first time Bakoush had gone on the record and said that not only did the Americans know because he told them about the impending coup, but that they helped Qaddafi overthrow the King. Bakoush's refusal to give names that might corroborate his theory does not help his credibility. It may be that the Americans did not jump on to his revolutionary bandwagon in 1969, or that they refused to back subsequent coup attempts against Qaddafi. There is no other evidence that the United States assisted

Qaddafi before his coup. But it is difficult to believe that the United States did not know about him. Colonel Lough finds the British and American government claims of ignorance incredible. The British had a fat file on Qaddafi as early as 1966 and they shared their intelligence on a routine basis with the Americans. If Abdul Aziz al Shehli knew about the plot and Qaddafi is certain that he did, it would be extraordinary if he had not, as chief of staff of the army, informed the King, the British and the Americans. Qaddafi's organization was so leaky that there were few in high positions in Libya who did not know that trouble was coming.

Colonel Aziz Shenib, number three in the Libyan army and deputy director of military training, says that he and other senior officers knew about Qaddafi's plot but 'did not take it seriously':

> We always thought it was rubbish, that Qaddafi and his group would never be able to do anything. One of his group came to me and explained everything about the plot. We didn't ignore it exactly but we didn't want to create a big row in the country at that time about discovering the plot, we didn't want to make a noise. We thought the best way was to send these young officers to courses outside. Then after a while they would come back and we would place them here and there in the army.

According to Wakefield, Qaddafi was one of these young officers and was due to go for his second six-month training session in Britain on 11 September. He had been chosen for special instruction on the new missiles that Britain was in the process of selling to Libya. 'That is why Qaddafi had to carry out his coup by the beginning of September,' says Wakefield.

Whether he enjoyed the tacit or active support of the US or not, Qaddafi was moving his coup attempt into top gear. It was in many respects a copy-book operation. In other ways it resembled a Keystone Cops movie. It was at first planned to take place on 21 March 1969 and his orders went out to his fellow conspirators. Then the plump Egyptian singer, Oum Kalthoum, inadvertently made her mark on political history. She was giving a concert in Benghazi and most of the royal and military figures due for arrest were going to the show. To interrupt a performance by the Arab world's most famous singer would have been bad taste and, worse, it was a benefit performance for the Palestinian revolutionary group, Fatah. With a fine sense of protocol Qaddafi called off his coup that night and rescheduled it for September.

5   The Coup

Peter Wakefield had spent all night in the embassy sending coded messages to the Foreign Office in London about serious disturbances in Libya which seemed, to him, the prelude to a *coup d'état*. He told London that he had arranged for a meeting with the Libyan Prime Minister that morning, 1 September, to discuss the crisis. At 5 a.m. he walked through the deserted streets of Benghazi towards his house on the seafront, turned a corner and bumped into a group of men wearing army fatigues and carrying guns. 'They were as surprised as I was,' said Wakefield. The armed men were courteous and asked Wakefield to go to the Benghazi radio station where he was introduced to a very young man wearing full army uniform and looking, Wakefield recalled, 'very dapper'. It was Qaddafi, and in this unceremonious way Britain became the first foreign power to know that Libya had a new ruler.

Wakefield explained that he was the acting British ambassador and asked Qaddafi what he intended to do. 'He was not very specific,' said Wakefield. 'He said it was time for a "rearrangement" of things inside Libya and that his "committee", which had taken power, would honour all international obligations. He refused to say who the committee members were.' Wakefield went back to the embassy and sent the historic news to London, although he admitted his message was pretty vague. He did not know how radical this new regime might be or that Qaddafi was the leader. 'In my telegram I merely said that he spoke with remarkable authority,' said Wakefield. He cancelled his appointment with the now deposed Prime Minister.

Despite Qaddafi's claim that the coup was ten years in the making, it ended up early on the morning of 1 September as a last-minute panic with a lot of chaos and just a touch of farce. Qaddafi, in an exuberant mood during a television chat show after the coup, described the night's events. He and his co-conspirators talked with enthusiasm, topping each other's stories about who made what mistakes that night like college students discussing a prank.

Qaddafi said that he had not told the others the exact time of the coup, or 'H hour' as he called it, because he was afraid of foreign intervention and because he knew that information had already leaked to senior officers in the army.

He ordered one of his key men, Omar Meheishi, to take an early-evening flight to Tripoli to organize the takeover of the army barracks in the capital. When Meheishi got to Benghazi airport he found the plane was overbooked. Luckily an airport official turned out to be an army friend and managed to squeeze him on to the flight. At Tripoli airport he grabbed a taxi to the Tarhuna barracks where other plotters were waiting for him. The unfortunate Meheishi rushed into the barracks, only to realize that he had left his gun and ammunition in the taxi, which had already sped off. (He got them back after the revolution.) In Benghazi Qaddafi, together with two army captains, Mohammed al Magharief and Mustafa Kharroubi, planned to begin their move to take over the Berka barracks and the radio station at 1 a.m. Just as they were about to set off, two military policemen came up and asked for their help in recovering a moped which had been involved in a motor accident just up the road. As the minutes ticked towards 1 a.m., the military policemen discussed the road accident and wondered whether it ought to be reported to higher authorities. Qaddafi lost his temper: 'Yes, yes,' he snapped. 'We'll do something about it tomorrow.'

As Qaddafi and Kharroubi set off again, another military policeman, who had been recruited as one of the conspirators but had lost his nerve at the last moment, rushed up to Qaddafi and said the game was up: they had been found out. Qaddafi said later, 'The bastard. I must confess I almost believed the operation had been discovered. In any case it was too late to turn back then. I said to myself, we must face up to it whatever the cost.'

Qaddafi gave a vivid, and candid, description of the next disaster:

> With the help of two soldiers I crammed my jeep full of munitions and light machine-guns, so convinced was I that we were going to meet resistance and that all hell was going to break loose. Kharroubi took command of the group which was to occupy the Berka barracks and off he went. I jumped into my jeep and drove to the head of my column. I took the Jilyana road as planned and then took a left fork. The vehicles following me, which were supposed to come with me to occupy the radio station, well they went straight on at full speed heading for Berka. I found myself alone in my jeep, bowling along the road to Benghazi, no lights, nothing.

Meanwhile, the officer with the task of taking the radio station in Tripoli returned to the barracks in panic. He had been driving around the city and could not find it. One of Qaddafi's closest colleagues, Lieutenant Abdul Moneim al Houni, jumped into a car and drove him there.

Another young officer, Khweldi Hameidi, led a group to arrest the Crown Prince in his palace. 'And naturally you made a hash of it,' Qaddafi said in the television debate.

'Come on, I didn't make a hash of it, whatever you may say,' said Hameidi. 'Let me tell you what really happened. First we went ahead and arrested the officials of communications and the police officials. Things did not go smoothly. For example, the office in charge of the depots was at the cinema and we had to go and seek him there. Then while we were driving along the Bir Miji road my car took a dangerous bend at too high a speed and the vehicle following me, with Lieutenant Musa Abdul Salam in it, crashed into it. Musa was injured.'

Then a police car arrived and the police, seeing the two wrecked cars, asked for the drivers' documents and papers. Musa kept his head and asked them to drive him back to the army barracks for medical treatment. When he arrived he promptly arrested them.

Hameidi continued his story, which was beginning to sound like a rollicking farce: 'When we arrived at the Crown Prince's palace things began to go wrong.' They climbed over the wall of the palace, alerted the sentries (who opened fire), then scoured the palace for the Prince, who could not be found. When he had heard the gunfire, he had run out of the palace and hidden in the swimming-pool. He was arrested next morning.

Jalloud, with Lieutenant al Houni, had to take over the anti-aircraft batteries around Tripoli and had 600 men at his command. That night he discovered that they had hardly any ammunition, and 1,050 rounds had to be rationed between them. His men had one and a half bullets each. As it happened Jalloud met no resistance.

On the whole it was a remarkably bloodless coup. The only real fighting that night was at the barracks of the Cyrenaica Defence Force in Gurnada where one member of the force was killed and fifteen were wounded.

By 6 a.m., as Qaddafi arrived at the radio station in Benghazi, martial music was playing on the radio from Tripoli and Libya was effectively in his hands.

At 6.30 a.m. Qaddafi went on the air with Communiqué One, the first message of the new regime. The broadcast was anonymous.

(Qaddafi did not announce his name, or those of the other officers, until a week after the coup. Uncharacteristically modest for Qaddafi, this was done for security's sake.) It was a shrewd statement, giving the impression that the rebels had taken power at the request of the Libyan people. It has been prepared hurriedly: Qaddafi had scrawled a few notes on a piece of paper and he ad-libbed the rest on the air.

People of Libya. In response to your own will, fulfilling your most heartfelt wishes, answering your incessant demands for change and regeneration and your longing to strive towards these ends, listening to your incitement to rebel, your armed forces have undertaken the overthrow of the reactionary and corrupt regime, the stench of which has sickened and horrified us all. At a single blow your gallant army has toppled these idols and has destroyed their images. By a single stroke it has lightened the long dark night in which the Turkish domination was followed first by Italian rule, then by this reactionary and decadent regime, which was no more than a hotbed of extortion, faction, treachery and treason.

In his final paragraph he tried to set the minds of Libya's foreign allies at rest:

On this occasion I have pleasure in assuring all our foreign friends that they need have no fears either for their property or for their safety. They are under the protection of our armed forces. And I would add, moreover, that our enterprise is in no sense directed against any state whatever, nor against international agreements or recognized international law. This is purely an internal affair.

There was immediate recognition from the more radical Arab regimes, Iraq, Syria, Sudan and Egypt, although none of them had the faintest idea what they were recognizing. Qaddafi's main fear on his first morning of power was intervention by Britain or the United States or both. If Bakoush, and other leading Libyans, are correct, then the Americans already knew about the coup attempt and were unlikely to oppose it.

The British gave Qaddafi more cause for concern. Would they intervene? The government certainly considered it, and in Benghazi Wakefield was weighing the odds. 'We didn't have a large number of troops in Benghazi but we had troops exercising in the desert, probably enough to do the job,' he said. But, according to Wakefield, the King, having decided to abdicate, seemed curiously uninterested in direct action. He did, however, send his counsellor, Omar al Shehli, to London to consult with the British Foreign Secretary, Michael

Stewart, who made it quite clear that Britain would do nothing; even agreeing to see the King's envoy was no more than an effort to do the decent thing: 'My motive in acceding to Idris's request to send an envoy to London was simply that it is not creditable in the long run to appear to cut off your old friends once they are down,' Stewart says. Idris, however, was down and out.

Wakefield, in retrospect, ascribes Stewart's inaction to lack of political will. 'It was too soon after Suez,' says Wakefield. 'The Labour administration [under Prime Minister Harold Wilson] was not the kind of lot who would have fought for anything.' But London had other reasons. According to a Foreign Office official, the British government, believing that Idris was doomed, did not see a coup by a young, dynamic leader as necessarily against the interests of Britain and the West. 'It was clearly not, at that time, worth fighting to keep a weak and unpopular king in power,' said the official.

Stewart said that the Foreign Office was concerned about the instability of Idris's regime, but had no knowledge of a coup and no intention of intervening militarily. His first impression of the new Libyan regime was not very hopeful. 'It was a new kind of dictatorship to replace the old, a monarch replaced by a military leader.'

Both the United States and Britain realized by 1969 that the days of practice bombing runs in the Libyan desert were numbered and the bases used as staging-posts had become less essential with the longer range of modern transport aircraft. Their military bases had become such a cause of popular resentment that even under Idris they would almost certainly have been closed down. The signs had been there for at least six years. On 30 November 1963, a secret memorandum for the President said: 'We need Wheelus base for quick deployments to the Middle East and India, but a weak Libyan government is letting our title be eroded.' A confidential report by the then US ambassador David Newsom, on 8 June 1967, at the time of the Six Day War against Israel which provoked widespread anti-US demonstrations in Libya, sounded the death knell for Wheelus:

We have numerous reports of possible demonstrations against embassy and Wheelus. . . . Wheelus just reported two efforts throw dynamite [sic] on to base. Government making maximum effort but we are not sure it will be enough. Feeling obviously running high. Accordingly we are reducing embassy staff to minimum tomorrow and removing last of classified files to Wheelus. Marine guards will remain on duty for final destruct crypto gear if necessary.

The United States put a 1970 deadline on its tenure of Wheelus. The British also decided, in 1968, to withdraw its own military presence by 1971. In the event, things happened slightly more quickly.

On 29 October Qaddafi sent the British a note asking them to evacuate their bases as soon as possible, and Britain did so by March 1970. The Americans agreed to go in June. Contrary to its expectations Britain, as a prominent supporter of the monarchy, suffered most. Barclays, Libya's largest bank, was nationalized and Jalloud cancelled King Idris's $1.5 billion arms deal with the British Aircraft Corporation for Thunderbird and Rapier missile systems. The US and British strategy was now limited to a single objective: to establish a working relationship with the new rulers of Libya so that their oil interests would be protected. The oil companies had seen the danger signals. Oasis, the second-largest producer after Exxon, prepared a memorandum shortly after the coup, which said: 'Once the regime is stable it will launch a frontal attack on the oil industry. Driven by its missionary zeal of absolute economic sovereignty the regime will use every possible means of persuasion. But it is unlikely that it will resort to outright expropriation.'

There was, at first, a slight hope that Libya's new regime would not be just another kind of dictatorship. It had been a remarkable coup in many ways: its leaders were all young, under thirty years old, inexperienced and virtually unknown. Not only had it been almost bloodless in execution, but its treatment of the old regime was extremely mild by the bloody standards of Middle East and African coups. Many of the key figures in the *ancien regime* were imprisoned, but none was executed. Some, like Bakoush, were imprisoned in luxury: 'I was treated very well,' he said. 'I had television, radio, books, good food. Friends could come and see me.' Others, like Colonel Aziz Shenib, were jailed under harsher circumstances, but later Shenib was released and given a key job in the foreign service.

On the evening of the coup Egypt sent Mohammed Heikal, the journalist and adviser to Nasser, to meet the young revolutionaries. He was greeted at Benghazi airport by one of Qaddafi's most senior colleagues, Colonel Adam Hawaz (the coup leader's other associates were mainly lieutenants and captains). Heikal immediately asked, 'Where is Abdul Aziz [al Shehli]?', the man both Nasser and Heikal presumed had taken power. Hawaz explained that Shehli was in prison. 'Who are you?' said Heikal. According to Heikal, Hawaz was non-committal. 'The brothers are eagerly awaiting you. They will be coming to see you shortly,' he said. 'Our leader is a sincere man, an Arab nationalist. Egypt should stand by him.'

When Heikal finally met Qaddafi later that night he was 'astonished'.

> I had written an article some months previously in which I said that the future of Arab unity should not depend on some young officer who gained control of a radio station. He had memorized every word of the piece. He told me it had caused him to hesitate in his plans for some time. Eventually he had decided to go against the advice offered in the article. I told him I was astonished that he had been able to repeat whole chunks of my article. But I got the impression that he would learn things by heart and not really digest them.

Heikal says that he was 'horrified' by Qaddafi's naivety, sincerity and intensity. Qaddafi said: 'We have carried out this revolution. Now it is for Nasser to tell us what to do.' Heikal spent most of the time calming down an excited Qaddafi, who repeatedly talked of his visions of Arab unity. 'I knew what Nasser would have to say about his unity plans. He was interested in Arab solidarity and co-ordinated action, but not unity.'

Qaddafi was to get his first lesson in the cold, pragmatic politics of the Arab world. 'I explained to him what I knew would be our policy line,' said Heikal. 'We would like maximum co-operation but unity would have to wait until after the war against Israel. I told him Libya, with its three thousand miles of Mediterranean seafront, was more important to Arab nationalism than Sudan. The important thing for him now was to protect his revolution. I told him we would help in this. But I stressed the importance of caution.'

When Heikal returned to Cairo he wrote about the leaders of the coup in glowing terms in the Egyptian newspaper *Al Ahram*: 'What I saw in Libya affected me more deeply than anything else I've seen. This is a different type of youth . . . the generation of young people whose upbringing and schooling were dominated by the sufferings caused by the setback in the Arab cause.'

Of more practical help to Qaddafi in consolidating his rule was Egyptian technical and administrative support co-ordinated by the intelligence officer assigned by Nasser to Tripoli, Colonel Fathi al Dib. Much of the day-to-day working of the civil service, as well as the medical and educational system, was carried out by the Egyptians. Although Gaddafi was later to stage a series of intellectual seminars where views were, in theory, to be freely exchanged, freedom of expression was stamped on in the earliest stages of the new regime. Executive power was concentrated largely in the hands of the new Revolutionary Command Council (RCC) composed of twelve of Qaddafi's closest colleagues, all military officers. In December the RCC was designated in the new constitution as 'the highest authority in the Libyan Arab Republic. Measures adopted by the RC may not be challenged before anybody.'

Within five days of the coup the council was petitioned by a group of Benghazi intellectuals who requested that democracy should be a priority of the revolution. They received no reply. In November they presented their nine-page memorandum again, asking this time for an appointment with Qaddafi. Again there was no reply.

To meet demands for some sort of political life, the RCC appointed a council of ministers, headed by Dr Sulaiman Maghribi, the Baathist-leaning lawyer plucked from prison where he was serving a sentence for leading a strike of oil workers. Maghribi led a cabinet of nobodies. The only important portfolios, defence and the interior, were given to the two soldiers in the council, Colonels Adam Hawaz and Musa Ahmed, who had played leading roles in the Free Officers' Movement, but were not actually members of the RCC. They had close contacts with the British and American embassies and were largely responsible for selling the new regime to the West. There was little else for them to do. With no real authority under the RCC, they regularly asked for permission to resign.

The true face of the new regime was expressed by the RCC's early ban on political parties. 'Henceforth he who engages in party activities commits treason,' Qaddafi said in October.

Libya's thriving press was brought under control by the removal of subsidies and then by suspension of licences. In January 1970 the RCC announced that only the official newspaper *Al Thawra* (The Revolution) would receive government advertising. By May 1970 a new labour law had banned all trade unions. People's courts, presided over by a member of the RCC, were established to try supporters of the old regime and suspected dissidents under the new one.

Qaddafi worked round the clock from his new headquarters in the Aziziya barracks. His most important task was ensuring the support of the army. The success of the coup had made a soldier's life a glamorous one with huge potential for promotion, even to president perhaps, and he had no trouble in doubling the army's size, particularly as he doubled the soldiers' pay.

The army's 600 officers were whittled down to 170, as most of those of the rank of major and above were arrested, posted abroad or pensioned off. Qaddafi, as commander in chief and head of state, promoted himself from captain to colonel. He quickly developed a political style, based on the rhetoric of Nasser, but with disquieting echoes of Benito Mussolini. His watchwords were liberty, socialism and unity, and always, incessantly, 'the people'.

In one not particularly long speech in Sebha on 22 September 1969 he used the word 'people' seventy-seven times:

> The armed forces are an integral and inseparable part of this people, and when they proclaimed the principles of liberty, social-ism and unity they proclaimed nothing new. It is the people which believes in liberty, socialism and unity and inspired them to the armed forces, its vanguard, which imposed them on the enemies of the people with the force of arms, thus, the people is the teacher, the inspirer and the pioneer.

As there were no elections, unions, free newspaper or even opinion polls, what 'the people' thought was entirely dependent on what Qaddafi decided they would think.

It was doubtful whether 'the people' fully embraced the puri-tanism of the young colonel. Symbols of what he considered decadent culture were attacked. At first it was all fairly innocuous. Alcohol was banned, as were traffic signs and advertising in Roman script, which were replaced by Arabic. One night, revolver in hand, the Libyan leader and his heavily armed entourage marched into Tripoli's Bowlerina night-club, where a mildly erotic floor show featuring foreign dancing girls was in progress, and ordered its immediate closure.

The regime's policies soon took a more unpleasant and xenophobic turn. A small number of Jews and up to 30,000 Italians, many with small farms, were expelled. The main Catholic cathedral of the Sacred Heart of Jesus was closed down and turned into the Gamal Abdul Nasser Mosque. On Nasser's advise Qaddafi did not immedi-ately attack Western economic interests. There was no reason to. Europe and North America, not to mention the Soviet Union, were falling over themselves to get along with the new regime.

It soon became clear that not all 'the people' supported Qaddafi. Only four months after he took power, a group of his fellow officers in the army were trying to take it away from him.

Colonels Adam Hawaz and Musa Ahmed, having helped set up Qaddafi's coup, suddenly became terrified it would mean Libya being 'taken to Nasser'. They were arrested by the security police and charged with plotting to overthrow the government. Since the coup attempt took place as the Anglo-Libyan talks on the evacuation of the military bases began, Qaddafi found a convenient motive. He said the plotters wanted imperialism to stay on in Libya. Ironically, the CIA is suspected by some, including John Cooley in his book *Libyan Sandstorm*, of tipping Qaddafi off about the coup attempt. There is more evidence that it was the Egyptian intelligence officer Colonel al Dib who first heard of the plot and passed the word along to Khweldi Hameidi, the RCC officer then in charge of the potentially dangerous (because of its strong royalist–Sennussi tradition) province of Cyrenaica.

The young officers were still jittery when, in June 1970, a second plot was uncovered. A prominent member of the Senussi family, Prince Abdullah al Abid, the nephew of King Idris and known as the 'Black Prince', tried to sneak a group of 5,000 mercenaries through the deserts of Chad into the Fezzan, where they planned to arm tribes still loyal to King Idris and march on Tripoli.

Prince Abdullah sent a small advance group on a scouting mission into the Fezzan, where they were immediately caught by Libyan security agents. Again there have been allegations that the CIA was involved, but they have little substance. In fact, a Tunisian opposition politician heard about the Black Prince's plot and told the French intelligence service, who in turn tipped off Qaddafi.

A general veto by Western governments on exiles' attempts to topple Qaddafi became even clearer towards the end of the year when a truly spectacular plot came to light. It was conceived by King Idris's former counsellor Omar al Shehli, whose brother Abdul Aziz's conspiracy to depose the King had been so rudely interrupted by Libya's new leader. This time Shehli, in exile in Geneva, tried to hire a British security firm headed by the retired British army colonel, David Stirling. The plan involved recruiting mercenaries to launch an assault on the main prison in Tripoli, code-named 'the Hilton' by the plotters, and to free hundreds of political prisoners including Abdul Aziz himself. These prisoners would then be armed and would storm Qaddafi's headquarters at the Aziziya barracks. The whole ludicrous episode is described in detail in *The Hilton Assignment* by Patrick Seale and Maureen McConville.

The plot thickened when Stirling's associate James Kent was approached by one of Qaddafi's closest colleagues in the RCC, Major al Houni, now in charge of counter-intelligence, with a project to assassinate Omar al Shehli. Kent fobbed the Libyans off by saying that he needed to do a feasibility study for the assassination at a cost of $60,000.

According to Seale and McConville, Stirling was warned off the coup attempt by the British secret service and he agreed to drop it.

Kent, however, decided to go ahead. He hired French mercenaries and bought a boat in Toulon. Kent was once again approached by British intelligence and told to lay off. But it was Italian intelligence, the Servizio Informazione Difesa, which finally pulled the plug on this unhappy operation.

The attack on 'the Hilton' had been planned for 31 March 1971. On 21 March Kent's boat was preparing to set sail from Trieste to pick up a cargo of arms in Yugoslavia when Italian police swarmed aboard and arrested the captain and the crew.

The only significance of this coup attempt is the message it sent to Qaddafi: that the Europeans were happy enough that he was in power. He could therefore go ahead with his own coup against the international oil companies, without fear of foreign military intervention.

Libya's oil negotiations, conducted by the young Major Jalloud, are still considered by one American oil executive, who was among the first casualties, to have been 'state of the art'. Jalloud, who had recently been appointed Prime Minister, became a perfect balance for Qaddafi. While Qaddafi was the theoretician of the revolution, Jalloud was its practical and worldly face. Jalloud spent long hours studying newspaper reports and theses on the workings of the global economy. He had taken a signals course in San Antonia, Texas, in 1966 while Qaddafi was having a miserable time at his training course in England.

Jalloud, on the other hand, took to the United States and liked to say that his trip had given him an insight into the minds of Americans, especially American women. He boasted to his envious colleagues in Libya of his exploits with American women, and of his taste and capacity for bourbon. It was not all fun. Jalloud was impressed by US technology and fascinated by its economy. 'The US always lies about its economic performance,' he said. 'The US economy is doomed because it is conducted by crazy people who don't know their business.'

Jalloud made sure he knew the oil business. During the 1960s power had been totally in the hands of the oil companies, who, despite the activity of the Organization of Petroleum Exporting Countries (OPEC), could pick off the producers one by one. Jalloud turned the tables. It was the oil companies that now became isolated and were forced to compete against each other for better terms – a strategy of divide and rule. His first move was to reach a technical and co-operation agreement with Algeria in October 1969. Algeria had recently been offering concessions to American independent oil companies which were prepared to pay more for their privileges than the major oil companies. In January the Libyan National Oil Company resurrected a demand of the old regime for a 20 per cent increase in the Libyan government's cut from oil production. The oil companies were naturally reluctant to hand over a higher proportion of their profits, so Jalloud concentrated on one of the indepedent companies in Libya, Armand Hammer's Occidental Oil. He demanded that Occidental cut its output by almost 50 per cent, a devastating blow to a company with no other sources of crude oil. As Jalloud confirmed in a television interview in 1986, '[Occidental] needed the oil and we used this weakness to achieve our historic victory.'

Hammer approached Esso, the largest company in the world, to supply its shortfall of Libyan oil at cost price. Esso refused. Jalloud then played his ace. If Occidental agreed to pay an extra 30 cents on a barrel of oil it could increase its production back almost to its old level. Occidental had no choice, and its capitulation had a domino effect on the other oil companies in Libya.

The timing of the Tripoli agreements could not have been better for Libya. In 1970 Syria had closed down the Tapline which carried Saudi crude to Mediterranean ports, and oil was at a premium.

Other countries began taking the Libyan lead, and at an OPEC meeting in Venezuela in December the oil producers vied with each other to come up with tougher demands to put to the oil companies.

US diplomat James E. Akins, later ambassador to Saudi Arabia, writing in *Foreign Affairs*, said:

> It seemed at the time, and still does, that they had little choice. Libya had $2 billion in currency reserves; its demands were not unreasonable; its officials could not be corrupted or convinced, and, most important, Libyan oil could not be made up elsewhere. The Libyans, it should be noted, did not threaten to cut off oil deliveries to the consumer countries; their only threat was not to allow the companies to have the oil unless they paid the higher taxes.

The Libyan demands, according to Atkins,

> demonstrated like a flash of lightning in a summer sky what the new situation was; to be sure it was Europe that was extraordinarily vulnerable and extraordinarily oblivious, the United States as a consumer was not yet affected. . . . But these points were incidental to the fundamental fact, which was that a threat to withhold oil could now be effectively employed to produce higher prices. Hindsight suggestions as to how that threat might have been

countered, either by the companies or by the American or other governments, seem to me quite unrealistic and the charge that the State Department by inaction was to blame for creating a new monster is, in simple terms, nonsense. The Libyans were competent men in a strong position; they played their hand straight and found it a winning one.

So far the Libyan policy had followed the dire warnings of the Oasis 1969 memorandum. At the end of 1971 the nightmare that had haunted the industry since the coup began to come true: Jalloud moved to expropriate oilfields.

His first victim was British Petroleum, and Qaddafi had a specific reason for making it a target: he had a grudge against the oil company itself. It was rather a dramatic gesture over what he saw as a slight by the British government, at that time the majority owner of BP, against the Arab nation. In their hasty withdrawal from commitments 'East of Suez' the British had that year granted independence to the sheikhdoms now known as the United Arab Emirates. However, three small islands off Sharjah, one of the emirates, had long been disputed between Iran and the rulers of the Arabian peninsula. The British arbitrarily gave them to the Shah of Iran, which Qaddafi saw as an intolerable piece of British arrogance and anti-Arabism.

On 7 December Qaddafi set in motion the nationalization of BP's 50 per cent share in the thriving Sarir oilfield which had reserves of 11 billion barrels of crude. Britain tried to retaliate by having the sales of oil from Sarir blacked by other oil companies. But the operation was impossible to police. There were always ready markets for the oil in the Soviet Union, Eastern Europe and, increasingly, Italy.

Over the next two years Libya demanded 51 per cent participation in the remaining Western oil companies operating on its soil. Those who refused, like Hunt Oil, Texaco and Shell, were nationalized outright.

Qaddafi had every reason to feel pleased with himself. He had taken on the Western imperialists and won a resounding victory. Foreign troops had left Libyan soil and the most powerful corporations in the world, the oil companies, had been forced to play his game. The Libyan national coffers, already packed with oil revenues, were overflowing.

The money paid by the West was to be used, in part at least, to undermine it.

6 Terror Inc.

The Nile Hilton in Cairo was, in the early 1970s, the only hotel in town. In the evening the staircases and the foyer were clothed in pink tulle for fashionable wedding receptions, and during the season it was full of American and European tourists. Men in Bermuda shorts and women in bikinis swatted the flies away as they lay by the swimming-pool while the illegal money changers, taxi drivers and touts swarmed around the rear entrance. On 22 September 1970 the Hilton had a very different clientele. The hotel was cordoned off by armed secur-ity men and even some of the guests – Yasser Arafat, chairman of the Palestine Liberation Organization, King Hussein of Jordan and Colonel Qaddafi – wore revolvers in their belts.

President Nasser had called this conference in a last-ditch effort to end the bloody confrontation between King Hussein's army and the guerrillas of the PLO in Amman, Jordan. He sat in his suite on the eleventh floor eating cheese sandwiches and trying to prevent his brother Arabs tearing each other apart. The strain was to kill him.

Qaddafi had been in power for a year and this was his first major international event. He did not win many hearts or minds as he strutted around the Hilton corridors, sporting his revolver and his clutch of bodyguards. In fact this pure young man from the desert got on everybody's nerves. He was one of the most outspoken leaders on the question of the Palestinian struggle, and, although the hotel was full of Arab rulers at each other's throats, he still lectured them about Arab unity:

> Palestine cannot be restored by negative means, nor by classes, nor by donations. It can only be attained by the march of the Arab masses, free of fetters, restrictions and narrow regionalism. We will arrive in Palestine, brothers, when we have pulled down the walls which impede the fusion of the Arab people in the battle. We will reach the holy lands only when we have removed our borders and partitions. We shall liberate Palestine when the Arab world has become one solid front.

This rhetoric did not go down well. Arafat, who has always disliked Qaddafi, called him the 'knight of revolutionary phrases'. According to his biographer, Alan Hart, one of Arafat's few amusements is telling jokes at Qaddafi's expense. The Palestinians were angry at the Libyan leader's forthright observation that only 10 per cent of the forty separate organizations within the Palestinian resistance had directed their efforts against the Zionist enemy, and the rest had been feuding with each other and Arab states. Nasser's aide, Gahazzen Bashir, found Qaddafi 'dynamic in an irritating way, like a little boy, very erratic'. A senior Russian diplomat was less generous. 'He is crazy,' he told Bashir.

Even Nasser sometimes found his young protégé slightly wearing and made fun of his naivety. He told Mohammed Heikal about Qaddafi's first confrontation with a shrimp. He was having dinner with Nasser and the first course was shrimp. Qaddafi looked at his plate with horror. 'What are these?' he said. 'Locusts? Do you eat locusts in Egypt?' 'They are shrimps,' said Nasser and explained that they were a kind of fish. Qaddafi refused to eat them: 'I can't eat fish. It is not killed according to correct Muslim ritual with someone saying "*Allahu akbar*" at the moment of slaughter.'

It was not only shrimps that confused Qaddafi. He had been wooed and flattered by the Arab world and by the West. As the former US Secretary of State William Rogers said: 'I guess we were kind of euphoric about him at first.' He was, the United States thought, young, malleable and virulently anti-Communist: in fact their kind of guy. They had offered to sell him Phantom jet fighters and the French were competing to sell him their advanced fighter plane, the Mirage.

His diplomatic efforts to gain his ideal of Arab unity had not gone as well as he had hoped. There had been an agreement in principle for unity between Egypt, Sudan and Libya in the Tripoli Pact, signed by Nasser, Qaddafi and President Jaafar Numeiri of Sudan in December 1969, but it existed more on paper than in reality and it was a long way from the total union which Qaddafi had suggested in the first moments of his revolution.

He had begun to see chinks in the revolutionary armour of his hero, Nasser, who, instead of fighting the Israelis to remove the stain of the 1967 defeat, appeared instead to be negotiating with the Zionists by accepting the Middle East peace plan of William Rogers to end the terrible war of attrition between Egypt and Israel along the Suez canal. Both Nasser and Hussein had supported UN Resolution 242 which proposed that territory cannot be acquired by force and then kept; it is still, in the 1980s, a key element in Middle East peace plans. The resolution proposed that Israel evacuate the Sinai, which it had conquered from Egypt in the 1967 war, and withdraw to permanent and secure borders; that a 'just settlement' be made for Palestinian refugees; and that the state of belligerency between Israel and the Arabs be terminated. For Qaddafi the resolution was a sell-out to the Israelis. The only solution, for him, lay in 'continuous war'.

Qaddafi toured the Arab world to explain his uncompromising view of the Middle East struggle. It did not go well. As John Wright points out in *Libya: A Modern History*:

> Gadafi was ready to prepare the Arab world for the annihilation of Israel. In May and June [1970] he and Foreign Minister Busair toured Iraq, Jordan, Syria, Lebanon and Egypt to propose a grand strategic plan for co-ordinated military action . . .
>
> The tour seems to have been something of a revelation to Gadafi. He found that the so-called 'eastern front' of Jordan, Syria and Iraq was little more than a name; he also found that his advice was not welcome, and was even resented.

In short, Wright points out, the other Arab leaders found Qaddafi's intrusion, as the leader of a country far from the war zone which had taken part in none of the Arab/Israeli wars, impertinent.

The Palestinians were beginning to believe that the solution to their problems lay not in diplomacy or even conventional warfare, but in terror. The Cairo conference was held in the shadow of a terrorist extravaganza, the most complex, co-ordinated quadruple hijacking in the history of air piracy.

On 6 September, just two weeks before the Cairo conference, Waddi Haddad, the late mastermind of the Popular Front for the Liberation of Palestine, staged what even he described as a 'spectacular' on Dawson's Field, a former RAF base in the desert outside Amman in Jordan. Haddad, who was George Habash's deputy, had arranged the simultaneous hijacking of four planes. An American and a Swiss jet were hijacked and flown to Dawson's Field. Then an El Al Boeing was boarded by Leila Khaled, a young Palestinian woman, and Patrick Arguello, a Nicaraguan sympathizer. Immediately after take-off Khaled announced that she was hijacking the plane, but El Al security guards managed to shoot and kill Arguello and overpower Khaled, who had hidden two grenades in her bra. She pulled the pins on both but neither exploded. The plane returned to London where Khaled was arrested. Two other terrorists who had failed to get on the El Al flight boarded a Pan Am 747 bound for New York with 170 people on board and hijacked it. They took it to Cairo where the hostages were released and the plane was blown up. Four days later, with the other two planes still at Dawson's Field, Haddad decided he needed a British plane to force the British authorities to release Khaled. Three PFLP members promptly took over BOAC flight 775 from Bombay to London as it refuelled in Bahrain. It too was flown to Dawson's Field.

The PFLP demanded that three of their members should be freed from Swiss jails, three from West Germany, Khaled from Britain and a number of Palestinian prisoners from Israel. The Israelis refused to negotiate, but the governments of Britain, West Germany and Switzerland agreed to release the prisoners. On 15 September Haddad ordered the 375 hostages, who had sat on the planes in the desert for four days, to be released. The planes were blown up in full view of the world's television and the Jordanian army.

It was a lesson for the Palestinians, the Arabs and the young Qaddafi that terrorism could work, although it went against the declaration of the Palestine National Council, under Arafat's guidance, that armed attacks on civilians were detrimental to the Palestinian cause and contrary to official policy. The Palestinian extremists not only ignored the edict, but increased their terror tactics. The PFLO claimed the Dawson's Field operation as a resounding success: the governments of three Western countries had been made to look feeble.

The negative side of this terror spectacular is rarely discussed by the PLO. King Hussein had faced a build-up of the PLO guerrilla groups in Amman. They had carried on cross-border operations into Israel which had brought the revenge of the Israeli Defence Force against Jordan, and they were on the point of creating a separate state inside Jordan. Crown Prince Hassan, who rules Jordan with King Hussein, described how he would have to drive through Palestinian road blocks as he went to his office in the royal palace each morning: 'I was often sniped at. The situation was getting out of control.' There had been several assassination attempts against the King.

Dawson's Field was the last straw. On 17 September the King unleashed his loyal Bedouin army on the Palestinian guerrillas, attacking their bases and headquarters. The fighting raged in Amman for eleven days and more than 1,000, mostly Palestinian, fighters were killed and thousands injured.

This battle went down in the annals of Palestinian military history as 'Black September'. It spawned a terrorist group of the same name, composed mostly of PFLP members, who would cause international havoc over the next few years. The Cairo conference was held during the fighting in an effort to stop it.

Qaddafi had no doubt which side he was on. Although Hussein argued persuasively that the PLO had been attempting to take over his country, Qaddafi supported the Palestinians. In his simplistic world view he associated all monarchs in the Arab world with King Idris, whose weak and corrupt regime he had deposed. It followed logically from the premise that all monarchs were like Idris that all kings should be deposed. It was a syllogism whose brute force both Hussein and King Hassan of Morocco would feel before long.

During the conference Qaddafi sat with Bashir, Nasser's adviser, in the Nile Hilton coffee shop on the ground floor. 'We were sitting at this very table,' said Bashir.

> Qaddafi said that in his opinion the Egyptian government should set up a gallows outside in the public square and hang King Hussein. I smiled. I really thought he must be joking. Qaddafi then said: 'Look, I'm serious. If you don't do it I will go on Egyptian television and announce myself that Hussein should be hanged and that the Egyptian government didn't have the courage to do it.' I tried to explain to him that it was not really possible for Nasser to hang the ruler of another Arab state and that it was not perhaps the best thing to do. I thought then that we were dealing with a dangerous young man.

Qaddafi continued his theme at the full session of the conference that day. Heikal, who was present, has chronicled part of the discussion in his book *The Road to Ramadan*.

> King Feisal of Saudi Arabia: 'I agree with your excellency [President Nasser] that all this [the battles in Amman] appears to be a plan to liquidate the resistance movement.'
> Gaddafi: 'I don't agree with the efforts you are making. I think we should send armed forces to Amman, armed forces from Iraq and Syria.'
> Feisal: 'You want to send our armies to fight in Jordan. It is not practicable.'
> Nasser: 'I think we should be patient.'
> Feisal: 'I think that if we are to send our armies anywhere we should send them to fight the Jews.'
> Ghadaffi: 'What Hussein is doing is worse than the Jews. It's only a difference in the names.'
> Nasser: 'The difficulty is that if we send troops to Jordan this will

only result in the liquidation of the rest of the Palestinians. I would like you to hear the contents of a message I received this morning from the Soviet Union. They are asking us to exercise the utmost restraint because the international situation is becoming extremely delicate and any miscalculation might result in the Arabs losing all the reputation which they have recovered over the past three years.'

Feisal: 'I don't think you should call an Arab king a madman who should be taken to an asylum.'

Ghadaffi: 'But all his family are mad. It's a matter of record.' [A reference to the mental illness of Hussein's father and brother.]

Feisal: 'Well, perhaps all of us are mad.'

Nasser: 'Sometimes when you see what is going on in the Arab world, your majesty, I think this may be so. I suggest we appoint a doctor to examine us regularly and find out who is crazy.'

On 28 September, after complaining of pains in his legs, Nasser had a massive heart attack and died. He was the only Arab leader who could, perhaps, have had a restraining hand on Qaddafi and guided him through the minefields of Arab politics. But it is doubtful. Nasser had found his reckless young friend hard to handle and he would not have been a willing student in the politics of compromise. Heikal gives a chilling example of Qaddafi's 'simplistic way of looking at questions of war and peace'. Nasser had been outlining to the Libyan leader the relative strengths of the Arabs and Israel in tanks, aircraft and artillery when the latter grew impatient. 'No, no, we should go straight to an overall war and liquidate Israel,' he said. Nasser explained that this was impossible. The international situation would not allow them to do it. Neither the Russians nor the Americans would permit a situation that might lead to a nuclear war. 'Do the Israelis have nuclear bombs?' Qaddafi asked. Nasser said that this was a strong probability. 'Have we got nuclear bombs?' asked Qaddafi. 'No, we have not,' said Nasser.

Within three months Qaddafi sent Jalloud on a visit to Cairo on Libya's first nuclear shopping spree. He went to see Nasser who asked him what he was doing. 'We are going to buy a nuclear bomb,' he said. 'Where are you going to buy it?' said Nasser. Jalloud said that he knew the Americans and Russians would be unwilling to sell one but maybe the Chinese would. 'We don't want a big atomic bomb, just a tactical one. We contacted the Chinese and said we wanted someone to go there and pay them a visit and they said they would welcome us,' said Jalloud. He set off under a different name, changing his Libyan passport for an Egyptian one, and travelled via India and Pakistan to Peking. He found he was on the same flight as Arafat's deputy who was on a shopping mission for more conventional weapons. Jalloud saw the Chinese premier, Chou En-lai, who explained courteously that atomic bombs were not for sale in China. It would not be Qaddafi's last attempt.

Nasser's successor, Anwar Sadat, had less patience and his relationship with Qaddafi moved swiftly from coolness to dislike and, eventually, to hatred. Sadat suspected that Qaddafi 'was not like other men' and had something seriously wrong with him.

Western leaders are inclined to see a kind of schizophrenia in Qaddafi's foreign policy. Qaddafi the diplomat carries out energetic and often successful initiatives, dealing with such issues as trade and oil competently and sometimes brilliantly. Then there is the Qaddafi who funds terrorists and revolutionaries. Qaddafi himself sees no contradiction, although he is often puzzled by the reaction of Western governments who criticize his policies, condemn him as a lunatic, but are still prepared to do business with him. He believes that conventional diplomacy and revolutionary politics can operate in a complementary, not a contradictory, way and be means to the same ends: Arab unity, a Palestinian state, and the overthrow of imperialist or monarchist governments. He believes that if other rulers do not take the revolutionary path then they should be overthrown. He has no doubt that the United States acts in a similar way in its efforts to destabilize such regimes as Castro's in Cuba and the Sandinistas in Nicaragua.

After Nasser's death Qaddafi accelerated Libya's twin-pronged offensive. On 9 November Libya, Sudan and Egypt announced that they had formed a 'federation to hasten and develop integration and co-operation'. The union had enormous potential, combining Libya's money with Egypt's population, military power and technical expertise and Sudan's potential for agricultural development. It would give Egypt strategic depth and create a power bloc, with a population of more than fifty million people, which might pull other Arab nations into its orbit. Syria joined the federation in April 1971 and there were plans to put the four armies under joint control, to have a single president over a sixty-member federal assembly. On 1 September, the second anniversary of the Libyan revolution, the peoples of Egypt, Syria and Libya voted for the merger of their countries, with an average of 98.3 per cent in favour.

Despite this expression of popular support the unity agreement never got off the ground. Sadat was more interested in 'co-operation' and getting his hands on some of Libya's oil money than in unity with a country led by a man he considered mentally unstable. The Syrians were concerned that Egypt would dominate the union and Syria would become a mere department of a new state. Qaddafi's proselytizing trip to Cairo in April 1973 when he lectured Egyptians on the new Libyan revolution was a disaster. Hamdi Saleh, a senior diplomat in the Egyptian Foreign Ministry, recalls: 'Sadat thought, "Qaddafi wants unity, okay, so come and talk to the people about it." Qaddafi lectured Egyptian women about how their place was in the home and that they should be wives and mothers in strict accordance with the Koran.' This did not go down well in Egypt which, by Muslim standards, is a fairly liberal society where women go to work and are not forced to wear strict Islamic dress, and where alcohol is sold and drunk. 'The women's groups and the intellectuals thought he was a primitive,' says Saleh. 'The women gave him hell. The whole visit was dreadful. Qaddafi left with a grudge, shocked by the opposition from his Arab brothers.' He consoled himself with the thought that he had only met the decadent bourgeoisie of Egypt, who would naturally oppose his abrasive new ideas. The real people from the slums and the villages would react differently.

In September 1973 he organized 20,000 Libyans to march 1,500 miles to Cairo where, he believed, they would be joined by vast numbers of the Egyptian masses clamouring for unity. It did not work out like that. The Egyptian government blocked the main road from Mersa Matruh to Alamein with a railway carriage and the 20,000 Libyans were stopped at the border. A pathetic little group of officials was allowed to travel to Cairo to hand in a petition.

Qaddafi's unity agreement with Tunisia had an even more ignominious end. On 22 December 1972 Qaddafi spoke at a popular rally in Tunis and called for union with Libya. This came as a shock to President Bourguiba of Tunisia, who was listening to the speech at home on his radio. He rushed to the rally, took the microphone and promptly rubbished Qaddafi's unity idea. He said that Arabs had never been unified and did not want to be lectured on the subject by the leader of a backward country that had its own problems of internal unity.

Qaddafi had more success with a campaign mounted from Tripoli which, by the end of 1973, persuaded thirty African countries to break off relations with Israel. Arab unity, however, was a mirage on Qaddafi's horizon: Israel still occupied Arab territory and there was nothing Qaddafi could see in the divided and spineless Arab world to dislodge them. He was not impressed by the leaders of the Arab world, who all seemed to him to be either monarchist, Western lackeys or tinged with ideological impurity.

One passage of his well-thumbed copy of Nasser's little book *Philosophy of the Revolution* had fascinated but eluded him:

> The pages of history are full of heroes who created for themselves roles of glorious valor which they played at decisive moments. Likewise the pages of history are also full of heroic and glorious roles which never found heroes to perform them. For some reason it seems to me that within the Arab circle there is a role, wandering aimlessly in search of a hero.

Qaddafi had inverted Nasser's parable. He was the hero, searching desperately for a role. And he was to find it not on the traditional stage of world politics, but in the shadowy arena of international revolution and terror.

Black September was a watershed for the Palestinians. John Amos, in his book *International Terrorism*, says that the 'confrontation doctrine' (attacking Israel from Jordan with conventional guerrilla tactics), followed by Arafat's Fatah guerrilla group, was sharply criticized on a number of grounds. Palestinian spokesmen were concerned about the high loss of life. Arafat estimated that there had been 30,000 Palestinian casualties, dead and wounded, between 1967 and 1970. Palestinian leaders were calling for more effective operations in which commandos returned to base safely. The Palestinian Research Centre produced a report in 1970 based largely on Fatah records which showed that the majority of commandos killed were 'both young and relatively well educated' and that the Palestinians' principle resource, educated young people, was being sacrificed with little to show for it.

In the report George Habash argued that Arafat was wrong to use Algeria or Vietnam as strategic models. First, the Arab states bordering Israel were not permitting Palestinians to carry out effective operations. Second, as long as this was true, it would be useless to continue engaging superior Israeli forces. Nothing could be achieved without the aid of conventional Arab armies, and this aid did not seem to be forthcoming. Third, Palestinian manpower was an extremely limited commodity. There were only a few thousand guerrillas and the total Palestinian population outside the occupied territories was less than two million. The conclusion was that cross-border raids were difficult and ineffective. The Palestinian resistance should carry out hit-and-run operations inside Israel, or should hit Israeli and allied targets anywhere in the world.

Qaddafi had found a role. In June 1972, on the second anniversary of the expulsion of the United States from the Wheelus airbase, he publicly offered to help any anti-Western revolutionaries, including the Irish Republican Army (IRA) and the Black Power movement in the United States, and to equip every Arab who was willing to join the resistance. Twenty-four hours later more than 500 Palestinians and other Arabs had contacted the Libyan embassy in Cairo alone to sign up.

Qaddafi was beginning to espouse an odd bundle of causes. Heikal attributes this to 'a terrifying innocence of how things worked in the modern world'. 'He was capable of gross oversimplification,' Heikal wrote. 'I myself at one time explained to him that the IRA was not a liberation movement in the sense that we understood the term – but in vain. Many times I tried to convince him that the Bangladesh problem was one of self-determination and that the new state deserved recognition from Libya. But he could not see this. To him Pakistan was the biggest Muslim country in the world and Bangladesh a disruptive, separatist movement.'

Although there was a bloody sequence of hijackings and assassinations between 1970 and 1973, it is wrong to blame Qaddafi solely for these incidents. It is true he funded a number of Palestinian groups, including Black September run by Waddi Haddad and George Habash. (For a time he stopped payments because he disagreed with Habash's Marxist philosophy.)

In funding the Palestinian resistance, however, he was merely continuing the policy of the Libyan monarchy he had overthrown. King Idris was a substantial paymaster, along with all the other Arab countries, of Arafat's Fatah. On a single visit to Arafat in 1966 Idris handed over $100,000. Qaddafi's coup had had to be postponed in March 1969 because the Libyan top brass were at a Fatah fund-raiser. If Qaddafi is to be held partly responsible for all the acts of Palestinian terror, then so must the leaders of the whole Arab world, including pro-Western Kuwait and Saudi Arabia who gave more money than anyone else. They, however, were less outspoken in their support, and they generally condemned, instead of supported, random acts of terror which their oil money made possible.

Qaddafi crowed, for example, at two assassination attempts (in July 1971 and August 1972) against his brother Arab King Hassan, the hereditary ruler of Morocco. On both occasions he applauded the attackers and called for Hassan's overthrow. The myth grew that he had been responsible, or had at least assisted, in the assassination attempts, but senior security officials in Rabat deny this. The assassins were fuelled by Islamic zeal and contempt for the King's wealth.

Claire Sterling in *The Terror Network* claims that Qaddafi played a crucial role in the kidnapping and murder of the Israeli athletes at the Olympic Games in Munich in 1972. However, Israeli intelligence officials, in long discussions with the authors on Libyan terror, have denied that Qaddafi had any role in the Munich massacre. 'This was purely a Black September operation,' said an Israeli official. 'We have no information that he took part in the planning or the logistics.' All that is known is that Libya received the bodies of the five Black September terrorists killed in the operation and gave them ceremonial funerals.

Qaddafi saw himself as godfather to terrorists of almost any creed. Tripoli became a sort of Club Méditerranée where international terrorists could always be sure of a welcome. Qaddafi allowed a group of Japanese Red Army and Palestinian terrorists who had hijacked a Japan Air Lines Boeing 747 *en route* from Paris to Tokyo to land in Libya in 1973. A woman hijacker was killed and several passengers were wounded when a grenade exploded just before the plane, carrying 145 passengers and crew, was taken. They called themselves the Sons of the Occupied Territories and demanded the release of Kozo Okamoto, the Japanese terrorist who was eventually to be released by the Israelis in the 1980s in a massive exchange of PLO prisoners and their supporters for a handful of Israeli soldiers captured during the invasion of Lebanon. This time the hijackers failed. They flew to Benghazi airport where they blew up the plane. On this occasion Qaddafi's welcome was muted. He allowed them to land but then condemned their actions and said the hijackers would face trial under *sharia*, or Muslim, law. Nothing more was heard, however, and the terrorists were apparently never punished.

Qaddafi was not alone in freeing terrorists. It was the international rule, rather than the exception. According to official Israeli figures, of 204 Palestinians arrested for terrorism outside the Middle East from 1968 to 1975, only three were in jail in 1975.

Of all Qaddafi's funding of foreign terrorists and revolutionaries, his backing of the IRA has been perhaps the most controversial. According to Ed Moloney of the *Irish Times*, the links between Qaddafi and the IRA began with the speech he made in June 1972 declaring support for the 'revolutionaries of Ireland who oppose Britain and are motivated by nationalism and religion'. The Provisional IRA, which badly needed arms and money, saw this correctly as a green light from Tripoli, and in August that year two members of the IRA's ruling council flew to Warsaw in Poland to meet a representative of Libya's Foreign Ministry at the offices of the Libyan trade delegation. Moloney describes the deal they made as 'quite extraordinary'. The Libyans suggested that the Provisionals should send full-time representatives to Tripoli and that they would be given semi-diplomatic status. They also agreed to give substantial economic aid. The new IRA diplomats, a teacher from County Monaghan, another teacher from County Down and an Iraqi–American married to an Irish woman, went to Tripoli under the cover of taking jobs as English teachers.

The senior of the three was housed in a large villa in the centre of Tripoli's foreign embassy area, next door to the Bulgarian embassy, and his bills were paid by the Libyans. He was also given a living allowance. His contacts with the Libyans were through a senior Foreign Ministry official. For three months the new IRA diplomats were kept incommunicado until in January 1973 they began the negotiations that were to lead to the *Claudia* gun-running episode.

In March 1973 the Irish navy intercepted the SS *Claudia* off the south-east coast of Ireland. Five tons of weapons – rifles, other small arms and a large number of anti-tank weapons – were found on board along with Joe Cahill, a member of the IRA ruling council. A German businessman, who was a middle man in the deal, revealed that the IRA had asked him to send the *Claudia* to Tripoli to pick up the arms. He said that three IRA men had been in Tripoli to carry out the deal but that 'something had gone wrong'. There were supposed to be 100 tons of arms on the ship but somehow 95 tons had gone missing.

According to Moloney, the *Claudia* was loaded not off-shore, as the German businessman maintained, but right next to the British embassy in Tripoli, and the men who put the gear on board were Qaddafi's elite 'red cap' regiment.

The story of who informed on the *Claudia* has never been revealed but Moloneys says that at the time the IRA suspected that Qaddafi himself, eager to make a reputation in the Arab world as a funder of revolutionaries, had deliberately left clues that something big was about to happen and therefore alerted Western intelligence agencies in Tripoli. The loading bay itself, so close to the British embassy, was perhaps clue enough.

As the *Claudia* steamed towards Ireland, the Libyan Foreign Ministry suddenly asked the three IRA diplomats in Tripoli to make lengthy broadcasts on successive nights on the radio arguing their revolutionary case. This aroused the suspicion of Western diplomats. They Libyan/IRA relationship was, therefore, flawed from the beginning.

Moloney maintains that, despite all the stories about other arms shipments and IRA training camps in Libya, the bulk of Libyan aid was financial. Moloney puts a figure of $3 million funnelled through a Libyan-owned bank in London. The liaison formally came to an end in May 1975 when the Libyan police publicly arrested the senior IRA representative at his villa with sirens wailing and lights flashing. He was taken to the airport and put on a Rome flight. One reason for the abrupt Libyan change of heart was, Moloney says, a row over money. The IRA had refused to account for the cash to the Libyans' satisfaction.

The amount of Libyan support is uncertain. Peter McMullan, a former British soldier who deserted to the IRA, then left it to live in the USA, told the authors that the Libyans had been giving the IRA 'millions of dollars a year'. McMullan is not, however, a reliable witness as his account of his activities with the IRA frequently proved.

A senior office with Scotland Yard's anti-terrorist squad dismissed McMullan's claim and said that Libyan support for the IRA had been 'very minor indeed. It can be counted in the thousands of pounds, but certainly not in hundreds of thousands and any talk of millions of dollars is ludicrous.' This officer said that the total Libyan funding equals less than one year's payments by Noraid, the US supporters of the IRA. This is supported by a secret British army intelligence report from Northern Ireland in 1978 which says: 'We doubt whether PIRA [Provisional IRA] receives financial aid from Libya or any overseas government.'

The IRA's rivals, the Protestant paramilitary force in Northern Ireland called the Ulster Defence Association (UDA), take some of the credit for preventing these payments during a visit four of their members made to Tripoli in November 1974. Glenn Barr, the leader of the group and the political head of the UDA, Tommy Lyttle, Andy Robinson and Charlie Chicken made their contacts with the Libyans simply enough by going to the Libyan embassy in London. As members of a paramilitary group they were given immediate permission to go to Tripoli. Their only problem was that the British Special Branch watched the embassy and followed them back to Belfast, and then all the way to Heathrow airport when they flew to Tripoli. 'It was quite comical,' said Lyttle. 'These Special Branch boys were everywhere, ducking in and out of doorways. Real cloak and dagger stuff.'

When the group arrived in Tripoli they faced the same problems which confront many of the revolutionary hopefuls who go to Libya for money or arms; there was no one to meet them. They waited at the airport for six or seven hours until these 'shabbily dressed blokes' turned up to escort them to the Libya Palace Hotel where, Lyttle said, they did not have reservations. There were more hours of confusion until the Libyans got them rooms.

'We didn't see Qaddafi,' said Lyttle. 'He was off in the desert meditating or something, but we did see some senior officials, including a minister, and they were very friendly and easygoing.' The UDA men found the Libyans had a strange and distorted view of the Northern Ireland problem. 'They had the impression that the whole of Ireland was occupied by British troops and they were surprised to hear that there was an independent Southern Ireland. We also got them straight about the Provos [Provisional IRA],' said Lyttle. 'We told them that the Protestants didn't want the British out at that time and that the Provos weren't just shooting military targets, but ordinary Protestant people as well.'

It was, on the whole, a miserable week. Barr got food poisoning and spent most of his time in his hotel room. Robinson caught sight of some IRA men in the Libya Palace Hotel. There was, of course, no drink and the UDA men were kept under tight security. It was also very hot. Lyttle did feel, however, that their trip was successful in opening Libyans' eyes to the scale of the Irish problem.

The IRA itself was never totally happy about its Libyan link. The old guard, who were committed Catholics and politically conservative, did not approve of dealing with a fundamentalist Muslim who was beginning to form strong links with Moscow, although the young turks disagreed with them. The IRA sent recruits to Libyan training camps but were not satisfied with the expertise of the Libyan and Palestinian instructors, who taught them about fighting in the desert, which is not a skill an urban guerrilla from Belfast needs to know. The IRA found that their own expertise in bomb manufacture and timing devices was far superior. The flow of recruits dried up, as did the funds from Libya to the IRA. Even the arms deals were a problem. There is a story in Belfast that the IRA received a batch of rocket launchers from Libya with the complex instructions written in Arabic.

Much later, in January 1986, the spectre of Libyan support for the IRA loomed again after 140 Soviet-made assault rifles in crates marked 'Libyan Armed Forces' were found in Ireland. Although this appeared to be conclusive evidence of Libyan arms shipments, a senior officer of the Irish Garda said this interpretation was 'simplistic' and pointed out that the original source of the arms and the end-user may have no direct connection at all. He said that Libyan guns have often passed through numerous Middle East and European sources before reaching the Provisional IRA. This view is shared by the Royal Ulster Constabulary in Belfast and by senior members of Protestant paramilitary groups, who believe that these weapons were bought on the illegal gun market in Amsterdam.

The total amount of money Libya dispersed to revolutionary groups throughout the world in the early 1970s is unknown, and cannot be accurately assessed because both Qaddafi and the groups he funds either refuse to say, or lie. A member of one Palestinian extremist group in Tripoli gave two figures for the amount of money Libya was providing. One day he said 'nothing', the next day he said 'billions'. His cynicism reflects Qaddafi's growing disillusionment with the Palestinian cause in 1973; the Libyan leader felt he was not getting value for money in terms of military action against Israel. He also disagreed with the Marxist slant of the Palestinian extremists. It is possible that his interest might have swung back to conventional warfare and diplomacy had it not been for Libyan Arab Airlines flight number LN 114.

The Libyan Arab Airlines Boeing 727 took off from Tripoli airport at 10.30 a.m. on 21 February 1973 with 104 passengers on board. It flew first to Benghazi, then on to Cairo. An hour and forty-four minutes after take-off the pilot noticed that he had made a navigational error. It was not, under normal circumstances, a grave one: he had overshot an air traffic control beacon by ten miles. But in the turbulent skies of the Middle East such an error can be fatal. The Boeing failed to make a turn towards Cairo airport and flew over Israeli-occupied Sinai. It did so for only nine minutes, but it penetrated Israeli airspace as far as Bir Gafgafa airfield in Central Sinai, one of Israel's most sensitive military installations. Despite a blinding sandstorm, the Israelis sent up Phantom fighter planes, marked with the Star of David, which flew at times only five yards from the Boeing and indicated that it should land immediately. An appalling series of errors occurred over the next few minutes.

From their radio conversations it is clear that the pilots of the Libyan plane thought the Israeli jets were friendly Egyptian Mig fighters. The Israeli pilots said they suspected the plane was about to make an attack on the military installation, although it must have been clear to them it was a passenger jet. In the last few seconds the Boeing pilot decided to fly on to Cairo airport and trigger-happy Israeli pilots opened up with three bursts of cannon fire. The plane crashed only one minute's flying time from the Egyptian border. All the passengers and crew were killed.

The Israeli action was universally condemned and Qaddafi vowed revenge. He was also bitter about Egyptian inaction. The Libyans believed that Egyptian fighters could have come to the aid of the Libyan passenger jet. The Egyptian air force told him that they could not scramble their planes because of the sandstorm, to which Qaddafi snapped back that the Israelis had managed to scramble theirs. The Libyans were not convinced, and a mob in Tripoli attacked Egyptian buildings including the embassy.

According to Heikal, Qaddafi then planned a terrorist attack which, had it succeeded, would almost certainly have started a major Middle East war. A group of wealthy American Jews had chartered the QE2 liner to take them from Southampton in England to Ashdod in Israel to celebrate the twenty-fifth anniversary of the founding of the State of Israel.

Qaddafi wanted to blow it up. On 17 April 1973 he summoned the commander of an Egyptian submarine which was stationed in Tripoli. Qaddafi was standing, as Heikal later revealed, with a map of the Mediterranean spread out in front of him:

> I speak to you as an Arab nationalist and as commander in chief of the armed forces of Libya. You are now working here with us. Can you identify the QE2 in the Mediterranean?' The commander said he could. 'In that case could you aim two torpedoes at it and sink it?' The commander said he could, but he would have to have a direct order. 'All right,' said Gadafy. 'I give you that order.'

The commander took his submarine out to sea and that night sent a coded message to the naval commander in his home base, Alexandria, explaining what Qaddafi had told him to do. He, in turn, informed the commander in chief of the Egyptian navy, who told Sadat. Sadat immediately recalled the submarine to Alexandria. He called Heikal that day and said: 'It seems that Qaddafi wants to put us on the spot. He is trying to sink the QE2.'

Sadat was less concerned with Qaddafi's revenge than with his own plans for attacking Israel in October 1973 – plans which were so secret that the Libyan leader was not told about them. In fact relations between Egypt and Libya had deteriorated almost irrevocably. In October the Arab leader who had argued most strenuously for war against Israel, stood on the sidelines as Sadat, supported by King Feisal of Saudi Arabia and President Assad of Syria, ordered his army into battle across the Suez canal.

7 The Green Book

In February 1973 thousands of mourners congregated in Benghazi's main public cementery at Ras Obeidah on the outskirts of the city to mourn victims of Libyan Arab Airlines' ill-fated flight LN 114. The ceremony was presided over by Benghazi mayor Abdul Wahab Zentani, in the presence of RCC member Khweldi Hameidi.

Knowing that there was resentment against Egypt for its failure to retaliate against Israel's aggression, Zentani, in his official address, made conciliatory noises, suggesting that Cairo had done its best and that Libyans should not be too hard on it. This was too much for certain sections of the crowd, who began to shout abuse. Zentani pleaded for restraint, but the student son of former Foreign Minister Saleh Busair, who had been killed in the crash, refused to be silenced.

Scuffles broke out. Zentani himself was assaulted. In no time a mob was surging through the streets of Benghazi, tearing down revolutionary posters. It quickly made its way up Sharia Gamal Abdul Nasser to the gates of the Egyptian consulate-general. Shouting slogans now not only against Israel but also against the Libyan and Egyptian regimes, complaining about their lack of resolution, the demonstrators burst into the building and looted it, contemptuously throwing out into the street official posters of Nasser himself.

Colonel Qaddafi was appalled. This was a savage and sacrilegious attack on the memory of his political mentor. However, he chose to read it not so much as an attack on him personally but as a show of his people's impatience with the slowness of moves towards Arab unity. He therefore decided to turn this setback of his advantage. Relations with other members of the Revolutionary Command Council had been strained for some time. Conflicts about the direction of Libya's revolution had arisen. Major Meheishi, for one, was voicing criticism of Qaddafi for spending too much time following his dream of Arab unity and too little thinking about Libya's own internal development. Meheishi criticized growing expenditure on arms and on terrorist activity abroad.

Qaddafi was unrepentant. Arab unity remained his goal. What was needed was simply an intensification of his revolution. Despite his reverence for its creator, he was beginning to feel that the model he followed – the softly-spoken Nasser approach, which had crawled to a snail's pace under Sadat – must be improved upon. Was that not exactly the message the Benghazi mob had been giving him? They, like he, wanted a new, more activist phase of the revolution.

The next two months show Qaddafi in one of his most accomplished roles – the political prima donna. He called a meeting of the Revolutionary Command Council and, as he had done in September 1971, announced his resignation. 'The revolution has been destroyed; there is no point continuing,' he moaned. Abu Bakr Younis was appointed head of the Council. Qaddafi summoned a helicopter and flew to Houn, a favourite oasis in the desert, south of the Qaddadfa tribal centre of Sirte. For two months he pondered.

Then on 15 April, the anniversary of the Prophet's birthday, Qaddafi returned to the fray in Zwara, a seaport west of Tripoli, close to the Tunisian border. Having reversed his resignation, Qaddafi made a fiery speech, known as the Zwara Declaration, calling for a clean break with the established political order. The revolution was in danger, he told his startled audience, which included most of the members of the RCC. (Jalloud sitting next to him was 'flabbergasted', according to a witness.) The root of the problem was lack of Arab solidarity, the Libyan leader asserted. He began to rail against Egypt and Syria for their pusillanimity over the downing of the Libyan jet. He said he had sent envoys to both countries to demand retaliatory action, 'but they returned empty-handed'.

Lack of Arab solidarity had not only failed the Palestinian movement, which, Qaddafi said, now 'exists only in radio broadcasts; it has been destroyed by the Arabs in co-operation with Israel'. It was also holding young Libyans back from volunteering for army service. Indeed the Libyan people as a whole were becoming lazy. They were not working in agriculture and in development projects in remote areas. They were being poisoned by ideas put forward by anti-revolutionary 'perverts', mainly in the universities.

The time had thus come for the revolution to be defended. In a five-point programme, which many commentators see as the blueprint for Qaddafi's entire period in office, the Libyan leader called for

– the suspension of existing laws: in future all civil and criminal cases would be judged on their merits, according to the precepts of *sharia*;
– the elimination of 'political illnesses' in the country, particularly Communism, the Muslim Brotherhood and Baathism;

101

- the arming of the population to secure 'the defence of the revolution';
- an 'administrative revolution' to bring the bureaucracy back to the people;
- a cultural revolution to purge universities of 'the demagogic spirit and foreign cultural influences'.

Several targets were identified for a special weeding-out process – the legal profession, political parties, the army, the bureaucracy and the intelligentsia; of the privileged sections of the community Qaddafi was to attack over the following years, only merchants were missing from this particular hit list.

On a practical level Qaddafi demanded that 'every village, town, college, factory and school must form popular committees under the control of the masses to fulfil the five points'. Predictably the Libyan leader threatened that if his demands were not implemented he would resign.

Speaking at Benghazi University shortly afterwards, Qaddafi referred to two factors which were holding back progress in Libya: arrogant officials and purveyors of false doctrines. Now both were going to be eliminated. 'Trample under your feet any bourgeois bureaucrat who closes the doors of government offices in your face,' he urged his student audience. 'Tear up all the imported books which do not express Arabism, Islam, socialism and progress. Burn and destroy all curricula that do not express the truth.'

Almost immediately the Zwara Declaration was pressed into operation. On 7 May people's committees were elected throughout the country to run everything from government offices, through schools and universities, to factories, businesses and even villages. Reuter reported from Tripoli that day that each committee had between sixteen and twenty members and that there would eventually be several thousand people's committees the length and breadth of the country. The election of the committees, according to Reuter, was supervised by 'neutral groups whose members have no right to stand for election themselves. After the elections the Revolutionary Command Council, the country's ruling body, sends a delegation to make sure the elections were freely held.'

A few days later on 14 May, at a gathering of Arab and European youth in Tripoli, Qaddafi talked for the first time of the Third Universal Theory which underlay his Zwara Declaration. He told participants:

> The Third Theory or ideology (which is an alternative to capitalist materialism and Communist atheism) is an ideology which calls

for mankind to return to the Kingdom of God. . . . It is our claim that mankind was never in greater need to rearm itself with faith than it is now in the seventh decade of the twentieth century. . . . Humanity now urgently needs a cry of justice which would return it to its senses and to its Creator who made it His successor on earth. We need to go back to God and to turn away from evil. . . . The ideology which we propose to the world is a humanitarian ideology and not an aggressive theory as the racial theories designed to bring destruction to the world. . . . When we speak about the Third Universal Theory we stress that it is not made by man nor is it a philosophy, but it is based on truth. There is a great difference between truth and theory: theory is liable to change by revocation or refutation, but truth is firm and unchangeable.

Never afraid of repeating himself, Qaddafi added, 'We call it the Third Theory to indicate that there is a new path for all those who reject both materialist capitalism and atheist Communism. This path is for all the people of the world who abhor the dangerous confrontation between the Warsaw and North Atlantic military alliances. It is for all those who believe that all nations of the world are brothers under the aegis of the rule of God.'

Qaddafi touched upon the economic aspects of the Third Universal Theory. The possibility of a solution to economic problems through socialism was officially admitted, but only in an Islamic, not a Marxist, context. For Islam and socialism are indivisible. Both allow for nationalization and limitation of property. 'Islam provides for the realization of justice and equity; it does not allow any rich person to use his wealth as a tool of oppression nor to exploit people.' However, private ownership could continue 'if it causes no harm'. Wealth and poverty

should not be allowed to exist side by side in any society, and it is the duty of the state to enact laws which would provide for taking away from the rich person and giving to the poor person.

Islam stands against poverty, and firmly stands by the side of the working classes.

After ranging over the ills of both capitalism and Communism, Qaddafi concluded, 'Chauvinism and selfishness are characteristics of godless government. The Third Universal Theory rejects both of these vices and calls for the brotherhood of mankind. For men and states without that shall be none better than the wild beasts of the forests.'

If this version of Qaddafi's Third Universal Theory showed rather more of its Islamic infrastructure than later appeared, it had been a long time gestating. The Libyan leader had first seriously begun to think about blending his ideas – with their subtle populist allusions to Nasserism, Islam and Sirtic Bedouin common sense – into a coherent whole a few months after he had taken power. Perhaps he felt that a heroic leader, as he was beginning to see himself, needed an ideology, like Nasser's *Philosophy of the Revolution*.

There had not been much time for political discussion in those first few months. The RCC had been too busy consolidating its rule and negotiating not only the evacuation of British and American bases but also radical new terms with the oil companies. So it was not until May 1970 that Qaddafi, together with five members of the RCC, and what the record describes as 'Libyan intellectuals, Libyan women (eleven) and other average Libyans', gathered in the Boy Scouts' Theatre, next to the fairground to the west of Tripoli, for the first session of what was known as the Libyan Intellectual Seminar.

The venue was curiously anachronistic. Vestiges of Western cultural imperialism such as night-clubs had already been closed down. But here at the local headquarters of the worldwide scouting movement, founded by the nineteenth-century British imperialist, the hero of the siege of Mafeking, Lord Baden-Powell, Qaddafi was preparing to discuss the ideas which underlay his regime. In other ways the Scouts' Theatre was surprisingly appropriate. It not only symbolized the schizophrenic basis of Qaddafi's political philosophy at the time. It also emphasized the fact that, like Baden-Powell's scouts, Libya's revolution had, until then at least, shown itself to be practical, reformist, militaristic and eager to clean up society with a dose of conventional morality – based in the one case on Christianity, in the other on Islam.

The first day of the seminar was devoted to defining 'the working forces of the people who have an interest in the revolution'. Debate was good-humoured, but strangely stilted and unproductive, as though participants indeed wanted to let their leaders know their feelings about a broad range of issues but could not do so since Qaddafi and his colleagues were determined not to let the proceedings become too serious.

Sadiq Nayhoum, a maverick intellectual with a reputation as an existentialist-style free thinker, was first off the mark with his attempt at a definition of the topic of the day. 'The Libyan people were like a herd of cows,' he declared. 'Now the cow wants to feel at one with freedom. The whole Libyan people have an interest in the revolution because they are all human beings.'

Nayhoum seemed to be saying that Qaddafi's revolution was the property of all Libyans, a theme which had often been stressed by the leader himself. But somehow this interpretation failed to meet the approval of the RCC members present. Captain Omar Meheishi, Qaddafi's old friend from Misurata, flew at Nayhoum, saying, 'What Mr Nayhoum said is a reflection of deformed opinion. Mr Nayhoum is not a revolutionary educated man. He is a reactionary element. He wants us to bring King Idris back because he is a human being and has an interest in the revolution like anyone else. . . . This is a revolution, and what Mr Nayhoum said is something which might be said by President Nixon or Johnson but not by a revolutionary intellectual.'

Nayhoum tried to set the record straight. He did not mean that the revolution was literally for everybody, including inhuman reactionaries like the King. 'President Johnson was never human,' he said. 'I believe I was misunderstood, perhaps because of the language I used.' This was the cue for Major Jalloud to intervene. 'Could the speaker use words that make sense? Could he avoid using flowery words?' On a point of clarification Qaddafi himself had a question for Nayhoum. What exactly had he meant by a 'herd of cows'? Who were the cattle and who the cattleman? Nayhoum was quite precise on this. 'The cattleman was King Idris and the Libyan people was the herd of cows.'

As the loudspeakers crackled (at one stage Qaddafi asked for them to be fixed), Abdul Moneim al Munir Mohammed must have thought it was time to get down to basics. 'Before we define the working forces, I think it would be appropriate to know which revolution we are talking about. If it is the Libyan revolution, then we should be able to throw some light on it – whether it was a socialist revolution or—' Mohammed al Marziq, the former director-general at the Ministry of Information, who was chairing the seminar, cut him off. References to politically controversial topics such as socialism were clearly not on the agenda. 'The aims of the revolution are clear and are not for discussion,' he stated forcefully, thus negating what many must have felt was the *raison d'être* of the gathering.

Qaddafi himself tried to defuse the situation. 'Pardon me,' he said with a smile. 'We are talking about the revolution which took place in Libya and, more specifically, the September 1st Revolution.' The Boy Scouts' Theatre erupted in laughter and clapping.

Abdul Moneim was not to be deflected even by Qaddafi's charm. 'There are two kinds of revolution – the revolution of the middle class and socialistic revolutions. The September 1st Revolution', he said provocatively, 'is a transitory event which will eventually turn into a socialist revolution.' Again the chairman was uncertain whether such sentiments did not cross the boundaries of what was permitted. 'Please come to the point,' he said officiously. (A speaker was later to describe his manner as 'peremptory'.) 'If you cannot speak your minds, please give others the chance to speak.'

However, Abdul Moneim had introduced an idea which was to occupy most of the rest of the day's proceedings: there was the revolution of the middle classes, who were the exploiters, and the revolution of the lower-middle classes, who were the exploited. When Jumaa al Fezzani elaborated on this theme, Qaddafi asked him to define his terms. 'The lower-middle classes are those whose monthly earnings do not exceed 100 pounds,' he answered definitively. 'Students, teachers and government employees are considered to be from the lower-middle class.'

Qaddafi still had some queries. 'You said the lower-middle class of people are teachers, students—' he was beginning to say, when Fezzani, feeling, perhaps, that he might have offended the Libyan leader by leaving out a crucial profession from his list, interrupted him, 'Army officers are also from the lower-middle class.' There were some titters from around the hall as Qaddafi completed his question: 'Do you consider the student who lives in a shack to be from the lower-middle class?' Fezzani refused to be wrong-footed. 'Well, if he believes in workers' theory, he will be considered a revolutionary element. If he does not, he may still be considered from the revolutionary forces, but should not assume a ruling position.'

Major Jalloud must have been getting bored, because his next question hardly raised the standard of the debate. 'Let's say we improved the living standard of those workers you talked about. . . . In which category of people will you put them?' he asked to the sound of laughter. Fezzani was still determined not to be ruffled by a member of the RCC poking fun at him. He knew his people's history. 'Mao Tse-tung, Castro and Ben Bella are from the lower-middle class,' he stated authoritatively. 'And they remain as members of the lower-middle class because they adopted and stuck to workers' principles.'

Now it was Qaddafi's turn for a bit of fun. Asked by his country's leader how much he earned, Fezzani, later to become an ambassador and one of the revolution's most articulate apologists, could only reply sheepishly, '117 pounds per month.' Qaddafi thought this hilarious. 'Oh,' he said, trying to stop himself laughing. 'You must be from the upper-middle class. Come to think of it, I make 192 pounds and 6½ piastres per month. This clearly makes me one of the upper-middle class.'

The first session of the seminar continued in this jovial and unproductive vein for some time. At the close, three messages of support – from Tarhuna elementary school, the Boy Scout headquarters and students from Tripoli University – were read out by the chairman. The Boy Scouts' message commended Captain Meheishi's intervention against Nayhoum, adding, 'We demand the striking down of any category of people that stands against the revolution. We didn't understand anything from Mr Nayhoum's speech, except his reference to the 'cattleman and the cattle'. We also demand that you avoid Byzantine debates.'

Over the next ten days the seminar reconvened for eight more sessions. The debates can hardly be described as Byzantine because the content was so lacking in substance. Speakers were continually steered away from controversial subjects. When one speaker called for scientific socialism, Major Jalloud said he would disagree 'if what was meant amounted to Marxist socialism'. The Major, generally more forthcoming than Qaddafi over the course of the seminar, had his own image of the social change since 1969: 'The previous regime was like a water spring watering a certain number of trees only. But now we have stopped the flow of water and changed its course so that the water can reach the greatest possible number of trees.'

One speaker told a joke which summed up the fact that the seminars were less about deciding Libya's future than an excuse for a general letting off of political steam. 'An army officer parked his car so that a wheel came to rest on a man's foot. Rather than scream, the unfortunate victim asked politely, "Are you a member of the RCC?" "No, I am not," came the reply. "Are you one of the Free Unionist Officers?" "No, I am not." "Then, why are you resting your car wheel on my foot, you bloody fool?" '

The serious business of establishing a political framework for the revolution came with the announcement – and there was little debate about it, apart from an officially orchestrated campaign in the press – of an official party in June 1971. It was to be a pan-national institution, known, like its model in Egypt, as the Arab Socialist Union. Membership was open to all forces of the revolution (defined, at last, as peasants, labourers, soldiers, intellectuals and national capitalists) over the age of eighteen. With committees of around ten people operating at a local level, the ASU was a hierarchical party with Qaddafi at its head as president. To ensure everyone knew where the power really lay, ASU resolutions at all levels had to be countersigned by an RCC member before they could be implemented and the RCC could dissolve any ASU organ.

Membership of all other parties and of existing trade unions was not only banned but declared treasonable, on pain of death. As Qaddafi said at the founding conference of the ASU in April 1972, 'Trade unions have nothing to do with politics – at no time and at no place. Trade unions and federations are professional organizations. It is ASU members who engage in politics.'

One speaker at this meeting bravely suggested that the duty of the revolution was to build freedom and democracy. Qaddafi told him categorically he was mistaken. Consulting workers, as in a democracy, he said, meant that the party would only take decisions in the interests of the working people. This was 'unfair for other sections of the people's working forces'. Showing the sophistry which was to become more marked over the next few years, Qaddafi argued, 'The larger the number of people consulted, the more it is done at the expense of revolutionary transformation.' He added that Islam had no concept of democracy. Allah had told the Prophet Mohammed to consult with his people, but, once he had decided on an issue, he was to go ahead with it, relying on God.

If the Intellectual Seminar shows Libya's lack of clear ideological direction and if the establishment of the ASU points to a need for some kind of formal political structure, Qaddafi was aware of these deficiencies.

By late 1971, with dissension in the RCC beginning to show, he was increasingly leaving the administrative side of government to Major Jalloud. Perfecting a technique he was later (as in March 1973, prior to the Zwara Declaration) frequently to use, Qaddafi would absolve himself of possible criticism by simply retiring from active politics. In September 1971 he handed in his resignation – 'to protest the shortcomings of the administrative apparatus in carrying out social, economic and industrial projects'. A month later he returned, declaring he had withdrawn his resignation 'in accordance with the wishes of the people' but would 'not remain at the head of the revolution for one more month if the present domestic situation persisted'.

But while the practical Jalloud had been running the show in his absence, the more reflective Qaddafi was using his retreats profitably to refine his own political philosophy – one that built on Nasser's, but took it further, in keeping with the changing circumstances of the time.

Qaddafi would invite Sudanese intellectuals, Lebanese clerics and Sorbonne philosophers to visit him in Tripoli. His Foreign Minister in 1972–3, Mansur Kikhia, who acted as an unwilling midwife to the development of Qaddafi's ideology, recalled:

Whenever new intellectuals arrived Qaddafi would tell me to invite them to visit him. Then as we talked he would take notes. He would ask them how to remedy this or that problem. The trouble for him was that he couldn't digest their ideas. He didn't have a basic scientific approach. When he himself offered an opinion, he came out with immature and confused analyses, such as were later to form the basis of his Third Universal Theory.

Qaddafi was also developing a more permanent ideological think tank. Hussain Mansour, a prominent Sudanese journalist, asked in his paper why Libya could not become the Israel of the Arab world, given that they had roughly the same sized populations. Qaddafi apparently seized on this idea. 'He called me to his office in the Aziziya barracks,' said Mansour. 'For four hours he asked me to expand on this idea. When I had finished he called one of his aides who handed me an envelope containing Libyan dinar notes. I can't remember how many were in there, but it was a large amount. I do remember feeling annoyed that he clearly saw me as a mercenary whose ideas could be bought for cash.'

Another regular ideas man was Abdullah Zakariyah, one of the many Sudanese refugees from President Numeiri's secular regime. There was even a place in the coterie for the iconoclastic Sadiq Nayhoum whose comments at the Intellectual Seminar in Tripoli in 1970 had caused such a stir.

Qaddafi used such thinkers to test and develop the ideology of his new order. It was hard going. For although something of an armchair philosopher Qaddafi was not a logical thinker. Mansur Kikhia recalled that the Libyan leader 'just didn't have a sound academic base. Qaddafi had only read two or three books though he knew all the speeches of Gamal Abdul Nasser by heart.' Others maintain that Qaddafi read more widely, and an Italian journalist who interviewed him saw his copy by the German author Heinrich Kleist. A passage had been underlined: 'A free man, capable of reflection, does not stay where chance happens to put him. He senses that he can raise himself about his destiny, that he can control his fate.'

If nothing else, Qaddafi was a good listener. Over the period 1971 to 1973 his ideas, which had been so amorphous at the seminar in 1970, became clearer. When the right blend of Nasserism, Islam and Bedouin lore had been established, and its political superstructure of people's committees had been thoroughly tested out in the Arab Socialist Union, Qaddafi was ready to set about his Chinese-style cultural revolution, as first announced in Zwara in April 1973.

By no means everybody was impressed. To some Qaddafi's personal political motivation was only too clear. A student at Benghazi University at the time, now a prominent member of the opposition National Front for the Salvation of Libya, recalled:

> Qaddafi had started to feel that Libya would never be changed and that he had to resort to power to keep control. His Zwara speech was specifically political, designed to warn certain sections of the power structure, particularly the technocrats and the intellectuals, that he intended to bring about their destruction and establish himself as the sole force in the land. It was the work of someone who wants to rule and keep power. It shows him as clever, highly motivated and innovative.

Qaddafi was not dissatisfied with his ideological synthesis. Much of the next few months he spent participating in a series of teach-ins on the theory and practice of his philosophy. The participants seemed to have been chosen to echo strands in his thinking – Muslim clerics in Tripoli, Egyptian intellectuals in Cairo, politicians and academics in Paris.

He did not always have an easy ride, even in Tripoli. According to Kalim Siddiqui writing in the *Guardian*, 350 Muslims from 103 countries came away from a two-week conference there in July having failed to be convinced that the Libyan regime's 'professions of Islam and Koranic piety, though perhaps sincere, were sufficiently well thought out or that the chosen path led where the regime claimed it was going'.

The main Libyan ideologues fielded at the conference were the ASU's Ahmed Shahati, later to head Qaddafi's Foreign Liaison Bureau, and Ibrahim al Ghwail. Shahati's 'headmasterly' speech strayed so far from the bounds of Islam that Libya's leading Koranic scholar present, Dr Mahmoud Subhi, jumped to his feet to protest about the dangers of 'intellectual terrorism'. 'The red-faced Libyans were furious,' reported Siddiqui. 'Subhi leads the second major prop of the regime, the Call of Islam Society, only marginally less important than the Arab Socialist Union. The inner conflicts in Libyan society were all too obvious to see.'

In Cairo the same month Qaddafi himself enraged President Sadat and put the impending union between their two countries further away than ever by calling on a gathering of Egyptian intellectuals to carry out their own cultural revolution. 'What you need here is a revolution too ... more democracy, more freedom of thought, speech and action. Egypt says it is ruled by the sovereignty of the law, but your laws are based on foreign regulations and not Islamic law.' The Libyan leader demanded, 'How do you permit all these bars and night-clubs and liquor and gambling? These are not the characteristics of a revolutionary society. How can a drunk make progress in his country? How can a drunk battle in Sinai against the enemy?'

A week later Qaddafi drew protests from feminists in an audience of 800 Egyptian women when he stated that, because of certain 'biological defects', a woman's place was in her home. When challenged that a woman was capable of any profession, the Libyan leader retorted, 'In that case you won't complain if we ask women in our army to parachute when they are pregnant.'

Qaddafi was clearly enjoying these opportunities to air his newfound ideas. In November he took his intellectual road-show to Paris to participate in a *colloque* with prominent French politicians and academicians organized by *Le Monde*, in collaboration with *The Times*, *La Stampa* and *Die Welt*.

It was shortly after the Yom Kippur War and many participants were keener to hear the Colonel's views on the Arab/Israeli conflict than on the Third Universal Theory. Qaddafi, who, according to the *The Times* correspondent Edward Mortimer, was one of the youngest people in the room, parried questions on disengagement and on UN Resolution 242. With ingratiating Parisian smoothness, one speaker likened the Colonel's political ideas, with their emphasis on resistance against superpower hegemony, to the late President de Gaulle's. When the Marxist orientalist Maxime Rodinson pointed out that some of the Theory appeared to have been derived from Marx, the Libyan leader retorted that, in that case, Marx must have been influenced by Islamic philosophers.

The following March Sudan's Minister for Information and Culture, Bona Malwal, visited Tripoli in an official delegation to celebrate the anniversary of the evacuation of British troops from Libya.

Malwal, a southern Sudanese Dinka, had not been too impressed with Qaddafi when he had met him in Sudan the previous year. Qaddafi had travelled to Wau in the south. The young girls of the town had spent three months preparing a dance in his honour, but Qaddafi had refused to watch the ceremony. He demanded to return to his guest house. When Sudan's President Numeiri later asked him, if anything had offended him, Qaddafi said he could not sit there watching girls who were topless. Malwal recalled, 'But they were just children, aged between seven and eleven. Qaddafi had negative feelings about either the culture or the autonomy of the south.' In other words, despite his hopes that his political theories were indeed universal and applicable to all countries, particularly those in the developing world, Qaddafi himself was not a great traveller.

However, when Malwal visited Libya in March 1974 Qaddafi went out of his way to take the Sudanese Minister to his side. He immediately gave him a draft of his Third Universal Theory to read and asked him to make comments on it. 'I didn't find an original idea in it,' said Malwal. Qaddafi was not deterred. He spent the best part of the next two days – flying from Tripoli to Benghazi, and then in Tobruk – trying to convince Malwal of the applicability of his Third Universal Theory to Sudan.

'You have a golden opportunity to have a cultural revolution in Sudan,' Qaddafi told Malwal.

'What do you mean?' the tall southerner replied.

'For a start you should stop all this Western garbage – music, plays, films – you put out on Radio Omdurman.'

'What makes you think I and my people don't like this kind of entertainment?'

Qaddafi was not amused. He stalked away. Malwal was soon recalled to see him on a nearby air force base. Qaddafi had a private room where he had surrounded himself with specially built customized electronic games. One involved American rockets trying to attack Libya, and Russian-made Libyan rockets fending them off.

Surrounded by this adolescent paraphernalia, Qaddafi talked about his ideas and their application in the world. Malwal recalled:

He touched on Arab unity, and its relationship to African unity. He made clear he saw Arab unity definitely happening in his lifetime. He felt all it needed was leadership. He made clear he did not see that coming from Saudi Arabia. It could only come from him.

I told him that the best example he could give to the Arab world would be to develop Libya itself. He said, no, Libya could take care of itself. What the Arab world needed was a series of revolutions.

We had a number of discussions. The most striking thing about them was Qaddafi's show of piousness. I know that in Islam you can defer your prayers. But Qaddafi would always stop a meeting to go and pray. That I thought was a bit too pious. We talked about Islam. He said he considered it the winning religion in the world.

Our meetings were not all serious. Qaddafi often talked slang. He joked about Libya and Sudan. I remember him telling me, 'Major Abul Gasim [the Sudanese Vice-President and leader of the delegation] tells me the revolution in Sudan is still alive. I thought it was dead.'

After hours of such discussion he clearly decided I was not the sort of person he could win over. Afterwards our discussions became much more general. He certainly left a strong impression on me. He was unlike most other leaders I've met. He knows what he wants and goes after it irrespective of what others think.

He didn't know much about Sudan, however. He admitted to Abul Gasim that he didn't understand why Khartoum hung on to the South. 'Why don't you let it go?' he asked.

While Qaddafi was honing his arguments in seminars and conversations, his intellectuals were still working away behind the scenes. Drawing now less directly on Islam and more on European philosophers of natural law such as Rousseau and on Libya's own rich Bedouin tradition, they were putting the final touches to the Green Book, a handbook for the implementation of the Third Universal Theory.

The Green Book's first slim volume, subtitled 'The Solution to the Problem of Democracy' and published in 1975, dealt with the practical business of governing according to the Theory. It sketched in some of the ramifications of Qaddafi's ideas. If 'all political systems in the world today are the product of the struggle for power between instruments of governing', then there always has to be a victor in that struggle – 'be it an individual, group, party or class' – and genuine democracy is defeated.

Qaddafi runs through the various political systems he sees in the world – parliaments, parties, classes and plebiscites – and concludes they are all fraudulent 'dictatorial systems'. The reason is that they deny the participation of the people in a democracy. In a parliamentary system, for example, people give up their sovereignty to representatives who then band together in parties – the very antithesis of democracy. 'For the members of parliament represent their parties and not the people. . . . Under such systems the people are victims, fooled and exploited by political bodies. The people stand silently in long queues to cast their votes in the ballot boxes in the same way as they throw other papers into the dustbin.'

'Representation is Fraud', 'No Representation in lieu of the people', says Qaddafi in two of the aphorisms which litter the volume. True democracy can only be achieved through the Libyan system based on popular congresses. The people form themselves into basic popular congresses at the local level. They choose people's committees to carry out their wishes. These popular congresses and committees then meet together annually in a General People's Congress to decide national issues.

The untutored might compare the General People's Congress to a parliament, but they would be wrong. For, according to the Green Book, there is a crucial difference. The General People's Congress is a collective body, incorporating, if you like, the general will, rather than a talking shop for individuals.

> [It] is not a gathering of members or ordinary persons as is the case with parliaments. It is a gathering of the basic people's congresses, the people's committees, the unions, the syndicates and all professional associations.
>
> In this way, the problem of the instrument of governing is, as a matter of fact, solved and dictatorial instruments disappear. The people are the instrument of governing and the problem of democracy in the world is completely solved.

The volume goes on to deal with other aspects of society such as the law. Clearly if a parliament is undemocratic it cannot draft laws. The trouble with most political systems, says Qaddafi, in a further allusion to the works of Rousseau, is that man-made law and constitutions have replaced the 'genuine law of society' which is defined as 'either tradition (custom) or religion'. Who supervises this law then? Well, no one. 'Democratically, there is no group whatever which can claim the right of representative supervision over society, "Society is its own supervisor".' It supervises itself through its system of congresses.

The final chapter of the first volume is devoted to the press. It is not difficult to predict Qaddafi's view. A newspaper owned by an individual only expresses his view, one 'issued by a trading association or chamber of commerce is only a means of expression for this particular social group'. 'The democratic press is that which is issued by a popular committee comprising all the various categories of society.'

The second volume of the Green Book, published in 1977, is the shortest – not much more than 4,000 words – and also the most full of waffle. It deals with 'The Solution of the Economic Problem'. Earlier obfuscations about socialism are left behind. The goal of society is now admitted to be a particular type of socialism – 'natural socialism', which existed in an idealized period when man conducted his affairs according to 'natural principles', including equality.

Turning to real history, Qaddafi reviews changes in the role and conditions of workers since the Industrial Revolution. He observes that not very much has altered in the crucial relationship between workers, as producers, and employers, who pay their wages. Whether in a private or state sector company, that relationship still amounts to slavery. The way round this is for wages to be abolished and for workers to become partners in the production process, sharing equally in the output or the income derived from it. As slogans festooned throughout Libya in the late 1970s used to say, 'Partners, not wage earners'.

The basic concept in Qaddafi's economic theory is 'need'. 'Man's freedom is lacking if somebody else controls what he needs.' Put another way, man should be self-sufficient. Basic needs, such as housing, transport, clothing, food and even an income, should never be controlled by another. Satisfying these needs, not the pursuit of profit, should be 'the legitimate purpose of the individual's economic activity'. Once basic needs are met, profit and even money are not required.

Sometimes Qaddafi's version of economic history has a curiously Marxist undertone. Although 'natural socialism' is contrasted with the evils of capitalism and atheistic Marxism, the Libyan leader talks about how 'the transformation of the contemporary societies from societies of wage labourers to societies of partners is an inevitable and dialectical outcome of the contradicting economic theses prevailing in the world today'.

The third volume, 'The Social basis of the Third Universal Theory', is the least noticed but most interesting part of the Green Book. In it Qaddafi is in his element. He ranges over the material of philosophers, not of politicians or economists. He talks about heroes and history, about women and the family, and about arts and sports.

The volume, published in 1978, starts with the obscure paragraph, 'The social, i.e. national, factor is the driving force of human history. The social bond which binds together each human group, from the family through the tribe to the nation, is the basis of human history.' The meaning of this becomes clearer as one reads on. Nationalism is a law of nature, like gravity, which binds people together and ensures their survival. 'Nations whose nationalism is destroyed are the subject of ruin.' They give rise to minorities, a subject tackled later in the volume.

What is this nation then? It is certainly not an empire or even a state – both anathema to Qaddafi. (Indeed much of Qaddafi's venom against Israel is derived from his concept of it as a Zionist-inspired European state on Arab soil.) To Qaddafi the nation is a natural phenomenon, a kind of extended family. It is made up of essential smaller social units – the family and the tribe. 'Societies in which the existence and unity of the family are threatened, in any circumstances, are similar to fields whose plants are in danger of being swept away or threatened by drought or fire, or of withering away.'

The family develops into a tribe through procreation. 'It follows that a tribe is a big family. Equally a nation is a tribe which has grown through procreation. The nation, then, is a big tribe. So the world is a nation which has been ramified into various nations. The world, then, is a big nation. The relationship which binds the family is that which binds the tribe, the nation and the world.' Qaddafi goes on, 'It is, therefore, of great importance for human society to maintain the cohesiveness of the family, the tribe, the nation and the world in order to benefit from the advantages, privileges, values and ideals yielded by the solidarity, cohesiveness, unity, intimacy and love of the family, tribe, nation and humanity.'

This can be read in many ways. It is Qaddafi in a blurry-eyed belated hippy phase. It is a curious Arab interpretation of Rousseau. It is even a sinister conservative or quasi-Fascist plea for the supremacy of family values. Some might add that this last idea gains credence in Qaddafi's subsequent chapter, entitled 'Woman'. This argues that because of her biology, and her need to menstruate, give birth and rear children, a woman's natural place is in her home. She must not work, for that is unnatural. 'The mother who abandons her maternity contradicts her natural role in life. She must be provided with her rights and conditions which are appropriate, non-coercive and unoppressive. . . . If a woman is forced to abandon her natural role as regards conception and maternity, she falls victim to coercion and dictatorship. A woman who needs work that renders her unable to perform her natural function is not free and is compelled to that by need, for in need freedom is latent.'

John Davis, Professor of Social Anthropology at the University of Kent, in his penetrating study, *Tribe and Revolution in Libya: The Zuwaya and their Politics*, points out what may be the real key to Qaddafi's political thought, indeed to his whole political system: it is an elaborate attempt to adapt the unanimity found in the Bedouin tribal unit to a wider stage. As Davis shows, Bedouin tribes do not operate according to any formal structure. They retain a strong sense of their own history and integrity. Like Qaddafi, in his theory, they have a vision of a naturally 'just society', where the individual is unfettered by constraints on his individual freedom. Authority is administered by consensus. 'The provision of services (welfare,

116

justice) is assured by the mutual loyalties and cohesion of descent groups,' says Davis.

This was something recognized by the British anthropologist E. E. Evans-Pritchard, who did most of his fieldwork for *The Sanusi of Cyrenaica*, published in 1949, while acting as British Political Officer in the province during the Second World War. He wrote: 'The tribal system . . . is a system of balanced opposition between tribes and tribal sections from the largest to the smallest divisions, and there cannot be any single authority in a tribe. Authority is distributed at every point in tribal structure and political leadership is limited to situations in which a tribe or a segment of it acts corporately.' Even after the overthrow of the monarchy, individuals readily identified with their tribes – in disputes, in demands for 'bloodwealth' and even in elections which officially did not exist.

However, by the late 1970s the Bedouins' image of themselves as stateless nomads was becoming anachronistic. Many of them were living in towns and participating, whatever Qaddafi might say, in the working of a modern nation state. In a strange way this made them cling to that image even more. In the late twentieth century the obligations of belonging to a tribe were hardly onerous. Bedouins did not have to ride for days over the desert to carry out their duties. They could jump in their Peugeots and drive to tribal assemblies; there was always surplus cash or kind to meet welfare and other payments.

Qaddafi made the same mistake. Perhaps realizing that his regime needed tribal support, he adopted the Bedouins' anachronistic image of themselves and made it the bedrock of his political theory – the proud individual must never give up any part of his personal sovereignty (through parliaments or man-made laws); he must retain the illusion of participating in all decision-making.

Referring particularly to the Zuwaya tribe, Davis says they 'found [that] those elements in their image which depended on solidarity among kinsmen, on the massing of cousins, on the exclusion of women, had rather more than an echo in the words of their head of state. And the high value which the Zuwaya placed on individual autonomy, on taking no orders, was elevated in Qaddafi's rhetoric to the touchstone of justice in political organization: Representation is Fraud.'

Both the tribes and Qaddafi were deluding themselves – the Libyan leader perhaps more so, because with his arcadian vision of the natural society he refused to admit to the concept of authority. As Davis explains:

The fundamental concept of the Green Book is that any claim on a person which diminishes individual sovereignty is unjust and oppressive. Hence, abolition of the state, of representative institutions, of parties and of all loyalties which derive from acts of political will and reason rather than natural kinship. Qaddafi writes of constraints, compulsion, oppression – but those are characteristics of states which are based on political rather than on social ('natural') bonds. The word authority and its cognates does not appear once in the Green Book (which is also silent about police, courts, armies and heads of state).

(Davis might have added taxation and finance to his list.)

It was as though these dark elements could not exist in Qaddafi's ideal state. The reality was somewhat different, as only the last paragraph of the first volume of the Green Book seemed to admit. 'Theoretically,' it said, 'this is the genuine democracy. But realistically the strong always rule, i.e. the stronger part in the society is the one that rules.'

8   The Revolution in Practice

On 9 February 1979 the people of Ajdabiya, a medium-sized town of 32,000 inhabitants, on the edge of the Cyrenaican desert, some sixty miles south of Benghazi, were preparing to go to the polls. They had not had a great deal of notice. Although they had known for some time that voting for sixteen people's committees, their local contribution to Qaddafi's political system, was imminent, confirmation of the date had come only two days earlier. Qaddafi's Green Book might pour scorn on the concept of elections, but no one in the town was in doubt what this voting process was about. Townspeople went around talking about the imminent election (*intikhab*); even the Ministry of Information Land-Rovers touring the area referred to it thus.

Under previous administrations Ajdabiya had been an administrative centre (notably for the Senussi). Now it had something of the atmosphere of a boom town. On the routes between Benghazi and Tripoli and Benghazi and Kufrah, it had a new role as a flourishing service centre for the oil industry. Despite the trappings of prosperity, the inhabitants of Ajdabiya saw the forthcoming poll as much more than an election. For them it was a tribal contest. Two distinct lists for the sixteen committees had been drawn up – one comprising candidates from the dominant Sa'ada tribe, the Magharba, the other from the more lowly Zuwaya.

Everyone seemed to recognize this basic reality. Two thousand, three hundred voters presented themselves at Ajdabiya football pitch on the morning of 8 February. At 10 a.m. the gates were shut to prevent any subsequent swing in the poll from late arrivals. The candidates for the first committee – on development – were presented. On the Magharba slate there was a young local primary school teacher, on the Zuwaya a professor of economics from Benghazi University.

The 'electoral' commissioner, a Captain Awud from Benghazi, proposed that, as the total number in the stadium was known, it was only necessary to count the number voting for one candidate. Those supporting the primary school teacher were asked to assemble on the northern half of the pitch, those backing the economics professor on the southern half.

The Magharba in the northern half were then asked to file past the goal posts, where a clerk touched each of them on the head, counting the numbers out loud as they went. When the total had reached 1,235, indicating a Magharba victory, the Zuwaya protested. They claimed that there were Magharba present who were not qualified to vote. After a check of identity cards, the electoral commissioner appeared to agree, for he ordered a recount.

The second process of 'choosing', as Qaddafi preferred to call it, got underway around 1.30 p.m. Everything was going well until, towards the end, a fight broke out near the Zuwaya goalmouth, where the counting was not taking place. The Zuwaya claimed that the teller, who happened to be a Magharba (although as secretary of the local people's assembly he was supposed to be above the fray) had counted 900 votes when there should have been 1,000. A policeman who was counter-checking agreed. The teller immediately climbed down; he said he would accept the revised count. But the Zuwaya were not placated. They argued that, in that case, he might have 'stolen' more than a hundred votes.

As Professor John Davis reports, stones were thrown and the teller was hurried away in a police car. In an ensuing discussion the Zuwaya suggested that because of the late hour the vote should be postponed until the next day. The Magharba protested that they had already proved their greater numbers; the Zuwaya were stalling so that they could muster more tribesmen at a later date.

Captain Awud left the pitch to find a telephone in order to call Tripoli for advice. He returned to say that the choosing process was postponed for a couple of days. However, for some reason, the Ministry of Information Land-Rovers circled the town that evening declaring that the election was to be held once more on the following day, a Friday.

The voting procedure of the previous morning was followed again. This time the Zuwaya emerged as clear victors by 117 votes. It was the Magharba's turn to complain. They did so vehemently. They attacked and overturned the election officials' desk, breaking Captain Awud's arm in the process. As he was rushed to hospital, the police intervened, placing a human barrier of officers between the Zuwaya and Magharba ends of the pitch. Surprisingly, however, after an hour this cordon sanitaire was removed. Within minutes the opposing tribesmen were at each other's throats again. Fighting spread to surrounding streets and lasted for several hours. Shots were fired, apparently by civilians, several people were badly hurt, and the vote was again annulled.

A third round of elections was scheduled for the following Wednesday, 14 February. The atmosphere was rather different from the previous week. The actual voting was to take place in the school playground where the electoral commissioners – not the single Captain Awud but a whole busload from Benghazi – had access to telephones and other modern communications which could be used to call help if the going got rough. There was just one access route to the playground which was ringed by troops, also bused in from Benghazi. Some of the soldiers took up positions, armed with machine-guns, on the roofs of buildings overlooking the venue.

Voters entering the playground were searched for knives, sticks and other possible offensive weapons. Eventually the Magharba candidate, the primary school teacher, was declared the new member of the local people's committee's development commission by just four votes, 1,261 to 1,257.

Predictably the Zuwaya protested. They said the Magharba had brought in new voters from the neighbouring districts of Bishr and Marada. The electoral commission was not to be moved. The Zuwaya left the playground *en masse*. As Davis reports, they 'sat in the streets near the school listening to the amplified announcements of successive unanimous votes for Magharba candidates, men – as one bank manager said indignantly and exaggeratedly – "without a school leaving certificate between them" '.

The whole process seemed a long way from Qaddafi's vision of 'natural' direct democracy. It bears more resemblance to those anachronistic ways of government the Libyan leader talked of in his Green Book:

> All political systems in the world today are the product of the struggle for power between instruments of governing. The struggle may be peaceful or armed, such as the conflict of classes, sects, tribes, parties or individuals . . . The result is always the victory of an instrument of governing – be it an individual, group, party or class and the defeat of the people, i.e. the defeat of genuine democracy.

In Ajdabiya, tribes had been in conflict. Whether there had been a victory of an instrument of governing is unlikely, if only because the phrase is gobbledygook. However, there does seem to have been a defeat of genuine democracy, though not for the reasons Qaddafi

121

himself gives. Rather the opposite: because Qaddafi's system refused to allow the concept of an election, there was no airing of issues, no opportunity for citizens to make up their minds on one side or another. Instead the election 'campaign' was concentrated into the few hours when voters congregated together to pass openly through the lists. (Secret ballots were of course outlawed; the Libyan system of direct democracy involved, at least in theory, a collective vote, in which each person was, as Davis puts it, 'answerable for his performance of his democratic duty'.)

Inevitably in such conditions there was little or no opportunity for rational discussion. Tribal allegiances took precedence over others. As Davis points out, the situation, if anything, exacerbated tribal feelings. 'As [tribesmen] did not have policy grounds for changing sides during the ballot, if they changed sides their action could only have been interpreted as a betrayal of tribal identity. For these reasons those Magharba and Zuwaya who were, so to speak, not tribally minded, stayed away: voters who regarded themselves as modernizing were silenced, and the turn-out was somewhat lower than would otherwise have been the case.' Such were some of the problems of trying to graft Qaddafi's idealistic political system on to what was still a fairly basic society, even in the late 1970s.

Qaddafi, the revolutionary, was in a hurry. But his people were lethargic and often jealous of their local rights. Qaddafi tried to assure them that their autonomy was respected in his system. Soon after this Zwara speech of April 1973 he was urging Libyans to take over their places of work, to root out foreign influences, to take their destiny into their own hands.

By late 1975 the basic structure of Qaddafi's new system was operational. People's assemblies made up of all adults met at regular intervals to discuss issues of the day (such as the siting of a local hospital) and to elect people's committees charged with sixteen areas of administration – finance, education, health, electricity, development, posts and telecommunications, agriculture, justice, municipalities, youth affairs, planning, housing, employment, water, transport and building. Crucially missing from the list were defence and petroleum. The people's committee chairmen became the executive committee charged with local administrative authority.

On what might be described as the consultative side of the political framework, the country's 187 people's assemblies, known from 1977 as basic people's congresses, sent three members (Qaddafi, in his rhetoric, refused to call them delegates or representatives) to an annual General People's Congress.

On the executive side the people's committee chairmen participated in national committees, corresponding to their sixteen areas of activity, which oversaw the workings of ministries, or what came to be known as secretariats of the General People's Congress. (Thus the Foreign Minister, for example, would be known officially as the Secretary of the General People's Congress for Foreign Affairs.)

The first General People's Congress was convened in January 1976 on a day previously scheduled for the third annual meeting of the Arab Socialist Union. Since the official political party had been struggling to find its feet for four years, it was killed off by this coincidence of dates. Similarly, not much more was heard of the Revolutionary Command Council. Qaddafi's close friend Mohammed al Magharief, the only aristocrat among the Council members, was killed in a car crash in August 1971. Mukhtar Gerwi, Mohammed Najm and Awad Hamza had backed out in one way or another. Omar Meheishi had attempted to stage a coup against Qaddafi in August 1975 and had fled to Egypt, where he was joined by Abdul Moneim al Houni. Bashir Hawadi, former secretary-general of the ASU, was detained in Libya for allegedly having a hand in the coup attempt, and remains to this day under house arrest. Apart from Qaddafi, only four members of the RCC survived – Major Jalloud, the trusted deputy, Colonel Mustafa Kharroubi, with a watching brief on intelligence, Colonel Khweldi Hameidi, who had a shadowy role as head of the people's militias, and Brigadier (as he later became) Abu Bakr Younis, the army chief of staff. From around the end of the 1970s, these five were being officially referred to as the 'historic leadership'.

By 1976 Libya was no longer looking towards Egypt as its political mentor. Relations with its neighbour had deteriorated rapidly after the October War of 1973. Although Qaddafi still hankered after the idea of unity with Egypt, he and Egypt's new President, Anwar Sadat, soon grew to dislike each other intensely. They harboured each other's opponents. They traded insults. Qaddafi called Sadat a friend of Zionism and imperialism, Sadat openly questioned Qaddafi's sanity. In July 1977 the two countries came to blows, as President Carter temporarily gave the go-ahead to Sadat to carry out a blistering series of air-raids and tank sorties into eastern Cyrenaica. After three days the Egyptian forces pulled out. The Libyans had been roundly beaten, though the official media gave no details of their losses.

Instead the Libyan media were concerned with reporting the latest phase of Qaddafi's revolution, the announcement of the Jamahiriya, which is often translated as 'the state of the masses', but literally it is rather closer to 'the state of massdom', a curious Qaddafi neologism in keeping with his concept of the people as an abstract generalized force. The Jamahiriya was officially inaugurated in March 1977. Libya became Al Jamahiriya al Arabiya al Libya al Shaabiya al Ishtirakiya, officially translated into English as the Socialist People's Libyan Arab Jamahiriya, often known by its initial letters, Splaj.

The average Libyan was confused by these changes, but he was not fooled. Despite the ubiquitous presence of the official media, he had ways of finding out what was really going on. One of the side-effects of the Libyan oil boom had been a phenomenal influx of Japanese consumer electronic equipment. No Libyan home was complete without its high-powered radio and cassette. As in the old days, people would regularly tune into Radio Cairo for information. They would balance this with what the news broadcasts from the BBC in London and Saudi radio in Riyadh were saying. Choice commentaries would be recorded on cassettes (usually directly from popular dual-function cassette radio machines) and distributed among friends. Armed with information, Libyans could generally keep the bruising rhetoric of the Jamahiriyah at bay. Within carefully described areas, they were jealous of their local rights.

Davis tells a couple of amusing stories. In the autumn of 1978 a Jordanian canteen manager at the Occidental Petroleum plant down the coast from Ajdabiya at Zuwaitina took delivery of a consignment of fifty-five gross tins of processed milk from the country's main importer and distributor, the Food and Dairy Products Committee in Tripoli. The Jordanian, employed by a subsidiary of the British multinational Grand Metropolitan Hotels, noticed that the expiry date on the tins had passed. He telexed Tripoli to say he could not therefore accept delivery. He then went on holiday. Some days later his deputy, a Scot, received a circular from the Food and Dairy Products Committee extending all expiry dates by a few weeks. He decided to use the milk in the canteen.

The Scot had not reckoned with what can only be described as an officious local policeman, who, eating in the canteen, happened to notice the old expiry date. The Jordanian manager was promptly issued with a summons for selling milk unfit for human consumption. When he informed the local police about the circular, they were profoundly uninterested. As far as they were concerned, the expiry date was that on the tin.

The issue escalated into a contest of authority between Tripoli and Ajdabiya district. The Jordanian appealed to the Food and Dairy

Products Committee to tell the police they had no authority to over-rule its circular. The committee wrote to the head of the executive committee of the people's assembly, the 'mayor', and he took the matter up with the chief of police – to no avail. The police insisted that only they had the authority to decide what was fit or unfit for consumption in Ajdabiya.

As the date for a court summons drew closer, local people cottoned on to the fact that this might be described as a 'constitutional' issue. The 'mayor' found himself in an alarming position. As a pragmatist who had backed the Jordanian and tried to get the police to see sense, he realized he might be called as a witness for the defence and have to argue that Tripoli's authority was superior to that of the local munici-pality and its police force. That could cost him votes. Alternatively, if he did not speak up for the defence, the prosecution might succeed and his standing in the capital would plummet. In the end a compro-mise was reached. It was discovered that the Scot had signed a form taking on legal responsibility for the canteen when the Jordanian went on holiday. The police decided not to bring a case against this unfortunate deputy.

In the following year, 1979, the local assemblies or basic people's congresses were called upon to debate Libya's relations with Malta. An important issue was whether the Jamahiriya should provide its smaller neighbour with economic assistance. One well-informed young man, who worked for an oil company, jumped up and declared that there was no point in discussing the issue. The *Financial Times* had reported the granting of Libyan aid to Malta and the establish-ment of Libyan/Maltese joint ventures six months previously. The same man queried the value of discussing salary rises for municipal employees because the municipalities' overall budget had not been disclosed and it was not therefore possible to take a rational decision on whether to apportion available funds to a pay rise or to something else.

However, demonstrations of local autonomy and individual spirit such as these were the exception rather than the rule in Qaddafi's Libya. The majority of the population was more interested in sharing in the fruits of the great oil bonanza which had hit Libya in the 1970s.

Economic growth and development in the years immediately before and after Qaddafi's accession to power had been so dramatic that figures become almost meaningless. In a population estimated at just 1.9 million in 1970 and rising by the most optimistic reckoning to only 3 million in 1980, oil production had increased from an average of 18,000 barrels per day in 1961 to 2.77 million barrels per day in 1968. Qaddafi immediately pushed output up to 3.31 million barrels per day in 1970. Subsequently, as oil prices began to rise and 'conservation' measures were introduced, pumping was cut back – to 2.76 million barrels a day in 1971, 2.2 million in 1972 and around 2 million for most of the rest of the decade. That was enough to assure the government of more than enough money for its domestic development programmes – and for its arms purchases and foreign military adventures. Revenues grew from $1.3 billion in 1970 to $2.3 billion in 1973, then took off, with the post-October War shake-out of the oil market, to $6 billion in 1974 and $8.6 billion in 1978, before showing another dramatic rise to $16.3 billion in 1979 and around $20 billion in 1980.

In line with these figures gross domestic product rose from $500 million in 1962 to $3.8 billion in 1969, $13.7 billion in 1974 and $24.5 billion in 1979. Average per-capita income which in 1951 was just $40 had grown to $8,170 in 1979 – more than the average in industrialized countries such as Italy and the United Kingdom.

Life for most Libyans had undoubtedly changed for the better. John Mason, a member of the international staff of the Co-operative Housing Foundation in Washington, made two visits to an isolated berber community in the oasis of Augila in the Sahara in east Libya, once before the coup in 1968 and again in 1977 to study how the community had changed during Qaddafi's revolution.

Augila consists of one main village and four satellite hamlets. In 1968 the population was about 2,000; by 1977 it had doubled. On his first visit most villagers found employment in the oil industry. The labourers commuted daily by truck to the nearby oilfields where the companies Exxon, Mobil and Occidental were drilling. The villagers worked as watchmen, kitchen help, porters and drivers. Mason said a fifth of the village labour force worked for the government, as teachers, religious functionaries, office workers, watchmen and messengers. About 10 per cent were merchants, shopkeepers and tradesmen. In 1968 there were schools, fully sponsored by the government, which offered the equivalent of ninth grade education, and Mason said that 'while Augila had emerged from both subsistence and peasant-type economies, it had not yet reached the point of sustained integration with the larger Libyan society'.

When Mason went back in 1977 there had been a lot of changes:

> The time it took me to get there from the coast was cut by three-quarters. The saving was due to an asphalt highway across the desert completed in 1972. . . . As I sped from the desert's edge

into the oasis . . . my first sight of dozens of new public buildings and literally scores of new homes struck like an unannounced sand storm.

It was as if the quiet village I lived in and depicted in 1968 had become a bustling town overnight. Five new educational centres had been constructed, including a Koranic school of which the secondary and girls school had been newly introduced to Augila . . . a large modern clinic had been completed.

He says that public housing had increased, there were new mosques and a cinema under construction.

In one fifteen-minute period there were more cars parked in the public square of the main village than I had counted in the oasis during my entire stay in '68–'69. In 1978 about a hundred families had a car compared to a total of only seven cars in '68. . . . More cash was available to everyone and there was much to buy. Internal plumbing was becoming a reality whereas traditionally water had to be laboriously pumped from wells and carried home.

For Qaddafi the most attractive feature of Libya's new-found prosperity, generated largely but not exclusively by the oil sector, was that it meant that, unlike most rulers in history, he did not need his people's consent for taxes to finance the workings of his government. Revenues came more or less directly to him, and he could do what he liked with them. All he needed to keep them coming in were some Western mercenaries working as oil technicians and considerably fewer dedicated Libyan bureaucrats willing to ensure that the country's bank accounts abroad were regularly credited with the right sums by oil companies and able to send telexes paying suppliers or repatriating funds from these accounts when required.

Of course, as a 'natural' socialist, Qaddafi also had to give something back to his people. Even King Idris had, in his desultory way, modernized parts of the Libyan economy – particularly housing and education. Now, with enormously greater wealth at his disposal, Qaddafi simply turned on the tap to all sectors.

In the eight years before the revolution expenditure on development was nearly $2 billion, with around 30 per cent going on housing. In the decade 1970–80 this total jumped nearly twenty times to $36.5 billion, of which 22 per cent went on agriculture and land reclamation, 20 per cent on industry, 12 per cent on housing, 11 per cent on electricity, 9 per cent on utilities, including water and roads, and 6 per cent on education. One measure of the effects of this policy is that the contribution of oil and gas to Libyan GDP declined from 63 per cent in 1970 to 45.5 per cent in 1980 as other sectors of the economy, particularly services, increased their share.

At the start of the 1970s government policies even helped create a new class of Libyan capitalist. State banks provided anyone who asked with up to 95 per cent of the cost of a commercial venture. As Omar el Fathaly and Monte Palmer record in *Political Development and Social Change in Libya*,

> A man could form a paper company, get a personal loan or use his savings to provide the necessary 5 per cent capital, receive his loan from the government bank, complete 10 per cent of the project by subleasing to a foreign firm, and start receiving a direct draw from the government which would be used to repay principles and interest and to reap a substantial profit. Procedures were even more generous for entrepreneurs wishing to initiate industrial ventures, with government banks offering 100 per cent financing. All that was required were remotely plausible ideas.

Certain industries, such as plastics, footwear, foodstuffs and metal goods, were exempt from taxation and custom duties. As a result in 1977, according to Howard Blutstein, writing in the American University in Washington's Libya area handbook, there were nearly ninety new factories, mostly in the foodstuffs industry, in various stages of completion. El Fathaly and Palmer report that in the coastal town of Sabratha, where before the revolution three firms shared government contracting work, thirty companies were competing for it in 1971. In Tripolitania alone, some 40,000 new grocery licences were issued in the first seven years of the revolution.

There was a similar bonanza in the countryside. Land confiscated from thousands of Italian farmers, mainly around Tripoli, was redistributed to deserving Libyans, many of them civil servants who wanted a weekend retreat. Landless farmers were provided with land and with all inputs, including machinery and livestock, at 10 per cent of value. Land purchases were interest-free and could be amortized over twenty years. In many cases, individuals would simply be given 25 acres of land and paid a salary to farm it until such time as it was profitable. Then they would be able to purchase the land through a mortgage on 10 per cent of its estimated value.

There was little incentive in this set-up to succeed. Despite nearly $78 billion pumped into it during the 1970s, at all levels, including the prestigious government projects in southern oases such as Kufrah and around Tripoli, agriculture was a spectacular flop. Its

Wearing traditional
Arab robes in London during
his army training course, 1966

Soon after the coup in September 1969, Qaddafi makes his first public
appearance at a rally with several of his Free Officers

With Presidents Sadat and Assad in Damascus, August 1971

Praying in the Sirtic desert with a close aide, 1973

Qaddafi's parents and members of his family
in their tent in the Sirtic desert, 1976

With his mother

Explaining a fine political point to members of a
people's congress in Sebha

Qaddafi, the statesman – Tunisia, 1983

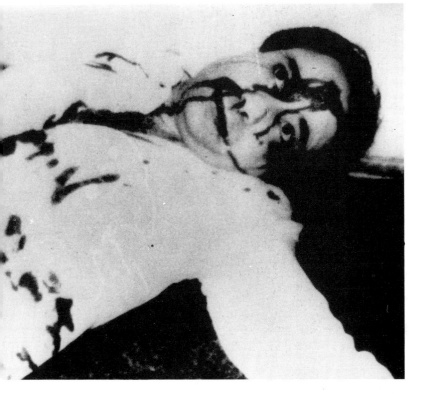

The photograph that tricked
Qaddafi into believing that
the assassination attempt on
former Prime Minister Abdul
Hamid Bakoush had
succeeded, November 1984

Qaddafi's right-hand man,
Major Abdul Salam Jalloud –
Tripoli, 1986

At prayer in his private plane

During talks at the Kremlin with Mikhail Gorbachov, October 1985

The flamboyant dresser: in Italianate suit
… and flowing cloak (with his wife Safiya)

Qaddafi's wife Safiya declaiming against US aggression following the raid on Tripoli, April 1986

Making his international political comeback after the US raid at the meeting of the Non-aligned Movement in Harare, September 198

contribution to GDP declined from 2.6 per cent in 1970 to 1.9 per cent in 1980 (when an admittedly succulent piece of Kufrah lamb in the Tripoli market cost five times as much as its imported frozen New Zealand equivalent) and, overall, Libya was more dependent on food imports than a decade earlier.

One early consequence of this redistribution of wealth was a boom in the Libyan property market. By 1973 capital formation in the housing sector – at around $500 million – was the largest in any sector of the economy (20 per cent of the total throughout the economy). Soon a class of *nouveau riche* capitalists mouthing revolutionary slogans could be found throughout Libya. This was not what Qaddafi's planners had intended. Greater state control of Libya's economy was progressively introduced from the middle of the 1970s.

Some sectors, particularly oil, were effectively nationalized early on. Libyan negotiators cleverly played to the junkie mentality of the foreign oil companies. In their eagerness for guaranteed sources of crude, the oil companies snatched at Libyan offers of access to an agreed proportion of the output of fields they operated (this was their 'equity crude'). A number of factories had come under government control during the first couple of years of the revolution , after large numbers of Italians were expelled. In 1969 around three-quarters of the industrial plants in the country had been privately owned. State control of the rest of Libya's manufacturing sector (estimated in 1973 at around 6,000 firms – everything from cement factories to motor-repair works – of which 5,400 were privately owned) was more gradual.

In 1973 the government started by legislating on profit sharing. All firms with more than ten employees were ordered to distribute a quarter of their profits to their workers – 30 per cent in cash, the rest in employee benefits. Private firms with a payroll of over fifty had to have two of its staff as directors. This type of edict helped distribute Libya's oil wealth more widely. As Omar el Fathaly and Monte Palmer note, 'Libya's lower classes, including some 50,000 door watchers, coffee fetchers, and similar individuals, were suddenly on their way to becoming comfortable members of the middle class.'

By 1975 Qaddafi was clearly worried about the growing economic power of the new capitalists. A series of laws introduced in September 1975 sought 'to curb exploitation and end unlawful parasitical incomes'. All foreign trade was taken over by public corporations. Three thousand housing units built with the help of government loans were nationalized. Following the introduction of the Third Universal Theory, calls for greater employee participation began to be made regularly. But it was not until September 1978, after the publication of the second volume of the Green Book, with its motto that workers should be partners, not wage earners, that the Libyan leader urged his people to take over the firms they worked for. By December 1978 some 180 companies, including farms, hotels, factories and construction firms, were in the hands of their employees.

Around the same time Qaddafi took further steps to restrict the real estate bonanza. A law on property ownership, issued in May 1978, laid down that Libyan families could own only one house. At a stroke thousands of tenants immediately became owners of their houses.

Most of these moves, while restricting the wealth of a small number of Libyans, had the effect of ensuring that many more eventually shared in a piece of the sizeable cake. Even those still without land or capital could benefit. As they were assimilated into the money economy, nomadic tribespeople began to drift towards the towns where they could call on all the trappings of Qaddafi's welfare state from free schooling and health services to subsidized housing, food and even cars.

Idris's visionary people's housing projects of the late 1960s were put in abeyance. Instead Qaddafi commissioned East European architects to run up anonymous-looking high-rise apartment blocks where deracinated Bedouins could be found cooped up in stuffy flats on the eighth floor, trying to tend a couple of sheep on the balcony.

It was not necessarily a good life, but it was not bad either. Undemanding jobs, offering an attractive minimum wage, could always be found for Libyans in the civil service or public sector. Employment involving some commitment, whether waiting in a restaurant or working in a hospital, was often reserved for foreigners. The non-Libyan element in the labour force rose from 16 per cent in 1972 to over 40 per cent, and probably significantly more, in 1980. In construction, it was as much as 70 per cent.

The average Libyan luxuriated, if it can be called that, in this welfare state. He played cards with his friends in street cafés. Otherwise his main recreational activity was careering around the streets of Tripoli or Benghazi in his brand-new car. Sometimes there were football matches or films to watch. Occasionally he might be dragged along to take part in a rally when Colonel Qaddafi was giving a speech. Until 1978, when travel restrictions were introduced, he could always pop over the border for a weekend of drinking and dancing in the rather more sophisticated environment of Djerba in Tunisia.

But there was little getting away from the fact that he was bored.

This showed, not only in occasional remarks to visitors, but also in statistics on such social phenomena as crime and marital strife. In 1974 there were 55 per cent more murders than in the previous year. Manslaughter cases were up 25 per cent, suicides 10 per cent. Although major robberies were down, smaller acts of theft were up 24 per cent from 3,619 to 4,500, while cases of car theft, a typical offence by a disaffected youngster, increased by 45 per cent from 378 to 547.

Qaddafi referred to the increase in violence, robberies and traffic accidents in a speech in Benghazi in April 1973, shortly after his Zwara Declaration. He berated his audience for not helping him disarm the police altogether. 'I wanted them to be like the British police, with a notebook, pencil or map to guide the people, not with a gun or a stick.' But Libyans had taken advantage of this enlightened hands-off approach to policing. 'The people of the Third World will need another 500 years to understand that a policeman, even unarmed, must be respected,' he said regretfully.

Libya's basic criminal code of 1954 was gradually extended. Laws such as those promulgated in October 1973 and September 1974 stipulating flogging and imprisonment for adulterers and homosexuals gave it a more moralistic and Islamic tinge. In 1975 a tough new law against corruption was introduced. The same year, following Major Omar Meheishi's attempted coup, a number of provisions in Law 80 laid down harsh penalties, including hanging, for crimes against the state. The law came to be used retrospectively. Two years later twenty-two soldiers and four civilians allegedly involved in the attempted coup were hanged – not only the first executions under Qaddafi but also the first for twenty-three years. While this was shocking to most Libyans – evidence that Qaddafi was cracking down harshly on sections of society which directly threatened his regime – the general approach to crime, punishment and rehabilitation was benevolent, in keeping with the East European-style social welfare system.

A 1971 decree provided for a rehabilitation centre for female criminals in Tripoli. The aim of the centre was 'to offer shelter to those minors and divorced women who are exposed to deviance, in order to guide them socially, psychologically and religiously. The aim is to improve their behaviour and enable them to return to a good family life and to adjust to society.' The Tripoli centre was followed by another in Benghazi in 1976 and a third in Tripoli in 1977.

Despite his patronizing attitude to women in the Green Book and in seminars, Qaddafi was very aware of the contribution they could make to the development of Libyan society. He encouraged them out of the home – into offices, places of work, hospitals, and eventually even into the army. In the early 1980s Qaddafi would often be seen with his bodyguard of female Amazon soldiers – a corps he laughingly referred to as his 'revolutionary nuns', though doubts have been expressed about their chastity.

Some Libyans say Qaddafi cynically exploited feminism to win the crucial support of women in his drive to radicalize society. Conservative males were often outraged at Qaddafi's encouragement to women to join the army and win better matrimonial rights. 'Divorce should not take place from one side only,' he said in 1976 in a reference to the traditional Islamic practice whereby a man need only pronounce the words 'I divorce you' three times to be freed from the marriage bond. 'Both parties should agree to it, and it should be done before a court of justice.'

Despite Qaddafi's support for their emancipation, women do not appear to have been much happier in his Libya than before. Marius and Mary Jane Deeb in *Libya Since the Revolution* point to the discontent with marriage exhibited by young women writing to the women's magazine *Al Mara* in the middle to late 1970s. Most common were complaints referring to their husbands' frequent absences from home and general lack of communication and affection.

Indeed an image for Qaddafi's Libya at the end of his first decade in power is of a surly and uncommunicative people, somewhat befuddled by his promises and rhetoric, putting up with doubts and inconveniences because their standard of living had grown so appreciably. Some were not so happy with this neurotically bustling but ultimately lethargic state of affairs. They challenged Qaddafi's Utopia and he cracked down on them hard.

9 Tightening the Screws

In July 1974 Mohammed bin Ghalboun, a stocky twenty-seven-year-old building contractor, was sitting in his house in Benghazi's al Fuwayhat suburb when two police cars drew up. An officer asked him to accompany them down to the local Ras Obeidah police station where bin Ghalboun was astonished to find himself being questioned in connection with an armed attack which had been made on an army building in the centre of Benghazi two days earlier.

The six-storey building on the town's major thoroughfare, Sharia Gamal Abdul Nasser, had special significance because it was the quarters where Qaddafi had chosen to house his first female army recruits. Like many aspects of the cultural revolution initiated by the Declaration, Qaddafi's plans for women soldiers antagonized the more traditional elements in Libyan society. There had been protests from the Muslim clergy against this particular act of emancipation.

In the assault on the girls' quarters in Sharia Gamal Abdul Nasser one guard had been killed and two others wounded in an exchange of fire. The only information about the attackers was that they were civilians. This was the first time civilians, as opposed to members of the military, had openly taken up arms against the regime, and the police determined to clear up the case quickly. Why they chose to arrest bin Ghalboun, the scion of a prominent Benghazi family, is unclear. He was able to hire the best lawyer in town, Omran Bou Ruweis, who was later to head an anti-Qaddafi dissident group based in Baghdad . When he was charged in court two weeks later, the case was dismissed for lack of evidence. 'That was when we still had an independent judiciary,' he says ruefully today.

However, the authorities were not satisfied with bin Ghalboun's acquittal. His file was passed further up. Almost a year later, in June 1975, bin Ghalboun was in his office in Sharia Ruwayfa Ansari when he was rearrested on an order signed by RCC member Khweldi Hameidi in Tripoli. This time there was no going to a police station, no pretence of a legal process. Bin Ghalboun recalls:

I was taken to Ras Obeidah supply station, where the police kept their weapons and equipment and where there was a small prison for military offenders.

Nobody knew where I was. My family and lawyer searched throughout the city. They went to court and obtained an injunction demanding that the authorities reveal where I was if they were holding me. But no details were given.

Inside the supply station I was being interrogated by two different groups of intelligence officers. They each operated like an investigating committee. The main one was headed by an intelligence officer, who told me I was now their property and that they had an order from the RCC to carry out my investigation until they had a confession. He told me they were going to torture me. He said, 'We're not asking you whether you carried out the attack or not. We know you did it. What we want to know is how you did it and with whom.'

They started to torture me. My feet were whipped with wire. Cigarettes were stubbed out on my back. I didn't know what to do. I had no information whatsoever about the attack. I was not involved. But I did know some of the details. In those days it was still possible to obtain official court documents on a case. My lawyer had paid 15 dinars for my file the previous year. I recalled some of the facts about the attack from it.

My interrogators seemed quite pleased. My corroboration showed their investigation had been along the right lines. They continued to torture me and asked me to sign a confession about my involvement in the incident. After three or four days of this, I was beyond caring. I refused to name any colleagues. I said I had carried it out by myself. I signed all the papers they put before me.

They then put me in a cell and told me they were going to keep me there for two or three months until my wounds had healed. Then they were going to bring me to court again. They seemed keen to have an open conclusion to the case so as to show everybody that such attacks could not go undetected.

My family and lawyer kept persevering in their attempts to find out where I was. After a couple more weeks they discovered where I was detained. They petitioned in the High Court for the supply station to confirm or deny I was there. A legal officer eventually came down to see me. He immediately called for a nurse to tend my wounds.

When my case came to court again two months later I had little difficulty proving that my confession had been extracted under torture. It became a big joke. I was able to show the judge the court record of the previous year and how my so-called confession matched it almost word for word.

The intelligence services hated me more for this. They rearrested me again the same week. This time they took me to Al Birka military camp where they kept me in solitary confinement. My lawyer and friends once again tried to petition the High Court. They concentrated their efforts on the authorities in Tripoli. Eventually the case came to the notice of Abu Bakr Younis and Qaddafi, and, for some reason, after I had spent two months in solitary confinement, they ordered my release.

However, bin Ghalboun was now a marked man.

I was followed, my phone was tapped and my car bugged whenever anything happened in the country. I couldn't live in peace. I decided I would have to get out of the country. But I didn't have a passport. That had been confiscated at the time of my arrest. I concentrated my efforts on trying to get my passport back. Eventually I came off the blacklist of people forbidden to leave the country. But then the authorities would not give visas to me and my family together. I had to convince them I was a trustworthy citizen. I had to make two business trips abroad on my own, and come back, before my family was allowed a visa.

Eventually in 1978, four years after his initial arrest, bin Ghalboun was able to leave the country, together with his family. He never went back. Today he lives comfortably in a suburb of the northern British city of Manchester where in 1981 he founded the pro-monarchist Libyan Constitutional Union and where Qaddafi's agents have frequently tried to seek him out and kill him.

Although relatively small-scale, bin Ghalboun's run-in with the security service in 1974 and 1975 came at a critical time for the Libyan regime. Qaddafi was beginning to meet with resistance against his concept of a cultural revolution as spelt out in his Zwara Declaration. He therefore redoubled his efforts to root out what he portrayed as foreign cultural influences. On one level this meant demanding that all visitors to Libya had details on their passports written in Arabic. On another it meant hitting at groups with overseas links. He started with obvious targets like Baathists and Marxists. But when Muslim Brothers started attacking initiatives like the recruitment of women to the army, the whole official Islamic clergy became suspect.

As Qaddafi's own ideas became more defined, anything that threatened their credibility and implementation was deemed suspect, whether it be an obdurate bureaucracy or the independence of mind and action which came from a private income.

At first Qaddafi thought he could rely on his people to support his policies – through their people's committees and their involvement in his Jamahiriya system. When their revolutionary zeal proved not up to the task, Qaddafi started training a special corps of ideological shock troops, the revolutionary committees, who, from around 1978, could frequently be found taking the law into their own hands, cajoling recalcitrant Libyans to keep to the Qaddafi path.

It is difficult to overestimate the importance of the Zwara Declaration. Prior to 1973 there had been arrests of associates of the old regime and suspected collaborators in a series of early coup attempts, but the trappings of a judiciary had been maintained. Despite Qaddafi's excesses, Libyans still believed they were living in a relatively civilized state.

Everything changed after the Zwara Declaration in April 1973. Mansur Kikhia, Foreign Minister at the time , recalled, 'it was then that the laws were abolished and the people were encouraged to take them into their own hands. From then on there was an inevitable progression to the calls to eliminate the opposition in 1979 and 1980.' Kikhia ascribes the dramatic change in Qaddafi's manner of dealing with power to the Libyan leader's 'desire for change'. Even 'his colleagues in the RCC could not agree about these things'. So Qaddafi was forced to set the pace himself.

Publicly Qaddafi had promised that the new, intensified phase of his revolution would at least be benevolent. Addressing students in Benghazi shortly after the Zwara Declaration, he said, 'From now on we are going to put in prison anyone who continues to talk in his sick way about Communism, Marxism or atheism.' He added reassuringly, 'There will be none of the police-state methods of other Arab regimes. We won't act in the dark, secretly throwing people in prison, breaking their necks and saying they fell off a wall. . . . People need not fear for their lives or security or property. We are Muslims – with the Muslim law.'

In reality things were rather different. Libya's Interior Ministry under Khweldi Hameidi, was boosted with the arrival of Karl Hans, at the head of a team of East German intelligence experts. The shadowy Hans, with his fabled knowledge of Arabic, theology, psychology and medicine, was reputed to report directly to East German intelligence chief Karlo Wolf.

During the summer of 1973 Qaddafi's Green Terror was unleashed as hundreds of covert members of the Baathist and Marxist parties were arrested. Among the detainees was Kikhia's own brother, Abdul Latif, a Baathist who headed Tripoli's chamber of commerce. Kikhia, who resigned shortly afterwards, recalled, 'I used to argue with Qaddafi about the escalating violence of his regime. But he used to laugh and tell me that there were some things I could not understand. He said the fact that the revolution had to be violent was one of the regrettable changes he had been forced to introduce.'

Sporadic acts of violence such as the attack on the women's army barracks in Benghazi, followed by arbitrary random arrests like bin Ghalboun's, and reports of torture by the regime's security forces, were becoming commonplace during 1974 and 1975.

Within the crumbling Revolutionary Command Council, dissident member Major Omar Meheishi began openly to take a stand against the regime's growing excesses. In May 1975, in a meeting of the Council, Major Jalloud called upon him to justify his position. Meheishi refused to rise to the bait. During the course of the summer he began talking in earnest with fellow RCC members Bashir Hawadi (who had chaired the revolutionary courts in the year after the coup) and Awad Hamza about getting rid of Qaddafi. Speaking to *Al Ahram* the following year Meheishi denied that he and his colleagues had been attempting a coup. He had simply wanted the Libyan leader, who, he said, had been fast becoming a 'despot' and a 'psychopath', to step down. Meheishi added that Qaddafi had been 'spreading intellectual terrorism by imposing his beliefs on the Libyans'.

Qaddafi himself clearly did not agree. He had Hawadi and Hamza arrested, along with twenty senior army officers, many of them close associates of Meheishi's from Misurata. Although he never publicly admitted a coup had taken place, Qaddafi, on 1 September 1975, announced a purge of the army, following an attempt by 'some felonious and Fascist officers . . . to introduce changes by force in Libya'. Over the next few months some 200 senior officers were arrested.

Meheishi escaped to Tunis and later to Cairo where he became Libya's public enemy number one. There was some justice in Meheishi's place of refuge since, according to the more credible interpretations of the alleged coup, he had been encouraged in his insurrection by Egypt, which wanted domestic difficulties to distract Qaddafi from marshalling opposition to the Sinai accord between Cairo and Tel Aviv, which US Secretary of State Henry Kissinger began negotiating in August 1975. The Egyptians then, so the story goes, got cold feet about the affair. They thought a coup against

Qaddafi in which they were implicated might turn the whole Arab world against their negotiations on Sinai. They also felt the neighbourly act of revealing a conspiracy to Qaddafi – something they had done in the past – would win his silence on Sinai, if not his eternal gratitude. So Cairo leaked details of Meheishi's plans to the Libyans, at the same time telling him that his efforts had been betrayed by one of his colleagues and that he should flee.

In the Egyptian capital later that year Meheishi was joined by another senior RCC officer, Major Abdul Moneim al Houni, formerly Libya's head of counter-intelligence (in that role he had attempted to recruit 'Hilton Assignment' mastermind James Kent to kidnap Omar al Shehli) and later Foreign Minister. Having discovered the whereabouts of his former colleagues, Qaddafi decided to strike at them. As was to become the norm over the next decade, he was none too subtle in his plans.

On 8 March Egyptian police revealed in Cairo that they had picked up seven Libyans sent by Colonel Qaddafi to commit 'sabotage, murders and kidnappings'. The Egyptians, who clearly had prior details of the kidnap team's programme, revealed that the Libyans all carried the same type of suitcase, and all wore identical underpants in which they carried $2,000.

Three more Libyans, who had come to Cairo with their colleagues some days earlier, had travelled on to Rome on a regular Alitalia flight. In transit at Rome's Fiumicino airport, they picked up a consignment of pistols and grenades delivered shortly after their arrival by a scheduled Libyan Arab Airlines flight between Tripoli and Rome. They were about to check in for their onward journey to Paris when they too were arrested. On the original passenger list for that same flight had also been al Houni. The pistol-toting trio had intended to hijack the flight and divert it to Tripoli. Police had alerted the former Libyan Foreign Minister to the danger and he simply travelled to the French capital on another carrier.

Qaddafi was infuriated by these setbacks. He immediately expelled 3,000 of the 300,000 Egyptians and 1,350 of the 50,000 Tunisians working in Libya. Following the establishments of the ominous-sounding Office for the Security of the Revolution in October 1975 (less than a year after Qaddafi publicly declared he had refused to open an office of state security because this was a 'manifestation of terrorism'), detentions of army officers were stepped up. Two more RCC members, Mohammed Najm and Mukhtar Gerwi, were put under house arrest.

Ideas, particularly foreign ideas, were still suspect, and this led

Qaddafi to identify as his main source of opposition at that time the students at Libya's two universities. During 1976 the larger of these, in Benghazi, with nearly 8,000 students, over 1,000 of whom were women, was renamed Gar Younis University, while the smaller, in Tripoli, with around 4,000 students, became Al Fateh University, commemorating Qaddafi's Al Fateh revolution, a pun on the Arabic word for both 'the first [of September]' and 'the conqueror'.

In January 1976, taking their tactics from Berkeley, the Sorbonne and the London School of Economics almost a decade earlier, students at Benghazi provoked a confrontation with the authorities. They claimed official interference in their union elections. Security forces were called on to the campus and there were reports – strenuously denied by the government – that between seven and thirteen young people had been shot and killed. Amnesty International was moved to cable Qaddafi on 14 January asking for clarification of the incident and urging, on humanitarian grounds, 'that details of those detained or wounded be made available to families concerned'. The Libyan leader was still conscious enough of his public image to ask his spokesman, Taher Sherif bin Amer, officially Minister of State for RCC Affairs, to reply, saying no police had been involved on campus, no arrests had been made and no one had been killed.

Student dissension flared up again during the first week in April. Qaddafi called for an intensification of revolutionary activity in the universities, which, following a spurt of enthusiasm shortly after the Zwara Declaration, remained sceptical of and relatively untouched by his ideas. In a speech at Benghazi University on 7 April Qaddafi himself reminded students of some of the successes of his regime. Since 1969 tens of thousands of houses had been built every year; families who had lived in huts and hovels for 500 years no longer had to do so. The Al Fateh revolution had meant handing authority over to the people, he said. In a throwback to his Zwara speech three years earlier, Qaddafi called once more for people's committees which would 'cleanse' the university of 'reactionary' students.

Taking their cue from Qaddafi, that very day revolutionary students attacked some of their less zealous colleagues at Tripoli University. Running battles immediately broke out across the campus, leaving around 250 people injured and, according to some reports, two dead. During the clashes Qaddafi's trusted lieutenant, Major Abdul Salam Jalloud, had come to the university and pulled out a pistol, firing five shots – according to Cairo radio, 'as an expression of what he called the beginning of popular revolution at the university'. By 23 April, following mass arrests in both Benghazi and

139

Tripoli, Amnesty International was again cabling Qaddafi for details about the alleged detention of 800 students.

As repression in the universities at home intensified, it was left to Libyan students outside the country to make their protests felt. There were demonstrations outside Libyan embassies in London, Washington and Bonn. On 19 April around 100 Libyan students in Egypt occupied the Libyan Relations Office, formerly the Libyan embassy, in Cairo. They denounced what they called 'autocratic rule in Libya and action by the authorities there against students in the universities of Benghazi and Tripoli'.

It was all too much for Maluk Siddiq, the inexperienced deputy head of the Libyan Relations Office, temporarily in charge of Libyan diplomacy in Cairo. Taking his cue perhaps from Jalloud, in a gesture of frustrations and defiance, which was to be mirrored, and with more fatal consequences, by another gunman in St James's Square, London, almost exactly eight years later, he grabbed a machine-gun from a safe, stepped out on to the balcony and fired at the shouting students. He did not shoot to kill. No one was hurt. Siddiq later claimed he had fired the weapon because he feared for his own life.

To Qaddafi student recalcitrance only proved that his cultural revolution still had a long way to go. Much of the rest of 1976 was taken up in establishing popular congresses and the political framework outlined in the first volume of his Green Book.

Opposition still troubled him though and, towards the end of 1976, what remained of Libya's legal system was called into play to put a stop to it once and for all. In December 1976 seventy-five officers accused of involvement in Meheishi's coup attempt the previous August were tried in camera by a military court. On Christmas Day twenty-five of them were sentenced to death – a figure increased to thirty-five on appeal.

In January 1977 a people's court was convened to try forty civilian detainees, including a number of students arrested during disturbances the previous year. When the court pronounced sentences of from four to fifteen years in jail, Qaddafi and what remained of the RCC intervened, in accordance with the Protection of the Revolution Law of 1969, and ordered the death sentence in two cases and life imprisonment for the rest.

Amnesty International immediately protested at the 'first death sentences to have been passed for a purely political offence' under Qaddafi. Apropos the overruling of a court decision by administrative decree, it added, 'Such disregard of the rule of law constitutes a danger to fundamental liberties and invalidates human and legal rights as guaranteed by the Libyan constitution.'

By now Qaddafi was not particularly interested in either legal niceties or the strictures of foreign observers. On 2 April he ordered the execution of twenty-two of the army officers involved in the 1975 coup. Hardly had the significance of this seeped into the public consciousness than five days later on 7 April, the anniversary of the disturbances at the universities the previous year, four civilians, including two of the students involved in those disturbances, were publicly hanged in Benghazi.

In subsequent years 7 April was to become a red-letter day on which Qaddafi's opponents, with their demonstrations, and his regime, with its acts of repression, appeared to compete with each other.

Qaddafi's obsession about ideas which he could not control is shown in his attitude to orthodox religion. It might be thought, given the emphasis on Islam in his Third Universal Theory, that he would try to work closely with the ulema, or Muslim clergy. However, he chose to see them as a potential focus for conservative opposition to his reforms. He feared their links with the Senussi order, which had been so powerful under the monarchy, and he suspected them of being close to the Muslim Brotherhood, a political party controlled from Egypt and Saudi Arabia. Already in May and June 1973 Qaddafi's police had rounded up 'several hundred' Muslim Brothers (according to a dispatch to *The Times* by Paul Martin), after some members had been caught tearing down posters announcing the 'cultural revolution' in Tripoli and Benghazi.

Qaddafi chose to deal with this threat by setting himself up as a reformer of Islam, as of society. He ordered the ulema to steer clear of political matters. In May 1975 he told Libya's clergy, 'Sermons on Fridays must deal with those matters which man has come to the mosque to seek, which are prayer and God's remembrance, only.' The Libyan leader also presented himself as a champion of Islamic Protestantism, challenging the authority of the clergy by his insistence on the individual's ability to commune directly with God. As he stated in a speech on the anniversary of the prophet in February 1978, 'The Koran is in the Arabic language and therefore we can interpret it ourselves without the need for an imam to interpret it for us.'

In keeping with this attitude Qaddafi attacked the Hadith, the vast commentary on the sayings of the Prophet Mohammed which orthodox Muslims relied on for their interpretation of the Koran. Together with the Koran, the Hadith comprises the Sunnah, from which derives the name of Islam's dominant tendency. Qaddafi took a

141

position more common among Shia Muslims – that the Koran was the word of God and no further textual guidance was necessary. According to his critics, Qaddafi feared the Hadith because its often contrasting opinions lent an element of intellectual uncertainty to religion. It left individuals and their consciences to come to decisions on moral, social and (Islam being a practical code) political issues. Qaddafi could not brook such liberalism. He needed official Islam to be a closed system, presided over by himself.

Qaddafi found compliant clerics to lend support to his ideas and to his Third Universal Theory through the official Call of Islam Society. However, even some of these ulema baulked when Qaddafi, from around 1974, began to press for the recruitment of women into the army. A decade later, in February 1985, opposition on this matter came to a head when the normally pliant General People's Congress voted against Qaddafi's express intention to conscript Libyan women.

Qaddafi accused the clergy of being too rigid in their interpretation of the Koran. His mentor on this theme soon became clear. He started praising the modernizing attitude to Islam of another soldier who had led his country, Turkey's Kemal Atatürk. He threatened the clergy with the observation that Atatürk's anticlericalism had resulted from the rigidity of the Turkish ulema of his time. In a speech to clerics in his own country in July 1978, Qaddafi reiterated his rejection of the Hadith, warning his audience that, if they continued opposing him, he would burn the Green Book and use Mao's Little Red Book instead. 'And this will soon happen,' he threatened.

Around this time imams in mosques throughout Libya began attacking Qaddafi directly from their pulpits. The Libyan leader's main opponent, particularly on his interpretation of the Hadith, was the venerated old Mufti of Tripoli, Sheikh Mohammed al Bushti. The sheikh was interrogated and accused of belonging to the Muslim Brotherhood. From the pulpit he replied,

> We are not party supporters. Nor do we know what the word party means as used by the authorities. However, Allah (God be praised) has let us know his party is the Muslimeen [the Muslim Brotherhood]. We do not know any party but this one. . . . We are servants of Allah, who gave us some knowledge, and it is our duty to teach it to the umma [the community]. . . . If this leads us to jail then we welcome that, for Allah's sake.

By 1980 the Mufti's intransigence had become too much for Qaddafi. On 21 November, just before Friday prayers, the sheikh placed in front of his mosque a blackboard inscribed with words from the Hadith: 'Those who condemn my friends, condemn me.' That day Qaddafi's security guards burst into the mosque and dragged the sheikh away. According to reliable reports, he was tortured, burned and finally killed.

Shortly afterwards, according to the English-language monthly magazine, *Arabia*, published in London, Qaddafi personally accused the sheikh of having been a Saudi agent. 'I asked the revolutionary committees to record a discussion with him so that people could hear and know the truth,' the Libyan leader is reported as saying. 'But they replied that they have relieved me of him by liquidating him physically.'

Sheikh al Bushti had taken over as Mufti of Tripoli from another critic of Qaddafi, Sheikh Tahar al Zawi, who, although nearly ninety years of age, was placed under house arrest.

Qaddafi did not stop at eliminating the ulema. He also sought the physical destruction of mosques thought to harbour dissident clerics. The Al Baida Islamic University and the five-century-old Abdussalam mosque at Zliten, which housed one of the country's most prestigious Islamic studies centres, preparing scholars for higher studies at Al Azhar in Cairo, were demolished. At three o'clock one August morning in 1979 Qaddafi ordered the destruction of the well-known Sidi Hammouda mosque in the centre of Tripoli – for no other reason than that he wanted to enlarge what had become known as Green Square (formerly Shouhada Square), on which the mosque stood, to allow tanks to take part in a military parade on 1 September.

Later, in October 1984, Qaddafi was to strike at Libya's principal shrine – the mosque and mausoleum of the Senussi family at Jaghbub, which still attracted an estimated half a million pilgrims each year on the anniversary of the death of the sect's founder, Sayyid Mohammed al Senussi. The Libyan leader argued that the Senussi were continuing to behave like kings with their private graves. He ordered the disinterment of the three principal tombs there – those of Sayyid Mohammed himself, and his sons Sayyid Mohammed Sherif and Sayyid Umran bin Bakr. He said these three were not Libyans and had to be buried outside Libya. The remains of the women and children of the Senussi were to be spread around the country.

At the same time as promoting his own brand of Islam, Qaddafi was enjoying a strange flirtation with a bizarre quasi-Christian religious cult. In September 1970 a Libyan diplomat came across an odd sect called the Children of God. It had been founded in California and then, having run out of good will in the US, had moved to Europe and set up 'colonies' in a number of countries. The leader was a forty-eight-year-old former pastor called David Brandt Berg who had alienated the established church with his exhortations to his converts to drop all ties with 'straight society' and join his army of God. In 1969 he divided his flock into twelve tribes and gave all his followers Biblical names. He called himself Moses David, or 'Mo'.

The colonies were presided over by 'shepherds', who were responsible for sending a tithe, or 10 per cent of their earnings, to Mo at his box number in Switzerland. From there Mo communicated with his followers through rambling missives known as Mo letters. In the mid-1970s the Mo letters became increasingly strange. Mo started urging his followers to take Jesus's message of love to its carnal conclusion and enter into sexual relations with their potential converts. He coined a phrase for this type of missionary work, 'flirty fishing', and produced a handbook which gave his female acolytes instructions on how to seek converts in bars and public places:

> There's no reason not to display the blessings of the Lord. Don't be afraid to wear low-cut gowns with very low neck-lines even to the waist or navel – no bras, see-thru blouses. Show them what you've got – that's the bait. . . . I want them to absolutely totally flip out and fall in love with you. In one night of love you can show what a love slave you are and how sweet and humble and unselfish you are.

Then Mo got to the real point: 'Fishing can be fun, but fun doesn't pay the bills. You've got to catch a few to make the fun pay for itself, so don't do it for nothing.'

Whether the Libyan diplomat was recruited in a night of 'flirty fishing' or was simply moved by Mo's sincerity is not recorded, but he arranged for Mo to go to Tripoli to meet Qaddafi in June 1975. Members of the Children of God had been to Libya in the intervening years. Moses David had told them about Qaddafi in Mo letters with titles like 'Qaddafi's Magic Lamp' and 'Qaddafi's Third World': 'Qaddafi is the only one sincere enough, godly enough, rich enough, persuasive enough, visionary enough and young enough to capture the youthful imagination and idealistic zeal, admiration, loyalty and aspirations of the youth of the world who are the life blood of every world revolution and cataclysmic change.'

When Moses David himself actually came to Tripoli it took him some time to achieve his goal of meeting his revolutionary hero. He tells in his Mo letters how:

finally after two months of waiting we had nearly given up and had made reservations to leave on the morning plane, thinking we might come back at a later date when it would be more convenient for him. . . .

Suddenly there was a knock at the door! We'd been waiting all evening for a long-expected guest. We had been there for two months expecting his coming daily and never knowing at what moment he might come. It reminded us of the Scripture, 'Watch and pray for ye know not in what hour your Lord cometh' (Mt. 24.22).

Moses David was taken to a house where the Libyan leader was staying.

Well, we were here and were soon in the living room together with him embraced in the first fond greeting of mutual admirers with the fervour of fellow comrades in the Holy War. With a fellow member of the RCC together with a Captain of the Security Forces and his civilian official of Islamic Affairs, as well as all the members of his own family and helpers in our first little colony in Libya in his own home, we began our three hours of dialogue and fellowship as follows. . . .

As Moses David tells it, he and Qaddafi then launched into a remarkable philosophical discussion about the similarity of their missions. The American cult leader certainly tries hard to highlight the common ground between them. He points out that both their revolutions started in 1969. He begins to call Qaddafi 'Godahfi' and 'Moamar'. The Libyan leader is keen to emphasize the parallels between Islam and Christianity.

However, Qaddafi does not seem overjoyed about the prospects of having the Children of God permanently on Libyan soil. He says,

Naturally we would be very honoured to have you here and to have the Libyan Arab Republic as the base for your movement. But I must be candid and say to you that you will have limitations on your movements if you are based here, because then it will be construed outside that you have become part of the Libyan Arab Republic, because then whatever you say will be thought to be Libyan, and this will make great limitations on your message and the cause for which you are fighting. Therefore it is best that this is not the case, only that there is a link between us intellectually and in understanding.

145

The letter concludes, 'it was a thrilling and historical event in our own history, and we feel undoubtedly in his history as well, as we join forces in God's work to lead the people of the whole world in God's path of righteousness against the forces of evil darkness and the enemies of God. . . . He provided a large beautiful two-storey new and fully-furnished colony house for our children whom we left behind as they established our first base in an Arab country.'

One of those left behind, a leader of the cult and now a successful businessman, recalled that Qaddafi was interested in using the Children of God's street-level distribution network to promote his own literature, including the Green Book, in Europe. Over the years the cult had perfected the art of selling their pamphlets (and later their bodies) on street corners, soliciting contributions for 'missionary work'. Qaddafi also wanted to show his ecumenicism to the world. The same former leader said, 'He made suggestions proposing to finance a meeting of all the Children of God in Libya. He would fly them in from all over the world, and give those who needed them Libyan passports.'

As flirty fishing became the accepted norm in the cult, many of the Children of God's women took Libyan army officers as lovers. However, Moses David's sought-after pact between his followers and Qaddafi's never really happened. By November 1978 he was writing a Mo letter entitled 'The Maltese Doublecross', giving details of the expulsion of some of his followers from Malta and blaming this on Qaddafi.

In February 1979 relations appeared to have improved once more, as Moses David was writing that he had received an invitation from Qaddafi to visit Tripoli again. He told his followers that he had replied, 'We have continued to support you and your work and express our sympathy toward your many endeavours around the world in the many good causes that you champion, particularly those of the poor, dispossessed Palestinians as opposed to the greedy, heartless, merciless oppression of the selfish Zionists.'

But the attractions of making love to what the British press came to term 'hookers for Jesus' had begun to pall among Libyan army officers. As part of their campaign against Qaddafi, Libyan clerics were beginning to sit up and take notice of this sacrilegious behaviour. Qaddafi could summon little enthusiasm for further dealings with the Children of God's sex-obsessed dictator. He had his own problems to attend to.

While most Libyans' energies were occupied in trying to make sense of the intensified rhetoric of the revolution and to make themselves useful in the artificial bustle surrounding the establishment of popular congresses, Qaddafi was busy building up a parallel structure where, those in the know quickly came to realize, real power lay.

The Libyan leader was particularly worried about continued dissension in the army. Meheishi's coup attempt in 1975 had unnerved him. The discovery in February 1978 of an attempt on his life organized by the head of his military intelligence, Captain Mohammed Idris Sherif, and his brother (air force) Captain Mohammed al Sayed, proved that his concern was not unfounded, particularly as the following month members of a top East German delegation headed by Werner Lamberz, regarded as the heir apparent to East German leader Erich Honecker, were killed in a helicopter crash in Libya. There was speculation that the crash was intended either for Qaddafi himself (his spokesman Taher Sherif bin Amer did indeed lose his life in it) or as a protest against the role of East Germans in Libya's increasingly repressive security apparatus.

Qaddafi's response, as the Egyptian press reports quickly picked up, was to entrust sensitive posts in the armed forces to members of his own tribe, the Qaddadfa. Close kinsman Colonel Hassan Ishkal was given command in Chad; Qaddafi's brother-in-law, Colonel Messaoud Abdul Hafez, in the Fezzan. His cousins, Sayed and Ahmed Qaddafadam, were active in military intelligence.

Meanwhile during 1978 Libyans became aware of a new force in the land. Citizens first in Benghazi and later in other towns and cities throughout the country found themselves being picked up for apparently trivial offences by scruffily dressed youths who described themselves as members of the revolutionary committees.

For a couple of years Qaddafi had been running special camps, like the Revolutionary Blooms Camp in Benghazi, to give special training in his principles to scores of teenagers who had known no education other than that provided under his regime. Recruits were usually from poor families who could be relied upon to see their future in terms of the success of his regime.

The revolutionary committees were the pick of these recruits – the fanatical shock troops of Qaddafi's revolution. Others before them had worked to root out 'unrevolutionary' influences. The revolutionary committees continued their work – only with ruthlessness and efficiency. They had their own buildings, their own organization, even (from the start of 1980) their own newspaper, *Al Zahaf al Akhdar* (Green March). Their leader was another Qaddadfa, Mohammed Maghgoub, though in other top members like Sayed

Rashid, a member of Major Jalloud's Mega'ha tribe, Abdul Salam Zadmeh, from the Awlad Suleiman, the revolutionary committee hierarchy reflected the tribal coalition on which Qaddafi relied.

The revolutionary committees provided the main thrust of Qaddafi's campaigns in 1979 and 1980 against the two sections of the community he continued to fear most – the army (because of its access to weaponry) and business people (because of their mobility, funds and potential for freedom of thought and action).

Revolutionary committees were set up within the army, enforcing petty regulations such as a ban on officers carrying personal weapons and a prohibition on officers entering barracks after working hours.

While Qaddafi's moves against the army were often little more than contemptuous, his implementation of the ideas put forward in the second volume of his Green Book, published in 1977, showed that he intended to reduce the merchant class to nothing. During 1978, the ownership of more than one house was forbidden, employees were encouraged to take over their places of work and in late 1978 all private retail trade was abolished. But Qaddafi was not finished in his campaign against independent sources of wealth. In 1980 he gave Libyans just ten days to gather together all their dinars and take them down to the bank to be changed. There Qaddafi had a surprise in store. All 100 dinar notes, the largest denomination worth $300, were confiscated. It is doubtful whether many of those who were hoarding large sums under their mattresses participated in this exercise designed to pinpoint the wealthy. A subsequent decree stipulated that an individual could cash only 1,000 dinars per month. All other business and financial transactions had to be by cheque. This acted as a further deterrent on the use of money and, as a bonus, helped boost deposits in banks.

But Qaddafi still had some tricks up his sleeve. During his first decade in power he had turned a blind eye to increasing corruption in his armed forces. Now, with the help of the ample dossiers compiled by his security services, he could kill two birds with one stone. For his officers had usually become wealthy by acting as middlemen for businessmen or accepting bribes from them. In late 1979, with the help of the revolutionary committees, Qaddafi turned the spotlight on these corrupt activities. Army officers and businessmen were hauled before revolutionary tribunals to account for their misdeeds. The whole process was filmed. The spectacle of colonels and merchants breaking down, weeping and pleading for mercy, provided a voyeuristic interlude in Libya's normally bland television fare in 1980.

Fathi Ezzat, boss of the Al Nasr Construction Company in Benghazi, helped drag down several senior army officers.

Mohammed bin Ghalboun, who, as a local contractor himself, says army projects were often costed out at between ten and twelve times their real value, recalls Ezzat well. 'He used to borrow equipment from me because he was small fry. Suddenly he was doing projects worth five or six million dollars. Within three years he had made $20 million. He owned a big yacht in Greece where officers used to go for a good time. It was all officially condoned. But some of these officers must have been ones Qaddafi wanted to get at. In 1980 Ezzat found himself on trial on TV, accused of corrupting the army. He was imprisoned and tortured until every penny he had made from corrupt contracts was paid back.'

When Qaddafi and his revolutionary committees wanted someone's blood any small incident would suffice, as the TV trials clearly showed. A Colonel Shebani, for example, the head of the military accounts office in Benghazi, had visited Ezzat's battery-chicken project outside the city and had ordered four birds for his family. Ezzat happened to be there and asked him to accept them as a gift. Shebani protested but Ezzat insisted that the chickens were 'on the house'. The court did not think Shebani protested enough and this incident became a key part of the evidence against him.

What Qaddafi was beginning to realize was that his campaign against business people and other sections of the community was driving more and more Libyans abroad where they were swelling the ranks of his opponents in exile.

10 Stray Dogs

When Barry Howson, a British arms dealer, entered the Libyan people's bureau in St Jame's Square, London, in November 1979 he knew immediately that something was up, Howson had been there the year before and, although he had read in the papers how Libyan embassies had been changed into 'people's bureaus' at the decree of the Libyan leader, he was not prepared for the stark change in the atmosphere of this beautiful eighteenth-century building which the Libyans had bought for £5 million in 1978.

A metal detector had been installed in the lobby; the first floor, where the former ambassador had a lavish suite and reception area, now looked dilapidated, like the campus of a radical university. A twenty-nine-year-old Libyan, a graduate of political science from Michigan State University called Musa Koussa, now sat in the ambassador's chair, and his new revolutionary-style diplomats, scruffy young men with open shirts, jeans and long hair, lolled around in the Regency chairs. The atmosphere was, Howson felt, distinctly sinister.

This did not deter him from the business at hand. Howson, whose wife was ill, needed money badly and Libya was the Eldorado for arms dealers. 'I needed £100,000. And fast,' said Howson. His first dealings with the Libyans had been in 1978, when he and a partner won an order to supply 8,000 flak jackets to the Libyan army. The jackets contained kevlar, a hard but light material developed for the US space programme. Howson signed the contract with the second secretary at the Libyan embassy and arranged to have the order made up by a firm in Daventry, England. There were the usual problems in finalizing details, not least over the payments. The jackets cost £200 each and, with 8,000 ordered, Howson and his partner stood to make a tidy profit.

At his November 1979 visit Howson thought he would be discussing the flak-jacket deal. Instead Koussa led him to the second floor of the embassy into a room in the middle of the building without external walls. The Libyans had constructed a secure room where they and their guests could talk without fear of being listened to. 'It was obvious they'd spent a fortune on debugging equipment,' said Howson. 'I understood Koussa was in charge of security at Libyan missions in northern Europe. He said that the Libyan bureaus around Europe were under fire from a number of sources, notably from the Israelis.' Then Koussa came to the point. They now needed defensive weaponry to protect themselves against the real possibility of armed attack from outside. Could Howson help? Howson said he was astonished to be approached so directly, but after getting some assurances from Koussa – 'I said the stuff was only for export, I didn't want it moving around, although I realize now that was a pious hope' – Howson clinched a deal. He would export 600 weapons, from 'baby Brownings' (small .22 handguns) to heavy-calibre .38 Walther automatics, to eight Libyan bureaus around Europe. 'I said I would supply them at normal retail prices, making a reasonable margin on them,' said Howson. Koussa asked him to go to Libya to finalise arrangements.

Britain's anti-terrorist squad, C13, is often criticized for its somewhat nonchalant approach to Libyan terror. This time, however, it was on the ball. Later that month Howson was summoned to Scotland Yard and asked if he was supplying the Libyan bureau in London with weapons. He answered, truthfully, that he was not. However, he did not mention that he was supplying arms for export. The interview shook Howson a little and, instead of flying direct to Libya to discuss the deal, he went to Malta, using a first-class ticket supplied by Koussa; there he caught a local flight to Tripoli. On his first night out in the Libyan capital he was taken to see Atef Maharab, secretary of the Shooting Club of Tripoli. Howson suspected it was more than a social club: 'I believe it was a euphemism for the place where they train guerillas.' During his ten-day trip he met Major Jalloud, who did not impress him – 'a weak character but a good administrator' – and then on 3 December he was ushered into the presence of Qaddafi at his office in the Aziziya barracks.

'We had a very amusing conversation, initially through an interpreter. He was very affable,' said Howson. It was extraordinary that Qaddafi should bother himself with such a small-time operator as Howson, and strange that he should be so friendly, even flattering. 'He talked about his admiration for the British royal family and for the British army,' remembered Howson; at other times, of course, Qaddafi has expressed a withering contempt for both institutions.

A week after his return Howson made the first arms delivery to a

Libyan diplomatic post in Europe. With an end-user certificate signed by the Libyan defence attaché at the Paris bureau Howson says he bought sixty Browning semi-automatic pistols and assorted ammunition from Fabrique Nationale des Armes de Guerre in Herstal, Belgium. He stowed them in a false bottom of his Fiat car and drove across the border into France. In Paris Howson went through a procedure which he would follow, almost exactly, during subsequent drops in other capitals. 'I would be given the name of someone to speak to,' Howson explained.

> From about a kilometre away I would telephone the Libyan people's bureau in the city. Having ascertained that I was speaking to the right person I'd say: 'I've got something from Musa Koussa.' They would know straight away what I was talking about. They'd say: 'Come along.' I'd drive up to the gates, they would be open, and go straight to the garage. I would wait in the bureau while they made a phone call (presumably to Musa), then they would pay me the money. They were always very generous, giving me expenses and often tossing in an extra $2,000. They would say: 'Go away and enjoy yourself.'

On one occasion, according to the prosecutor at his subsequent trial, Howson, his wife Claire, who suffered from multiple sclerosis, and a friend drove to Greece, ostensibly on holiday, carrying a hidden cargo of weapons for Libyan bureaus in Athens and Istanbul.

By February 1980 Howson had made three weapons drops, the flak jackets had been delivered and the Libyans were clearly pleased with him. Koussa suggested he took another trip to Libya:

> Musa told me there was other stuff they wanted but he hadn't been specific. When I got there I found the atmosphere in Tripoli had changed dramatically, rather like it had in the bureau in London. Now when I met the low-level procurement people in Tripoli they wanted offensive rather than defensive weapons. They asked for Sterling machine-guns with silencers, and Heckler and Koch machine-pistols. They even showed an interest in the Israeli-made Uzi machine-pistol. They were keen to get spare parts for C130 aircraft, they wanted detonators – all sorts of rubbish that I could not do.

Howson agreed to supply Maharab, the secretary of the Shooting Club, with 200 Ruger .22 rifles and 600 Walther .32 PPK pistols. Maharab obviously wanted them for more than sporting purposes. He asked for the Walthers with silencers, the assassin's weapon.

Howson asked him why he wanted silencers. 'Maharab said, "Because of the noise inside the shooting range," and laughed.' Howson 'played along with the game' because it was 'a jolly nice order'.

On this trip Howson again met some of the key figures in the Libyan leadership, leaving no doubt that the smallest deal is approved by the highest authority. He met Ali Treiki, the Foreign Minister, and the head of military procurement, Colonel Sherif bin Amir. He also met Qaddafi again. This time the leader was in a curious mood. 'He told me a story about a nephew of the King [Idris] who used to go to Beirut to visit a European girl friend, who was also being courted by his younger brother. One day the girl told the older brother that she could not sleep with him because she had a venereal disease. He immediately rang his brother and told him he was finished with the girl. He could have her. 'I thought Qaddafi was going to explode with laughter,' said Howson. 'Then he quietened down and said that this was what used to happen under the old regime, it couldn't happen today.'

Qaddafi then pressed Howson on whether he could do anything to expedite the delivery of Boeing 727s he had ordered for Libyan Arab Airlines. He said he knew why the Americans were baulking at the sale of Hercules C130 military transport planes but could not see why they were taking the same course with 727 passenger planes. (Although Howson had no influence with the US administration, and it was absurd of Qaddafi to think he had, the Americans later relented and allowed the delivery of two 727s. The planes were soon ferrying troops to Chad and Uganda.) 'Qaddafi was very bitter about the planes,' said Howson. 'He thought the Americans were taking an unnecessary and illogical stand against his regime. I had to listen to a ten-minute tirade against America. I could see the real man working then.'

Howson had realized that this 'jolly nice order' for guns and silencers was not just for the benefit of the weekend sportsmen of Libya. Soon after his return from Tripoli he knew what the true purpose was. Howson was called into Scotland Yard again. At the start of April 1980 a Libyan journalist, Mohammed Ramadan, an opponent of Qaddafi's regime, had been killed in London. Ramadan worked for the BBC World Service and was known less for his verbal attacks on the Libyan regime than for his criticism of Nasserism and militarism.

On 11 April, a sunny spring afternoon, he walked out of the mosque in Regent's Park after Friday prayers. He was approached by two young Libyans. One of them, bin Hassan Mohammed al Masri, shot him at point-blank range and killed him instantly. Al Masri had been sent from Tripoli to assassinate him. The police now told Howson that one of his guns, an East German Rech .22, had been found in the car used by Ramadan's killers. Howson told them that the Rech had been in a consignment he had supplied to the Libyans in Belgium. The pistol had not been fired but Howson was furious that it had filtered back into Britain. 'I went storming off to the Libyans. I told them, "You've broken the rules. One of my weapons has turned up in Britain. You swore to me it wouldn't." '

Howson's outrage did not last long. He continued his arms deliveries to the Libyan people's bureaus. After Paris there had been Brussels; now he delivered to The Hague, Athens, Istanbul, Belgrade, Sofia, Madrid and Rabat.

Keeping to his agreement with Maharab, in September Howson claims he obtained a licence from the British Department of Trade to supply the Tripoli Shooting Club with its 200 Rugers. But the Department baulked at condoning the export of 600 murderous Walther pistols with silencers to Libya. However, the weapons had been ordered and paid for (from Accuracy International, the Walther agent in Britain), so Howson resolved to find a way of getting them to Tripoli via a circuitous route. He still had his export licence for the Ruger .22s. This he changed to read .32, the calibre of the Walthers. Then he had 200 Walthers crated up and a greasy Lotus engine put on top.

When the shipper put the requisite IMCO code on this consignment to indicate its danger, Howson changed it to suggest that the package was more innocent than it was. The Walthers, screwed for silencers, were then shipped via Paris and Madrid to the people's bureau in Morocco. However, Howson forgot that he had bought the Walthers without VAT pending receipt of the requisite export licence for Tripoli. Since he had attempted to ship to Morocco illegally there was little he could say when the British Customs and Excise asked him where he had sent the consignment. Howson was arrested. Although he was originally charged on fourteen counts, most of which related to exporting weapons to Libyan people's bureaus abroad, he was only convicted (and fined £4,000) in December 1982 on two – changing the export licence and the IMCO code on the airways bill on the shipment to Morocco. The judge trying the case described Howson as, 'a confidence man and an adventurer.' By that time two more of Howson's weapons had turned up on the scene of Libyan terrorist incidents in Europe. In December 1981 Swiss police discovered a cache of weapons, including five originally from Howson, hidden in a wood near Zurich. Howson claims that the guns were part of a consignment delivered to the Libyan people's bureau in Brussels.

In February 1982 one of the Walthers sent by Howson to Morocco turned up in Frankfurt, where it had been used in a petty murder by a Moroccan. Howson says the weapon had been 'sequestered' by the Moroccans from his shipment to Rabat. It was traced to him because it had been screwed for a silencer. The number had been erased but it had been positively identified as one of Howson's after an ultra-violet test.

Thus some of Howson's weapons were implicated in what Qaddafi came to call his campaign to eliminate 'stray dogs', his dismissive term for members of the Libyan opposition who fled abroad. The campaign had an international impact out of all proportion to the number of its victims. It led to a direct conflict with the United States and disrupted Libyan relations with many countries in Europe. But, as Howson's story shows, it went on under the nose of the British anti-terrorist squad. The Libyans had reason to believe that foreign governments were prepared to turn a blind eye when the Libyan government murdered Libyan dissidents on their soil.

Qaddafi had dispatched hit squads to kill key dissidents as early as 1975 and 1976, when he had launched two unsuccessful attempts to kill the former RCC member Omar Meheishi after he defected from Libya. In 1979 secret assassination became overt policy when Qaddafi said he intended to 'follow these people [Libyan exiles] even if they go to the North Pole'. On 6 February 1980 the revolutionary committees held their second annual conference at Gar Younis University in Benghazi and issued a communiqué which sent a shudder through the 30,000 Libyans living abroad. It stated: 'Physical elimination becomes the end stage in the conflict of the revolutionary struggle for a final solution when removing economic, political and social weapons from the counter-revolutionaries fails to put an end to their activities.' It said that the committees would set about 'the elimination of the enemies of the revolution abroad'.

Why was Qaddafi taking the opposition so seriously? In 1980 he was at the height of his power. The world oil glut had not begun. Libya and its three million inhabitants were grossing $20 billion a year in oil revenues. Domestic opposition had not been totally wiped out, but it was kept in check by Qaddafi's use of his security services to hit ruthlessly at any centres of privilege or power.

The opposition abroad began to haunt him. 'It is his weakest spot,' said Bruno Kreisky. 'I have talked to him about it and cannot get a real answer. He is paranoid about this opposition, he cannot think about it logically.'

Some influential figures had recently fled Libya: the former Foreign Minister, Mansur Kikhia, the ambassador to India, Mohammed al Magharief, and the ambassador to Austria, Ezzedin Ghadamsi. And the opposition had begun to pool its resources. Early in 1980 the Libyan Democratic Front, led by former journalist Fadl Messaoudi, linked up with the Libyan National Rally to form the Libyan Democratic National Rally, the nearest thing to a coalition in Libyan opposition politics. The General Union of Libyan Students, dedicated to avenging the April 1976 hanging of two Benghazi students, was active wherever Libyans took courses abroad. The Islamic Association of Libya took root in the United States in 1979, as did another opposition group, the Libyan National Movement, in Baghdad. Within a year Bakoush's Libyan Liberation Organization the National Front for the Salvation of Libya and the Libyan Constitutional Union would be active in Cairo, Khartoum and Manchester.

Like Qaddafi's army this opposition looks impressive on paper, but in reality it does not add up to much. None of these groups had the cohesion, the means or the manpower to take over in Libya. They were not a threat to the Libyan state, but they were a blow to Qaddafi's self-esteem. He saw that opposition literature was being read by the thousands of young Libyans sent to study abroad. Their pamphlets, and more ominously their seditious tape cassettes, were filtering back into Libya.

Qaddafi decided to go on the offensive. The man he entrusted with the job of hunting and eliminating his opponents abroad was Colonel Younis Bilgasim, a tall, rather handsome man with a shock of white hair and two small green tattoos, one on each side of his forehead. He had a diffident manner and indifferent health: his heart disease and rheumatism were treated by doctors in Europe. He owned a house in Wiesbaden, West Germany, where his two sons were educated, and often, in subsequent years, when European governments became concerned about the excesses of Libya's diplomats, Bilgasim would be wheeled out as a kind of elder statesman to reassure them. He often succeeded. He would explain that Libya was only indulging in domestic political squabbles and meant no harm to the interests of that particular European country. The iron fist under the glove was that Libya would pull out of lucrative contracts with that state if an undue fuss was made.

He was a career police officer under King Idris, and became a passionate supporter of Qaddafi after the coup. His revolutionary fervour and violent anti-imperialism dated back to his terrible experiences during the war, when he fought with the British against the

Italians. He was captured and put into an Italian concentration camp in Libya where his mother and two brothers died. He was number two in the Ministry of the Interior when Qaddafi picked him as the co-ordinator of Libyan intelligence operations at home and abroad.

It was a tough job, one of the most powerful in Libya. He controlled a plethora of agencies: the Jamahiriya security, directly under his command and, related to it, the general internal security run by Mohammed al Ghazali, military security under Abdullah Hejazzi and revolutionary security headed by Captain Abdul Salam Zadmeh.

Bilgasim loved gadgets. Abdul Hamid Bakoush, the former Prime Minister under Idris, went to see him in the late 1970s in one of his offices, near the Udan Hotel in the centre of Tripoli with a view of a modern mosque with a minaret shaped like a rocket. Bilgasim tapped a microphone on the table in front of him and asked Bakoush what it was. 'A microphone,' answered Bakoush. 'Wrong,' said a gleeful Bilgasim. 'This is the microphone,' and he pointed at an ashtray which had a microphone embedded in the base and which Bilgasim said he had bought in Amsterdam. In another room he had an array of gadgets: microphones hidden in cigarettes, a transmitter disguised as a pen, a telephone which fitted into a chair and popped up when a button was pushed, and a telephone hidden in the breast of a plaster statue of a woman.

It was a strange meeting. When Bakoush defected from Libya, Bilgasim hunted him relentlessly and ordered five assassination attempts against him. In a way Bakoush was to be Bilgasim's undoing, because all the attempts were ill designed and badly executed by a cast of characters so clumsy that they might have been selected by Inspector Clouseau. The plots were often so absurd, a hallmark of Libyan terror, that foreign intelligence agencies did not take them seriously. It was a fatal mistake.

Bilgasim had no excuse for fumbling the job. He controlled a huge intelligence empire. He could call upon a number of Libyan front companies spread across the world from Ethiopia to Peru. He could use the people's bureaus at will to provide funds, false passports and weapons for the Libyan agents. According to one former Libyan ambassador, between a third and a half of the staff of any Libyan embassy reported not to the ambassador but to Bilgasim. 'They were intelligence agents under the flimsiest cover. They would have continous contact with Tripoli,' he said. 'They would pass all sorts of things through the diplomatic bag: laser systems, infra-red night sights for weapons, bugging devices and, of course, guns.'

Libyan hitmen were recruited in Tripoli and Benghazi by five or six revolutionary committee leaders under the general control of Captain Abdul Salam Zadmeh. Qaddafi allowed them a generous budget. After basic training the hitmen, operating in twos or threes, would be sent to a western capital armed only with wads of $100 bills. They would take an expensive flat and check in with the local people's bureau where the revolutionary committee or the Jamahiriyah security liaison officer would provide them with logistical help and weapons. On the whole he would keep his distance, emphasizing that the assassins' role was a freelance one which could be officially fêted, or denied, as Tripoli thought fit.

The murderers would live well for a couple of weeks, going to nightclubs and dating local girls before visiting the victim in his office or luring him to his death in a public place. Some of these victims were obvious targets, the leaders of opposition groups who could be deemed to pose a threat to the regime. Others were random, picked at the whim of the hitmen, perhaps because they were soft targets. Although the stray-dog operation was ordered by Qaddafi, who took a personal interest in some of the attempts, the pattern of attacks shows that the hitmen were allowed considerable discretion.

A Libyan lawyer, Mahmoud Abu Nafa, was shot dead in the offices of a legal firm, Arab Legal Consultancy and Translation Services, in Ennismore Gardens, London. It was just round the corner from the education office of the Libyan people's bureau, which could be one reason why Nafa's name appeared on the hit list. It was a strange killing. Nafa, who left Tripoli in 1974, disliked the regime but remained on friendly terms with many of its officials. He was close to Qaddafi's cousin, Sayed Qaddafadam, and had been a guest at his rowdy London parties in the late 1970s. In January 1980 Qaddafadam invited Nafa to Tripoli for his wedding and Nafa afterwards said he had had 'an enjoyable trip'. In April Nafa was killed. It seems that he was a victim of a clash of personalities within the ruling group in Tripoli and that Abdullah Hejazzi, the head of military intelligence and a rival of Qaddafadam for the leader's favours, accused Nafa of using his trip to Tripoli for smuggling anti-government literature and tapes into the country. He suspected him of working for a foreign intelligence agency and told Bilgasim to put his name on the list.

Without trial, evidence or even very much discussion, Nafa was eliminated. The day after his murder, and in apparent approval of it, Qaddafi issued another threat in Tripoli: dissenters were to return home by 11 June, the anniversary of the evacuation of the American bases in Libya. If they did not they would be 'liquidated wherever they are'.

Qaddafi did not wait for his deadline to expire. On 21 May a wealthy Libyan timber merchant was murdered in Rome in his hotel bed. A note pinned to his body said: 'Whoever flees from the country will be followed wherever he goes. An enemy of the people.' It was signed 'The Libyan revolutionary committees in Rome'. The following afternoon Salem Fezzani, a naturalized Italian of Libyan birth, was shot at in the Rome restaurant he owns. The assailant, a twenty-five-year-old Libyan, missed, and was caught by the police. He told them: 'I was sent by the people to kill him. He is a traitor and an enemy of the people.'

Between early April and mid-June 1980 twelve Libyans were murdered in Europe. It is not unusual, especially in the Middle East, for a state to order the assassination of its opponents. Israeli agents have murdered PLO leaders in their homes in Beirut, the Syrian government had made its point known to its opponents in Lebanon with the indiscriminate use of the car bomb. Governments also use terrorist groups to carry out their dirty work.

The extraordinary thing about this campaign is that the Libyan government admitted, and even boasted about, the murder of its fellow citizens. President Hefez al Assad of Syria, whose involvement with terrorism is considered to be more substantial than Qaddafi's, has always publicly denied any complicity. It was Qaddafi's bragging about his murderous activities, rather than their effectiveness, which made him the number-one target for the US administration. In an attempt to put a statesmanlike gloss over the killings, Jalloud told an Italian newspaper on 4 June 1980:

> Ours is a profound revolution. We are passing through a phase which Europe lived through centuries ago. You have had the French revolution. You have struggled. Now our people are struggling. Europe should not judge everything as terrorism. Many people who fled abroad took with them goods belonging to the Libyan people. . . . Now they are placing their illicit gains at the disposal of an opposition led by Sadat, by world imperialism and by Israel. But they are not guilty as a consequence of political crimes. They are thieves and for this reason they must be extradited through Interpol.

Western governments began to react to this wave of killings. Between April and June West Germany deported four Libyans. Britain sent Sir Antony Acland, a senior member of the Foreign Office, to Tripoli to tell the Libyan government to keep its internecine squabbles off British soil. The United States demanded that four Libyan diplomats accused of intimidating Libyans studying in US colleges should return to Tripoli. At first the four denied they were diplomats, insisting that therefore they could only be deported after an appeal to an immigration tribunal. Then they locked themselves in the people's bureau and claimed diplomatic immunity. Finally, when the US administration made clear it was serious about wanting to get rid of them, they were recalled to Tripoli.

Generally speaking, however, the West was loath to take action which might hold their exporters back from Libya's buoyant market. In 1980 Libya was drawing up its second five-year 'socio-economic transformation plan' and proposed to spend $62.5 billion between 1981 and 1985. This made Libya the West's third most important Middle East market after Saudi Arabia and Iraq. In 1980 Libya's main suppliers were Italy (28.6 per cent of the market share), West Germany (14.1), France and the United Kingdom (7.5), Japan (5.9) and the United States (5.7).

One Western European ambassador, who arrived in Tripoli in 1980, says that 'the first indications of a common European position towards the Libyan government were beginning to emerge around this time.' One difficulty, he found, was to weed out which threats Qaddafi really meant and which were just rhetoric. The Israeli intelligence service, the Mossad, says that it 'always takes what Qaddafi says seriously. However outrageous it sounds there is usually something behind it. Sometimes, but only rarely, the words are empty. But we cannot take any chances. We have to repeat to the Americans: "This man is not a fool, he is serious." '

The Western diplomat disagrees: 'If you were to take the words of the revolutionary committees seriously all the time, you would drive yourself crazy.' He and other European ambassadors adopted the same approach to the Libyan government: 'We all used the same wordings. We warned that if more killings happened in our countries we would take concerted action. We used similar threats. We said we would make it very difficult for Libyans to enter our countries and we would be scrutinizing the activities of their bureaus.' The Libyan reaction was incredulous. 'What do you care if these are not your citizens?' the ambassador was asked. 'I said: Look, we look at these things very seriously.'

He believes this joint appeal had some effect:

In some ways I felt this message got through. On 11 June Qaddafi addressed a parade at the former American airbase at Wheelus just outside Tripoli. Around him was the full complement of Libyan dissidents who had decided to come home and be pardoned. He said: 'We have been killing abroad. Now we must stop.' I had the distinct impression that, as far as he was concerned, the whole operation had been a show. He needed to give his people the impression that the campaign was working. He was saying to his people: 'Look, these are what the results have been.'

Either the message did not get through to the Libyan hitmen abroad or, the more likely explanation, Qaddafi made his public speech for the benefit of the diplomats present and gave an entirely different set of instructions to his people's bureaus.

The killings did not stop. On the day Qaddafi spoke Ezzedin al Hodeiri, a fifty-six-year-old Libyan living in Bolzano, northern Italy, was shot dead at Milan railway station, while in Rome another Libyan was wounded in an assassination attempt. On 12 June the Libyan's total disrespect for the laws of their host countries was expressed by Musa Koussa, the head of the London people's bureau. He stood on the steps of the office in St James's Square and told a reporter that the revolutionary committees in London had decided to kill two more of Qaddafi's opponents in Britain and that he approved of it. This was too much for the British government. Koussa was ordered to leave the country. He returned to Tripoli, where he took charge of liaison between the revolutionary commit- tees and the liberation movements abroad.

The plan for one of the assassinations in Britain was already in motion. The victim was Farag Ghesuda, who, while a cadet in the Libyan navy in the early 1970s, had been sent to the English south- coast town of Portsmouth for training. There he met and married an English girl, Heather. Together they returned to Tripoli, but did not like it there. In 1974 they moved back to Portsmouth, where they lived in a small colony of Libyans with their two children, a son Karim, and a daughter, Soad. Drawing on his training, Ghesuda obtained a well-paid job as an electronics engineer.

His assailant was Hosni Farhat, who had also been in the Libyan navy and had studied in Portsmouth. He had returned to Tripoli where he got a low-paid job as a clerk in the national airline until he was selected for more important work.

Farhat first met his victim in 1980 at the flat of a mutual friend in Wimbledon. He gave Ghesuda the standard speech on why he should return home to Libya; his country needed his technical expertise and it was his 'duty' to go back to the Jamahiriya. Ghesuda said that he did not like Qaddafi, or Libya under Qaddafi, and that he intended to

161

stay in Portsmouth. There was a furious row and Ghesuda walked out. Farhat did not forget.

He returned to London in July and went to meet the new head of the Libyan people's bureau in London, Mohammed al Gayed. Discussing the stray dogs in Portsmouth, they considered the idea of hiring a hall in the city where Farhat and a diplomat would address the Libyan community on why they should go back to Libya. Farhat had a better idea which he explained to a colleague as he drove to Portsmouth that night. He would poison Libyans who refused to go home. He would also carry out random poisoning in British pubs and dance halls and announce that they would only stop if the British government released the Libyans held for the murders of the two stray dogs, Ramadan and Nafa.

In November Farhat put the first part of his plan into action. He had obtained a small bottle of poison, which he may have brought from Tripoli or from the people's bureau in London. He bought a packet of KP peanuts in a bingo hall, made a small incision in the packet and poured into it a few drops of a poison so secret and deadly that at Farhat's subsequent trial the judge refused to allow it to be mentioned by name. He drove to the Ghesudas' house in Portsmouth and knocked on the door. He apologized to them for his behaviour the previous May, chatted briefly and said that he had brought a packet of nuts for the children.

The next morning Karim and Soad opened the packet of nuts and shared them. It saved their lives. Some of the poison fell on the ground and each child had only half the nuts. Within minutes the children were violently sick. They were rushed to hospital in Portsmouth, then to the National Hospital for Nervous Diseases in London.

The children's hair fell out as a result of the poison and for a time both had to wear wigs. But they survived. Their Pekinese dog, Foo, which had licked up some of the poison from the floor, died. Farhat was caught and sentenced to life imprisonment.

The Libyan government denies involvment in Farhat's attempted murders. In Tripoli the case is dismissed as yet another smear campaign by the British, in league with the CIA and the Mossad, to discredit Qaddafi's revolution. There is no evidence that Farhat received instructions from Bilgasim in Tripoli or from Mohammed al Gayed at the people's bureau in London to kill Ghesuda and his children, and it is unlikely that the family would have been named on any Libyan hit list. Farhat was, however, working under the broad rules laid down by Qaddafi that stray dogs should be liquidated wherever they were, and Farhat had sufficient official status to be received late at night by the most senior Libyan diplomat in Britain.

Senior British police officers believe that the image of Libyan terrorist activities as a vast and deadly network seriously over-estimates their real abilities. One senior officer described it as an invention largely of the American media; its only real danger, he said, is that it boosts the confidence of the Libyan government. The reality is less glamorous: the agents are a bunch of ill-trained and badly organized zealots or mercenaries who pick soft targets and even then usually manage to bungle the jobs. The almost ludicrously inefficent assassination attempts against Bakoush, who is a prime target for the Libyans and heads the stray-dog hit list, supports the cynical view of the Metropolitan Police.

At the time of writing, the Libyans have tried and failed to kill him five times since he left Libya in 1977; in Morocco, in London, in Paris and twice in Cairo. On three occasions the squads were infiltrated or exposed long before they attempted to make their hit. On 2 November 1985, when Bakoush was living in Cairo, four hit men were sent to Egypt over the Libyan/Egyptian border. They went to Alexandria and rented a furnished flat and began planning. Bakoush says that their intelligence was good, but not good enough. They knew that Libyan dissidents met in a villa a dozen miles west of Alexandria. They did not know that their team had been spotted by Egyptian intelligence when it first arrived in Alexandria and had been watched until it was poised to make the hit.

On 2 November Bakoush went to the villa for lunch with twelve other Libyan dissidents. He always travels with a bodyguard pro-vided by the Egyptian police, and as he entered the grounds of the villa he noticed a police car parked under some bushes. At 3.15 as they sat down for lunch Bakoush heard machine-gun and automatic rifle fire outside. He rushed out and saw three of the four Libyan hitmen lying on the ground injured and the fourth held by the police. 'The next day my phone rang at home and it was Abdul Salam Zadmeh, the head of revolutionary intelligence. He cursed and swore at me, called me a bastard, then hung up. It is hard to imagine how stupid these people can be,' said Bakoush.

Zadmeh had reason to be irritated. He and Bilgasim had failed, once again, to kill Bakoush. They were still smarting from an earlier fiasco in November 1984, which must rank as one of the worst operations in the annals of international terror.

This attempt on Bakoush's life involved two English businessmen, Anthony Gill, a former salesman whose ambition was to export large amounts of children's clothing to Libya, and Ronald Shiner, who sold engineering valves, mechanical seals, marine hoses and ropes to oil companies in Libya. Gill first became involved in the shadier side of Libyan affairs when he helped organize the escape from Britain of a Libyan, Mohammed Shebli, a distant relative of Qadaffi who was awaiting trial for smuggling drugs. He escaped in a private plane, although it was nearly shot down as an enemy aircraft as it approached Tripoli airport (Gill and Shiner stood trial for 'perverting the course of justice' at the Old Bailey in London in 1986. Shiner was acquitted. Gill was sentenced to five years.)

Shiner had a house near Rugby in England, and a 46-foot yacht called *Charlie Uniform* moored in Malta which acted as a second home. He spent eight months a year in Libya and had been working there for six years. He had occasionally been approached with what he describes as 'daft suggestions' by Libyan officials about importing arms. He says that Shebli once asked him if he could get hold of F16 US fighter planes. 'I thought it was a joke and I said to Shebli, Sure, I've got a couple of F16s in my back garden in Rugby. Do you want them?' Shiner says his joke did not go down very well. Shebli was serious.

Gill was also approached. The Libyans gave the hosiery salesman a surreal shopping list which included an F16, ground-to-air missiles, Mirage 2000 and 4000 fighters, tankers for refuelling jets, a private plane and 'special cigarettes' with microphones in them, silencers for guns, gas guns and cameras with lasers. Gill said, in his later confession to the Egyptian police. 'I still have the list of those and other items that I know nothing about. And in fact have done absolutely nothing about it. I was not asked about it again.'

Gill was out of his depth, but he was interested when a senior official of a Libyan ministry mentioned a different sort of contract. 'I was given a photo with a name of a man in Egypt and a diagram of a house with an address and instructions to arrange a liquidation. I was not told who the man was, I did not know how to achieve this sort of operation.' The man was Bakoush. The Libyan official first mentioned $150,000 but then dropped to $75,000 for the hit. He would get $10,000 expenses. Two other men, both Maltese, would help him carry out the job.

Gill went to Cairo, met the contacts arranged for him by the Libyans and began recruiting local men to carry out surveillance on Bakoush's house and then to perform the murder itself. One of the first people contacted was an Egyptian police informer. Gill subsequently recruited a hit squad composed entirely of Egyptian security police. He had stumbled into an Egyptian 'sting'.

Shiner was lured into this fiasco by Gill, who phoned him from a Cairo hospital and asked him to come there immediately to lend him $4,000 because he had been hurt in a car accident. In fact he was fine. Egyptian security had arranged Gill's hospital room so that he had a legitimate reason to delay his hit and so could bring Shiner in. Shiner says that he went out of the kindness of his heart and was never, at any time, a party to the conspiracy. The plot had become so confused at this point that even the Egyptian security police were uncertain what was going on. They seemed to think that Shiner was the 'Mr Big', the brains behind the assassination attempt.

Shiner went to the hospital in Cairo with only £1,000 because the rest had been stolen. While Egyptian security men filmed the meeting secretly through a small hole bored in the wall, Gill told Shiner that he had come to Cairo to do a 'hit job'. 'I didn't pay much attention,' said Shiner. 'I went back to my hotel. I remember saying to my wife on the phone that Gill was acting very strangely. There's nowt so strange as folks, I said to her.'

The Egyptian police, convinced that Shiner was the key link with Libya, took elaborate precautions. Shiner's taxi driver was a security man. 'I remember he was a bit suspicious,' said Shiner. 'He wouldn't take any money from me. I'd say I want to settle up and he would always say, "No, no, tomorrow, tomorrow." In the end I insisted on paying. He charged me ninety Egyptian pounds. Afterwards I realized he had overcharged me.' Shiner had been conned again.

The plot came rapidly to a Hollywood conclusion. The police told Bakoush about the assassination attempt and asked him to co-operate so that Qadaffi would be fooled. He agreed with alacrity. He was taken to a tomb in the City of the Dead, a huge graveyard in Cairo, and made up by an expert from the Egyptian television drama department. A bullet hole was painted on his forehead and blood made to drip down his face and over his shirt. 'The make-up expert insisted on real blood and they got some from a hospital,' said Bakoush. 'I looked terrible.'

The police photographer took a Polaroid picture of the 'dead' Bakoush which was delivered to the Libyan people's bureau in Malta as proof that the hit had been completed. Then the unsuspecting Shiner was taken into the tomb to see the body. Bakoush says that the Egyptian police put on a good show to convince Shiner that a real assassination had been carried out. 'I was lying on the floor, dead, with my hands tied. They pretended to be nervous. One of them shot a gun in the air and two of them had a mock fight. I was nervous. I thought someone might actually shoot me,' said Bakoush. Shiner was convinced: 'Gill took me to the City of the Dead. I saw a man lying on the ground with his hands tied. It was Bakoush, although I didn't know his name at the time. I was terrified. Gill kept saying to me, "Relax, Godfrey, relax. Don't blow it." I went icy cold.'

Shiner, who believed that a man had really been murdered, spent a clammy week in a Cairo airport hotel while Gill pretended he was waiting for the money to pay the hit men. A week later as Shiner waited to catch a flight out of Cairo, a doctor from the hospital where he had first met Gill arrived at the hotel and offered to show Shiner the sights of Cairo before the plane took off. Shiner had been conned once again. The doctor was an Egyptian policeman who took him straight to the central police station and arrested him. Both Gill and Shiner were eventually sent back to London for trial.

The sting worked beautifully. The Polaroid picture of the bloody Bakoush reached Tripoli, and Gill phoned his contacts in Libya to say that the job had been carried out successfully. The Libyans fell for it. On 16 November Jana, the official Libyan news agency, broadcast a statement announcing that 'the sentence of execution on Bakoush, who had sold his conscience to the enemies of the Arab nation, has been carried out by a revolutionary force, thereby implementing the resolution of the basic people's congress which formed suicide squads to liquidate the enemies of the revolution internally and externally'. The next day the Egyptian Interior Minister, Ahmed Rushdi, held a press conference to reveal the hoax and presented a living, breathing and smiling Bakoush. Qaddafi's humiliation was complete.

11 Pursuing the Revolution Abroad

His Excellency the Secretary of the Libyan people's bureau in Jordan received an urgent telex in the autumn of 1982 summoning him back to Tripoli for an audience with the leader of the revolution, Colonel Qaddafi.

Aziz Shenib took the next Libyan Arab Airlines flight with some trepidation. There is little job security in the Libyan foreign service and Shenib ran through the ways in which he might have offended his master. Perhaps he had seen through Shenib's reliance on digests of the *Economist*'s Foreign Report and the local Arab press for his assessments of Jordan's domestic and foreign policy, or perhaps he had not been keen enough in recruiting Palestinians to the Libyan cause. Shenib's position was precarious. He had been number three in the Libyan army under King Idris and had been wedded to the monarchist cause. Qaddafi had imprisoned him in the first hours of the revolution in 1969 and he had spent more than four years in prison in Tripoli and another year under house arrest. Then, in 1978, Qaddafi had pulled him out of the wilderness and asked him to be a foreign envoy. Shenib was not unduly flattered. He realized that Libya had few people of education and experience to serve abroad and most of them were in prison. He went first as ambassador to Romania, then to Jordan.

Shenib drove to the Aziziya barracks and walked from the security gate across the football pitch to Qaddafi's tent. As he went in a group of Polisario rebels, who were receiving Libyan aid in their guerrilla war against King Hassan of Morocco, came out. Qaddafi came straight to the point. 'I want you to arrange the assassination of King Hussein,' he said.

After four years in the foreign service it took a lot to surprise Shenib. The role of Libyan ambassador is an odd one and has little to do with conventional diplomacy. In Amman his main function was to recruit Palestinians to serve as Libyan agents. 'Qaddafi wanted to concentrate on the fanatics,' said Shenib,

167

the PFLP-GC the PFLP, the DFLP. The Libyan embassy would pay the salaries of some of the leaders of these groups. Also anyone who left the Arafat group to join the extremists was paid a lump sum. The real job of the embassy was to go into the Palestinian refugee camps in Amman and recruit people. It was very difficult because most of the Palestinians didn't want to be recruited. It was risky as well because Jordanian intelligence is very good, very tight. We had some success and a number of Palestinians were persuaded to go to Libya for training in one of the seven military training camps there. They would be given basic or senior courses, with some special courses in explosives, camouflage, reconnaissance, ambush and weapon firing.

The assassination of Hussein was to be his second special assignment. The first was in 1981, after the Israeli attack on the Iraqi nuclear reactor, when Qaddafi had asked him to arrange for the destruction of the Israeli nuclear reactor at Demona in the Negev desert. Qaddafi told Shenib to obtain a Syrian Skoda rocket with a range of thirty miles, transfer it secretly (because the Jordanians would have stopped the operation if they had learned of it) to the mountains of eastern Jordan and fire it at Demona. Shenib thought the plan absurd and so did the Syrians when he contacted them. Abdul Halim Khaddam, the Syrian Foreign Minister, 'thought it was a big joke', remembered Shenib. 'He said that Qaddafi wanted not just to hit the nuclear reactor but to knock out the whole area. This would start a war and Syria was not ready for a war with Israel. The senior military circles in Syria were all laughing.' How, they asked, could an 80-foot Skoda rocket to be transported without being seen by the Jordanians or the Israelis?

Shenib prepared a report, of which he is still quite proud. 'It was done with great style and the detail of the reconnaissance was really very good.' He suggested that the Demona complex was not a target area but a point target, and a point target cannot be taken out with a missile. 'It would have to be a bomb planted exactly on the target. That would involve commandos and details of the construction of the nuclear site, its depth, width, etc. I sent my report to Qaddafi and made the point, politely, that the method he suggested was not practical. I suggested other ways of doing it.' The report was consigned to the dustbin of terrorist schemes, where the plans to attack the QE2 had lain for eight years.

Qaddafi was serious about killing King Hussein, although, according to Shenib, the method seemed more carefully worked out than the reason. Qaddafi waffled on about 'it being a good time to strike against the moderate Arab countries and how he had wanted to get rid of Hussein since 1970. He said that with the crisis in Beirut after the Israeli invasion the Arab world needed new leaders, not the moderate, pro-imperialist kings like Hussein.' For anyone wishing to wreck any possibility of a negotiated solution to the Palestinian problem Hussein was the target. He was poised, after the military defeat of the PLO in Lebanon, to launch his own Middle East peace initiative. Hussein is the key figure if only because more than half the population of his country is Palestinian, and it was the King who lost the West Bank, the site of any future Palestinian state, to the Israelis in the 1967 war.

Qaddafi said that Hussein's private jet should be shot down as the King flew from Amman to his residence in Aqaba, as he often did at the weekend. He said the plane should be attacked by a ground-to-air missile which, like the weapon sought for the abortive Demona operation, could be obtained from the Syrians. 'You are a good friend of Khaddam,' Qaddafi told Shenib. 'Go and talk to him about it. I want this to be a joint Libyan/Syrian operation.' There were to be two hit teams, one in Aqaba and one in Amman, both armed with missiles. Qaddafi had obviously done his homework. He told Shenib that the missiles should not be fired at a low level when the plane was coming in to land because Hussein might survive. They should be fired just as the plane lowered its undercarriage and began its descent. 'Go and arrange the people and the weapons,' Qaddafi told him. 'I said, "Yes, of course." I couldn't say no. Nobody ever said no. I had spent more than four years in a Libyan jail and I didn't intend to go back.'

As Shenib flew back to Amman, he decided to defect from the Libyan foreign service, but he needed time to get his family out of Libya: 'This really was too much. I was horrified at what Qaddafi wanted and I have a lot of respect for Hussein.' In Amman he informed Hussein about the assassination plot, then, with the agreement of the Jordanian secret service, flew to Damascus to see if the Syrians would take the bait. He went to Khaddam's house to explain Qaddafi's plan and says he was surprised by his reaction. 'He was astonished but said it was a good plan. He said that if we had shot down Sadat's plane before he went to Jerusalem then Camp David and the other problems we have in the Arab world would never have happened. He told me that he would speak to President Hafez al Assad the next morning.' The following day he met a chastened Khaddam who reported that Qaddafi's plan had not gone down well

169

with Assad. In fact Assad thought the scheme 'ridiculous and child-ish. If it succeeded then every Arab leader would have to fear for his life every time he took off in a plane.'

The plot was aborted. Hussein, who had been the first person whom Qaddafi had expressed a public desire to kill at the Cairo conference in 1970, remained high on the Colonel's hit list. Both Nasser and Heikal had hoped that Qaddafi might mellow with age and experience and look for more sophisticated solutions to the problems of foreign affairs than the quick kill, but they were to be disappointed.

Qaddafi would always strenuously deny that any of his actions could be defined as 'terror'. The Libyan government took out a half-page advertisement in the *Guardian* in August 1986, headlined 'The Truth About Terrorism'. It said:

> The American Administration is trying to distort the People's struggle by branding it as terrorism. For example the Liberation movements all over the world, such as the Palestine Liberation Organization, SWAPO and the Organization for the Liberation of the People of South Africa are all regarded as terrorists. The American Administration has also considered as terrorists all those who support the struggle of these people for freedom. Natu-rally, as long as the Libyan people are the main supporters of the People's struggle for freedom they have to be dismissed as terror-ists by such an Administration.

The Libyan government explained that it wanted to 'expose this lie and immoral distortion of the People's struggle' and demanded that the US submit its allegations to the International Court of Justice. If such a court case ever took place, many of the allegations against Qaddafi would almost certainly be dismissed for lack of evidence.

The greyest area would be the funding of terror, the extent to which Qaddafi has pumped his oil revenue into the coffers of organizations which carry out acts of terror. The statistics from the analysts of terror, and from the British, US and Israeli intelligence reports, are so vague as to be meaningless. Qaddafi has certainly given money to a wide range of organizations, but, as in the case of the IRA, it is often much less than is popularly thought. The US State Department has given the figure of £100 million in 1985 alone, although it gives no accurate breakdown of how the cash was spent. James Adams, in his book *The Financing of Terror*, underplays the role that states like Libya play in the funding of extremist Palestinian groups and says that the total state sponsorship of the PLO, the most moderate group of all, is £100 million a year, although he does not provide a figure for the Libyan contribution. Claire Sterling, in *The Terror Network*, says Libya's contribution was $40 million a year in the early 1970s. John Wright, in *Libya: A Modern History*, suggests the lowest figure of all £150 million (less than $250 million) for Libya's entire contribution to terror and international causes. The Israelis in an intelligence document ('Libya's Support for International Terror and Libyan Subversion in the Arab World'), says the total contribution is a billion dollars, The truth probably lies somewhere between these last two figures.

The Israeli Defence Force (IDF) produced a document in January 1982 giving details of Libyan financial support for the PLO before the breakdown in relationships following the Israeli invasion of Lebanon which occurred later that year. The document says that at the Baghdad Arab conference in October 1978 Libya promised to provide the PLO with $39.3 million a year, and also offered support for such Palestinian factions as the PFLP-GC, headed by Ahmed Jibril. Jibril said, in an interview with a Lebanese paper in July 1981:'From the outset the Libyan revolution declared its national and popular character and made Jerusalem a symbol and a goal. Libya never concealed its stand on the Palestinian issue, which it regards as an urgent national obligation. On this basis it has provided full material support to the Palestinian revolution since 1969.' The statement is, however, heavier on rhetoric than fact and Jibril neglects to mention the degree to which the tap had been turned on and off. Another Lebanese newspaper reported in June 1981 that the first portion of Libyan financial assistance, resulting from the Baghdad conference decision had reached the Fatah movement, but that the amount was only $10 million. If this figure is correct Libya owed the PLO approximately $100 million on its Baghdad pledge. Qaddafi did, however, seem prepared to give much larger sums of money to fringe organizations if the Jordanian Prime Minister, Mudar Badran, is correct; he said in December 1980 that 'a Palestinian organization consisting of only thirty people had received $6 million from Qaddafi'.

The Israelis monitor Qaddafi's machinations from an old, ivy-covered building in Tel Aviv, the headquarters of Israeli military intelligence, and from the Foreign Ministry intelligence unit which works from a group of prefabs in the ministry compound in Jerusalem. They are considered to be the experts on Middle East terror, with networks of agents in most of the Arab countries and huge teams of analysts who listen to radio, telephone and telex traffic throughout the Middle East. The Americans are to a certain extent dependent on

Israeli intelligence-gathering. According to another Israeli intelligence report given to the authors in 1986, Qaddafi spreads his money thin and wide:

Gadafy supports some fifty terror organizations and subversion groups, in addition to more than forty radical governments in Africa, Asia, Europe and America. Libya also helps almost all the terrorist and radical movements in the Middle East including several Palestinian organizations like George Habash's PFLP, Ahmed Jibril's PFLP-GC, Naif Hawatmeh's Democratic Front, the Saiqa, the Popular Struggle Front, and Abu Nidal. Other Middle East organizations include the Armenian ASALA, and underground groups operating against reactionary Arab regimes in Egypt, Sudan, Iraq, and Saudi Arabia. Libya also maintains close links with West European underground movements including the IRA in Ireland, ETA in Spain, Action Directe in France, the Red Brigades in Italy, Baader–Meinhof in Germany, the SIM group in Sardinia. In Latin America they support Colombia's M19, the Tupamaros in Uruguay, groups in El Salvador and the governments of Surinam, Cuba and Nicaragua. Support is also extended to extremist opposition movements in Asia, like the Moro in the Philippines, opposition groups in Indonesia and the Japanese Red Army. In addition to all these Libya encourages and supports underground and opposition groups in Africa, operating in countries where the regimes are identified as pro-Western or against regimes who do not back Libyan foreign policy in the continent such as Chad, Senegal, Uganda, Zaire, Tunisia.

Gadafy resorts to various methods in order to attain his goals in Africa. Foreigners working in Libya are being recruited and sent to training camps for missions inside their homelands. Islamic centres are built in Togo, Niger, Chad, Rwanda, Burundi and other countries to be used as centres of Libyan influence. These centres spread Gadafy's personal cult and his Green Book and recruit citizens for Libya's service. In the past, Libya also supported opposition groups in Somalia, Ghana, Nigeria, Mali, Mauritania, Morocco, Algeria and Sudan. All these subversive groups and organizations have received financial aid from Libya. They have also received weapons and help in planning operations, hiding runaway terrorists and training for terror warfare in Libyan training camps. Some of the instructors in these camps are Syrian intelligence, and also Palestinians, Cubans, East Germans and Russians. According to information some 7,000 terrorists are training in Libya now [1986] from many different nations. Here is a list of part of the terrorist training camps in Libya:

Al Hilal camp 250 km west of Tobruk; Al Jadayim camp west of Tripoli; Al Jaghbub camp 30 km west of the Egyptian border; Ghadames camp at the confluence of the Libyan, Algerian and Tunisian borders; Beda camp 200 km south of Sirte; Kufrah camp in the Kufrah oasis; Misurata camp in Misurata; Aouzou camp in northern Chad; Sidi Bilal camp south of Tripoli; Sebha camp (this is a special training camp for professional assassins); Sabratha camp west of Tripoli; a camp on the outskirts of Benghazi near the beach; the April 7th camp in the Benghazi area.

There is no doubt that the tremors of Qaddafi's underground activities are felt across the world. The exact details of his role are more difficult to establish. The US intelligence community is divided about how great a threat Qaddafi poses to the West and how to deal with it, and in the same way there are differences of fact and opinion among the various Israeli intelligence organizations. The Foreign Ministry intelligence analysts consistently downplay the risk posed by Libya and say that if there is a mastermind behind inter-national terror, it is President Assad of Syria.

According to a senior British police officer, most of those he has dealt with, including the claim that Libya played a key role in the massacres at Rome and Vienna airports in December 1985, 'would be thrown out of a British magistrates' court for lack of evidence'. The alleged link with Libya in those two incidents rests on the claim that the passports were taken from expelled Tunisian workers by the Libyan government and given to the terrorists who carried out the two attacks. On this occasion the British police agree with Qaddafi, who said after attacks: 'They say the passports were provided by Libya, but where is the proof? Passports can be forged or stolen and provided by any government, even the US or the Israelis. This is not proof.'

It is important therefore to look at three specific cases of Libyan terror which would keep Qaddafi's defence lawyers in any inter-national court case very busy indeed.

In the spring of 1977 Qaddafi's dream of unifying the Arab world for a military assault on Israel was shattered. He chastised the Palestinians for what he saw as their consistent failure to confront the Zionist enemy, and according to Arafat's deputy, Salah Khalef, relations had reached such a low ebb that Libya had stopped paying its contributions and owed the PLO between $80 million and $90 million. Relations with Egypt had reached the point where a border war between the two countries would break out that summer. Sadat was poised to make what Qaddafi and other radical Arab states believed to be the greatest betrayal of all: his historic trip to Jerusalem in November that year.

Qaddafi decided to put some muscle into his attempts to disrupt Egyptian/US relations by murdering the US ambassador to Cairo, Herman Eilts. He planned the assassination with some of his closest aides, working late into the night at an office in the former US base at Wheelus outside Tripoli.

Qaddafi had recruited two teams of two Egyptians to do the job, and he told one to enter Egypt across the Western desert, and the other to go across the Sudanese border. Meanwhile a team of Libyan agents was watching the movements of Herman Eilts. They took photographs of his residence and of his armoured car entering and leaving the embassy in Cairo. They even obtained pictures of Eilts's office inside the embassy, which subsequently caused a US internal inquiry into how the Libyans penetrated a 'safe' room. Two Libyans from the reconnaissance team rented rooms in a high-rise building which overlooked the entrance to the embassy.

The plot had two elements. One of the teams of Egyptians would roll a high-percussion grenade under Eilts's official car as he drove out of the embassy gates. Simultaneously the other team would open fire with a machine-gun from the apartment block opposite. If the shrapnel didn't get him, the bullets would. It was a good plan, and the US embassy security agents believed that the grenade would have killed the ambassador outright. But it had one fatal flaw: the United States knew every detail of it.

In the early spring of 1977 a senior Libyan had approached a member of the CIA attached to the US embassy in Tripoli and said that, for a large number of US dollars, he would give the Americans all the details of a plot to assassinate Eilts. The official provided what Eilts describes as 'a wealth of detail because he was present at all the planning sessions at Wheelus'.

After one of the hit teams had been picked up by Egyptian security, President Carter decided not to cause an international incident at such a crucial period in the Middle East peace process. Instead he sent a secret protest note to Qaddafi via the Libyan mission to the United Nations. 'It was not a strong protest,' said Eilts. 'It said that the US knew the attack was being planned and that Carter took a dim view of Qaddafi bumping off an American ambassador.' Qaddafi sent a note back through the same channel saying that he took an equally dim view of these vile and untrue allegations and that if the US thought he was planning an assassination then it should provide the evidence.

Against the advice of the intelligence community, which wanted to keep the official in place as an active US agent, Carter decided to give Qaddafi all the facts. The Libyan was told the bad news by the CIA station chief in Tripoli and, within a week, was flown out of the country. He now lives in Cairo. Carter prepared his second detailed note to Qaddafi which included every minute detail of each planning session at Wheelus, the names of all the Libyans involved, details of the plot itself, the names of the assassins, the proposed date of the assassination attempt, with the extra sting that all this information had been given to the United States by one of Qaddafi's closest advisers. It was one of the most devastating notes ever sent by one head of state to another. 'When Qaddafi saw that, we heard that he hit the ceiling,' said Eilts.

In March 1984 Qaddafi attempted another dramatic intervention in the affair of a neighbour, this time the Sudan. The residents of Omdurman, a town at the confluence of the Blue and White Niles next to Khartoum in Sudan, heard the rumble of a large plane. It flew low, and very slowly, over Khartoum, crossed the river and then circled Omdurman as if it had lost its way, which it probably had, until the pilot spotted the large aerial of the Omdurman radio station and made his bombing run.

One bomb landed outside the radio station and killed a Sudanese vendor at a food stall. The plane then flew off in a north-westerly direction. It was a Libyan TU22 bomber from Kufrah, in southern Libya, not far from the Sudanese border. If Sudanese air defences had been more alert, the plane would have been shot down long before it reached the suburbs of Khartoum. But the Sudanese army made every mistake in the book. Their radar did not work and so the first the anti-aircraft batteries knew of the plane was when it appeared overhead; their missiles were not ready for firing and if they had been, as a report subsequently established, they would not have worked. The anti-aircraft gunmen could not explain their problems to the army high command in Khartoum because their telephone line was down.

The point of this military escapade had been simple and absurd. The Sudanese allowed Libyan dissidents to use the Omdurman radio station to broadcast anti-Qaddafi material into Libya. Whereas most leaders would try to jam the airways or send a stiff diplomatic note to the radio's host government, or, if these actions failed, merely dismiss the whole thing as a minor irritation, Qaddifi enjoys the dramatic gesture and sent off a Libyan bomber to silence the radio station permanently. However, the attack failed, the radio broadcasts continued; the only victim was an innocent Sudanese selling meat balls.

Shortly afterwards, on 9 July 1984, a Russian cargo ship, the *Knud Jespersson*, was ploughing its way innocently through the placid waters of the Red Sea heading for the Suez canal when there was an enormous explosion under the bows. The baffled Russian captain managed to take his ship, although badly damaged, into port. Three weeks later in the same area a Japanese ship, the *Meitho Maru*, felt an explosion thunder beneath it. During the next few days ships of different nationalities at either end of the Red Sea were damaged by explosions which appeared to be caused by small mines. By 15 August the mysterious explosions in the Red Sea had claimed their seventeeth victim, a Cypriot cargo ship, the *Theopolis*.

The Red Sea explosions created an international panic. A flotilla of British mine-hunting ships, equipped with sonar and remote-control miniature sub-marines, accompanied by French, Egyptian and Russian mine-sweepers scoured the sea. US helicopters towing mine-sweeping sledges roared to and fro across the water. It was a nerve-racking job, as an expert on one mine-sweeper said: 'You crawl along the surface never quite knowing if something is going to blow up underneath you.' What puzzled observers was the small size of the explosions. 'They are such weedy mines,' said Anthony Preston, of *Jane's Defence Review*. A normal mine would break the back of a large tanker but these mines were causing only minor damage to the hulls.

Iran was the first suspect, but the experts were too busy mine-hunting to cast their eyes back through the speeches of Colonel Qaddafi. At the Arab summit five years before in 1979 he had made a speech which most observers shrugged off as the usual Qaddafi rhetoric. He accused the Palestinians of 'surrendering' to the demands of the Arab moderates and declared that 'the best tactics to be adopted by the Arabs would be to threaten navigation in the Suez canal and at the entrance to the Red Sea'. He said that ships carrying goods to Israel should be hit and Arab oil 'should be destroyed if it is not used for the liberation of Palestine'.

On 6 July an innocuous little ship had passed through the Suez canal and entered the Red Sea. It was a roll-on, roll-off ferry called the *Ghat* owned by the General Maritime Transport Company of Tripoli and normally used for transporting trucks. It was also ideal, with a rear door that can be lowered to water level, for rolling small mines into the Red Sea. The *Ghat* steamed south to the Ethiopian port of Assab at the bottom of the Red Sea, close to the narrow strait Bab al

Mandab. Strangely for a cargo ship it did not go into port but stayed at sea for three days. It docked at Assab on 14 July, sailed on 22 July and was clocked out of the Suez canal on 27 July, according to the computers of Lloyd's Shipping Information. At this point it disappeared from official maritime view into the territorial waters of Libya, which does not report ship movements to Lloyd's.

The *Ghat*, commanded by Lieutenant Zuheir Adham, head of the navy's mine-laying divisions, and with a crew of specially picked intelligence officers, laid a few mines on its trip south to Assab, sowed a lot in the southern straits of Bab al Mandab and then dropped more on its return through the gulf of Suez. The mines in its cargo were Russian and of new design. They were sophisticated 'acoustic' mines, triggered by the noise of ships' engines, but they were not 'front-line Soviet material' according to the experts.

One mystery remains about Qaddafi's foray into maritime terror: although he intended to create panic in the shipping lanes and cut the amount of traffic through the Suez canal, the mines were carrying less than a quarter of their normal weight of explosives. 'If someone intended to sink a ship with these things it is like shooting a rhino with birdshot,' said Preston. Egypt's revenue from the canal dipped marginally during August as the rash of bombs exploded, but picked up again at the end of the month. 'Qaddafi is trying to make a diplomatic point rather than take lives,' said a British Foreign Office official.

A pattern emerges from Qaddafi's direct use of terror. First, more often than not it does not work. Second, the targets are usually not Western or Israeli. There is a myth that Qaddafi's primary victims are Israel, the United States and Western Europe. They are more often the targets of his rhetoric than of his terrorism. A report by the US State Department, *Libya Under Gaddafy: A Pattern of Aggression*, published in January 1986, says Qaddafi is not particularly hostile to Israel and the US. The report shows that his hostility is directed in the opposite direction, at his own citizens, moderate Arab countries, African countries which do not fall into line, and moderate Palestinians. Its chronology of Libyan support for terror from 1980 to 1985 shows that Libya has carried out five acts of terror against the West in this period as opposed to forty-six against Arab and African targets. The attempted assassination of Ambassador Eilts was exceptional, and one of only two or three attacks aimed directly at US targets. This attack was aimed more at Egypt than at the United States. 'It was nothing personal,' said Eilts. 'The real target was not me but President Sadat and US/Egypt relations.'

According to analysts at Tel Aviv University in a report called *International Terrorism in 1985*, Libya's contribution to international terror is rather less than is popularly believed. The report say that out of a total of 408 incidents in 1985 Libyan hit teams were responsible for eleven. Eight of the victims of these eleven attacks were Libyan. The Libyans lagged well behind the Shiite Islamic Jihad, which, according to this report, was responsible for thirty-five attacks, as well as behind Abu Nidal's organization (responsible for twenty-four attacks) and 'unknown Lebanese groups' (twenty-two attacks).

Another survey, *Middle Eastern Terrorist Activity in Western Europe in 1985*, by Dennis Pluchinsky, European expert in the Threat Analysis Division of the Bureau of Diplomatic Security in the US State Department, reveals a strange statistic. He records more than seventy-five attacks which resulted in sixty-five deaths and more than 529 injuries. Most of the attacks (forty-two) were against Arab or Palestinian targets; thirteen against Israeli or Jewish, fifteen against Western and five against American targets. Pluchinsky's analysis shows that there were more attacks aimed against Libyan targets (six) than against American (five).

The terror campaign against Qaddafi and the Libyan regime itself is shadowy and mostly unreported. It is largely the work of a group calling itself Borkan (Arabic for volcano). There is speculation that Borkan has been backed since 1984 by Israel or the CIA in attacks on Qaddafi's supporters overseas. However, an investigation by *Stern* magazine in 1986 revealed a bizarre terror network which has links with Berlin and London. On 21 January 1984 the head of the Libyan people's bureau in Rome, Amar al Tagazi, was shot dead in front of his home. The killers, who had used silencers, escaped. In a call to the Associated Press news agency Borkan emerged for the first time and claimed responsibility for the shooting. Diplomatic observers were curious at the professional nature of the assassination – clearly not just the work of some of Qaddafi's disaffected opponents as had been at first suspected.

On 14 October 1984, in Bonn, West Germany, two Molotov cocktails were thrown against the front door of the Libyan people's bureau, which thereby caught fire. Again the bombers escaped, this time in a Mercedes. Borkan claimed responsibility again in January 1985 when a Libyan diplomat in Rome, Farah Omar Makkyoum, was shot leaving his home.

According to *Stern*, who traced the weapons used in these attacks to a German arms dealer, one of the key figures behind Borkan was a Libyan sent by Qaddafi to the United States with funds of a million dollars and instructions to keep an eye on the ideological purity of Libyan students in the US. Instead, *Stern* says, he set himself up in an import/export business and became a target for Qaddafi's assassins. The Libyan decided to turn the tables, although his motives for starting Borkan are still obscure. According to court testimony in the trial of a German involved in providing handguns and silencers for Borkan, London was a key site for the hand-over of weapons, and one of the meeting places was the royal Lancaster Hotel.

Although Qaddafi harangued other Arab countries and the Palestinian groups for getting embroiled in inter-Arab feuds, Libya is one of the worst offenders, and the waves of one of Qaddafi's actions can still be felt in the Middle East. In August 1978 the Immam Musa Sadr, the spiritual leader of almost a million Shiite Muslims in Lebanon, disappeared in Libya. Sadr had been invited to celebrate the anniversary of the Libyan revolution on 1 September, and he travelled to Tripoli on 25 August with two companions, Sheikh Mohammed Yacoub and Abbas Bedreddin, a journalist. All three subsequently disappeared.

Libyan officials still maintain that Sadr took a flight from Tripoli to Rome on 31 August. His name was on a passenger list for the Alitalia flight; however, his luggage arrived in Rome but he did not. The Shiites believe he did not leave Tripoli and that he was murdered on the instructions of Qaddafi. His body had never been found, but the murder theory is now accepted by Shiites, Libyan dissidents and Western intelligence agencies. There are many suggestions why Qaddafi would want to kill such an eminent Muslim cleric as Musa Sadr. One is that Qaddafi viewed the Imam as a threat to his own aspirations as a religious leader. Another is a good deal less esoteric: that Qaddafi and Sadr fell out over money which Qaddafi had given the Imam to finance the political and military activities of the Shiites in southern Lebanon. Yet another says that Qaddafi felt Sadr was not militant enough and did not use this money to attack Israel. Bakoush, the former Prime Minister, believes Sadr was killed in a murky dispute over money.

Younis Bilgasim, the head of Libyan intelligence, has given the most bizarre version of Sadr's disappearance: he accuses the holy man of being a drug dealer and an agent for the secret police of Iran:

> When Musa Sadr got to Tripoli he wanted to be treated like a head of state and to have a chair at Gadafy's side. When those in charge explained that they were seats reserved for heads of state, he got angry and decided to leave the country. We insist that Sadr

disappeared in Italy. When someone disappears and nobody knows how, you have to expand on every theory possible. We know that Musa Sadr was an agent of Savak [the Iranian secret police under the Shah] and we know that when he left that country, he was hunted down by the secret service. There is also another theory. The area where he lived in Lebanon [in the southern Lebanese port city of Tyre] is rich in hashish and this could explain the power and money which he accumulated in such a short time. He could therefore have been liquidated because of a war between the drug dealers.

Bilgasim's theories hardly help the wounded pride of the Shiite community. The Imam's fate is a subject the Libyans would prefer to forget. Sadr had haunted them since 1978, harming links with the Iranian Shiites under Ayatollah Khomeini and damaging Libyan efforts to achieve influence in Lebanon. Relations with the Amal militia, founded by Sadr, are bad and likely to remain so. In 1984 Amal militiamen kidnapped all the Libyan diplomats in Beirut and burned down the embassy. Amal leaders have branded Qaddafi as a 'CIA agent'.

Qaddafi's most recent terrorist link is with the group headed by Abu Nidal, *nom de guerre* of Sabri al Banna, a Palestinian orginally from Haifa. Nidal is the most secretive of the Palestinian guerrillas. He rarely gives interviews to the press and even his existence has been held in question. He has been reported both dead and chronically sick with cancer. However, his organization, which has perhaps 200 active members, continues to be the most feared and effective terrorist group in the world. Nidal used to base himself in the capitals of Iraq and Syria, where he had an office in Damascus. It was an awesome sight in a residential street in the centre of the city. The windows were blocked with sandbags against car-bomb attacks and the front door was made of steel and electronically operated. A remote-control camera fixed on the wall just above the door observed any visitors. Inside, however, it was more like a doctor's surgery. There was a waiting room where, during the visit of one of the authors, conservatively dressed ladies sat, chatted and flicked through Arabic magazines as they waited for an appointment. A smartly dressed and well-educated young man offered the visitors tea or coffee and biscuits on a china plate. He spoke impeccable English. 'I am really terribly sorry,' he told one of the authors. 'I am not authorized to give any information about our organization. You understand we have to be, well, cautious about what we say. However, I will take your telephone number and try to contact Mr Issa [Nidal's deputy].' He phoned the author's hotel a number of times with regrets: 'Mr Issa is very busy.'

That is not surprising, Nidal's group has carried out a large number of attacks on moderate Arab, Palestinian and British targets. Britain was high on Nidal's hit list after three of his followers attempted to murder the Israeli ambassador to London, Shlomo Argov, in 1982 – an attack which triggered the Israeli invasion of Lebanon. The assassins were caught, tried and imprisoned, and Nidal has made many subsequent assaults on British targets in an attempt to force their release.

Nidal is thought to have been expelled from Baghdad after US pressure on the Iraqi government, and he settled in Syria in 1983. In 1983 Nidal reportedly co-operated with the Syrian government in attacks against Jordan, but he was dissatisfied with what he saw as a Syrian/Jordanian *rapprochement* in 1985 and opposed the Syrian support of the Shiite Amal militia in their battles with the Palestinians in Lebanon. His links with Syria were weakened though not completely broken. Nidal looked for other backers, among them Libya, a country, Israeli sources say, he first co-operated with in 1983 in attempts to subvert the Egyptian government of Hosni Mubarak.

Nidal is a man after Qaddafi's heart. Both of them despise compromise on the Palestinian issue and believe in the military solution. The Israelis believe that a meeting in September 1985 in Tripoli between the Libyans, Syrians and various extremist Palestinian groups, including Nidal, was critical in establishing a new era of Arab co-operation on terrorism.

This dangerous liaison seems to have borne fruit in the attacks, in December that year, in Rome and Vienna. However, around that time the Jordanian journalist Nezar Hindawi was visiting both Libya and Syria seeking support for terrorist ventures in Europe. In Tripoli he was fobbed off with $5,000; in Damascus he found enthusiasm and logistical support for his plan to blow up an Israeli jumbo jet. In April 1986 he tried to hoodwink his pregnant Irish girlfriend into carrying a case lined with explosive on board an El Al plane at London airport. He was discovered, and later sentenced to forty-five years in prison in Britain.

British anti-terrorist specialists from Scotland Yard believe that despite this merger of terrorist expertise Qaddafi has grown more circumspect in his funding of revolutionaries. 'He doesn't give a blank cheque any more,' said a senior officer from Scotland Yard. 'He wants value for money.' And, the British police have long and bitter experience of Libyan terror.

12   Murder in London

When Britain's Minister of Health, Kenneth Clarke, arrived back in London at the end of a five-day official visit to Libya in February 1983 he was met at the airport by the Libyan ambassador, Adam Kwiri, who presented him with a large bunch of flowers. It was an ironic gesture, given the overall state of Anglo-Libyan relations. But in the circumstances it was touching and strangely appropriate. A lot of people in both Britain and Libya had been determined that Clarke's trip should go well.

Relations between the two countries had been cool since two of Colonel Qaddafi's opponents had been killed on British soil in 1980. Libya had continued to keep up its attacks on stray dogs, which it appeared genuinely to feel were being shielded and even aided by Britain. The threat of further incidents had never been far away. Yet wiser counsels in both London and Tripoli knew that in many ways, particularly economic, their countries needed each other. Diplomats had worked hard to improve ties.

Most responsible Libyans looked on Britain as an ideal cultural and trading partner. Traditional links with Italy might be stronger, but English was now the second language in Libyan schools. Ambitious young Libyans regarded it as essential for mastering technology and commerce in the modern world. In 1983 around 8,000 of them were studying (mainly practical and scientific subjects) at colleges, polytechnics and universities throughout the United Kingdom – more than in any other foreign country. Increasingly, as they returned home and climbed the bureaucratic hierarchy, they looked to British consultants to assist them in the serious business of developing their country.

This state of affairs suited Britain well. It now wanted to cash in on these valuable contacts and win more meaty export orders and contracts for British companies. The oil-price decline had begun to hit the Libyan economy, and Qaddafi's original $62.5 billion five-year development plan covering the years 1981 to 1985 had been trimmed. Total OECD exports to Libya had dropped dramatically from $12.3 billion in 1982 to $6.7 billion in 1983. But Britain's market share had held up well at around 7 per cent, making it Libya's fourth-largest supplier after Italy, West Germany and Japan. There was no reason to doubt that, with Libya's planners becoming more sophisticated and selective in keeping with their straitened economic circumstances, this percentage would increase.

Health care was a potential area for co-operation where Britain could best press home its advantages. Libya needed hospitals and, perhaps even more importantly, equipment and staff to run them. Britain's financially hard-pressed National Health Service would be delighted to help train and advise its still relatively rich and developing Libyan counterpart.

Kenneth Clarke, as Minister for Health, would have been the ideal senior politician to lead any British mission to Libya. Youngish, outgoing and unstuffy, he had the advantage, as a rising star in the Tory party, of having the ears of Mrs Thatcher, the British Prime Minister. No other senior British Minister had visited Libya since Mrs Thatcher came to power in 1979. Britain's Foreign Office, while recognizing that Clarke's main object was to foster bilateral economic relations, was keen that he should lose no opportunity of making a political point or two amid the general *bonhomie* surrounding his trip. The Foreign Office was particularly concerned that Qaddafi and some of his closest followeres were still making public pronouncements about the need to get rid of stray-dogs dissidents, may of whom, they made clear, were resident in Britain. On 17 February, only a few days before Clarke's departure, the General People's Congress in Tripoli had declared that 'every citizen is responsible for the liquidation of the enemies of the people and the revolution'. The Foreign Office hoped Libya could be encouraged by the prospect of beneficial trade relations to desist from making these kind of statements. The Office briefed Clarke along these lines.

Adam Kwiri, for his part, was also determined to capitalize on Clarke's trip. He sent along one of his trusted young political counsellors. Hamed Zlitni, nephew of the Minister of Education, to accompany Clarke, as well as his private secretary and an adviser. Clarke recalled that Zlitni was armed from the moment they left Heathrow and he got the impression that the young Libyan had a subsidiary role as a bodyguard.

Once in Libya, Clarke, as expected, spent most of his time with his opposite number, the Minister of Health, Dr Murad Ali Langi, who took him on a tour of Libyan health services. Clarke was unimpressed by a vast concrete hospital he saw being built by North Koreans. 'No British contractor could have built it so cheaply. It looked destined to become one of the largest empty concrete block in North Africa unless there were people to man it.' However, seeing it did cause him to redouble his efforts at selling British expertise to the Libyans. He was more struck by the Czech-built and -staffed polyclinics which provided health care in city suburbs. These were 'bleak, efficient and well run, though they would have got better quality out of us'.

Clarke was quite clear about what he was trying to do. 'The Libyans still had a substantial health expansion programme planned. We were keen to encourage them to send their doctors, nurses and technicians for training in British hospitals. We were also trying to interest them in [British] consultancies for building and managing hospitals.'

Dr Langi was a surgeon in his own right, not a politician. For this reason Clarke kept his discussions with him off political matters. 'I was trying to keep relations on an even keel. My motives were commercial. I was acting on behalf of UK Ltd.' Within his restricted area of responsibility Dr Langi was out to impress. Clarke was taken to Benghazi, where they ran into Mohammed Sherlala, the Treasury Minister, the man responsible for Libya's budget, in a supermarket. Clarke took this opportunity to strike up an acquaintance. 'We walked round the corner to a fairground, and I remember sitting in a big wheel chatting to the Minister and him telling me about the virtues of state-run supermarkets.'

Clarke then had a day off as the Libyan Minister of Health, ever hospitable, flew him down 'in his private plane' for some sightseeing at the picturesque whitewashed Berber village of Ghadames, in a strategic area of the desert to the south-west of Tripoli, close to where Libya borders both Tunisia and Algeria. Back in the Libyan capital, Clarke said, 'We had let it be known I wouldn't mind meeting Qaddafi. But the summons never came. If it had come off, I would have been fairly cagey. I would have stuck largely to platitudes – talked about the need for good relations and perhaps expressed some anxiety about the activity of some of his people overseas.'

In the event the British Minister's only substantive political discussions were held with Heavy Industry Secretary Omar Muntasser, a well-connected graduate of Egypt's exclusive British-style public school, Victoria College in Alexandria. 'I gave him a bit of my Foreign Office briefing. I said it was time for Libya and Britain to get on. I said I would appreciate the help of his government in curbing any excesses abroad.' But Muntasser refused to be drawn. He was more interested in telling Clarke about his proposed steel mill, which the

184

British Minister thought was not a bright idea, in view of world overcapacity in that product.

Assessing his visit Clarke said, 'I suspect it was taken on both sides as a genuine attempt to improve things.' However, the Foreign Office was prepared to read rather more into it. On 13 April junior Foreign Office Minister Douglas Hurd reported back to the House of Commons,

> The government have . . . made their views known to the Libyan authorities at a high level in recent months. My honourable and learned friend, the Minister of Health, discussed the matter when he was there in February. He received assurances which were important to the government. The government had trouble in this regard in 1980. Three members of the people's bureau were asked to leave at that time. I trust there will be no repetition.

Traditional diplomacy appeared to be working. Britain was even encouraged enough to allow Colonel Younis Bilgasim, head of the Libyan intelligence service and the man with much of the logistical responsibility for campaigns against Libyan dissidents abroad up till then, to visit London during April. According to opposition sources, Bilgasim was in Britain to meet a top American envoy in an attempt to mend fences between their two countries.

Clarke himself had no illusions about the people he saw in Libya. 'I was dealing with technocrats not politicos.' However, in their eagerness to improve relations with Qaddafi, Hurd and the Foreign Office were naive enough to think that pleasantries exchanged with the ministerial frontmen seen by Clarke in Libya were heavy with political significance. Indeed, real decision-making in Libya was slipping further from Ministers and their civil servants than ever. A Western ambassador in Tripoli at the time observed that Libyan Ministers, or Secretaries, as they preferred to be called, were like the director-generals of Western European ministries. He adds that they realized this and were always ready to tell him when a matter was outside their competence.

Nowhere were the technocrats more out of their depth than in dealing with the topic of exiles abroad. On this, more than anything, the revolutionary committees had consolidated their position as a state within a state. In 1983, after a period of quiet, they were returning to the offensive against stray dogs. Qaddafi had given responsibility for striking against dissidents to five select revolutionary committee commanders – his own cousin, Ahmed Qaddafadam, two of Major Jalloud's fellow tribesmen, Sayed Rashid and Abdullah Senussi, and the former London people's bureau chief, Musa Koussa, loosely co-ordinated by Captain Abdul Salam Zadmeh.

These revolutionary committee leaders saw London in quite a different light from the technocrats. They saw it as the centre for opposition activity abroad. As the downturn in the price of oil began to tell on the Libyan economy, they considered that Libya's 8,000 students in Britain were at risk from the increasingly sophisticated ideas and propaganda of groups like the National Front for the Salvation of Libya, who they were convinced were backed by Britain and the CIA. They now resolved to bring their own carefully nurtured organization in Britain into operation. They were determined that anti-Qaddafi sentiment should not be allowed to develop among Libyan students there.

For this the revolutionary committees relied on twenty-eight-year-old Dr Omar Sodani, their man in London since early 1980, when he arrived to pursue his medical studies at the Royal College of Surgeons. With the expulsion of fellow revolutionary committee chief Musa Koussa in June 1980, Sodani was drafted in to head the people's committee which ran the Libyan bureau and keep it to the revolutionary straight and narrow – as determined by Qaddafi, with whom Sodani was in constant touch. Qaddafi had followed and promoted Sodani's career with interest for some time. Intelligent, personable and apparently without means, Sodani, a negro from the south, was a star among Qaddafi's meritocrats.

Born, according to his own version of his life story, to poor and illiterate parents in a desert village in the Fezzan in 1955, Sodani liked to say that he would have had no chance of advancement under the previous regime. In 1975 his secondary education was completed in one of the exclusive schools which came to be reserved for revolutionary committee members. At these establishments (there were a dozen round the country), about 2,000 hand-picked young Libyans were specially trained in the thoughts and revolutionary aims of Colonel Qaddafi. While the general educational system was tied to the Green Book, these revolutionary committee training schools (such as the famous Revolutionary Blooms school in Benghazi) were considerably more intense. Children selected to attend often came from poor families who could be relied upon to see support for the Qaddafi regime as their only passport to power and prosperity.

In 1977 Sodani went to the medical school at Gar Younis University in Benghazi. Over the next three years he became prominent as foreign affairs spokesman of the Libyan Students' Union. But his real role was as a revolutionary committee member. In that capacity, he 'ran the college'. He even allegedly presided over the execution of two counter-revolutionary students and won the nickname in certain circles as the 'butcher of Benghazi'.

Once he had taken charge of the people's bureau in June 1980, Dr Sodani quickly set about shaking things up. Arms dealer Barry Howson, who had been introduced to him by Musa Koussa, says that before Dr Sodani arrived 'you could go to almost anyone in the bureau and they would give you American Express travellers' cheques'. Dr Sodani clamped down on this. A Pakistani accountant was brought in from Tripoli to take care of the bureau's finances. Henceforward funds could be provided only by the accountant, Sodani or Muftah Fitouri, the highest-ranking career diplomat.

After organizing the people's bureau, Sodani, with his reputation for having the ear of Colonel Qaddafi, set about establishing the requisite infra structure for the revolutionary committees to operate in Britain. In spring 1982, after considerable opposition from local residents, he succeeded in opening a Libyan school in Glebe Place, Chelsea. The school, formerly the Kingsley School, bought from the Inner London Education Authority for £1 million, was to become an important meeting place for Libya's revolutionary committees over the next two years.

Then Sodani began to make contact with Libyan student groups around Britain. He made it clear they had to toe the Qaddafi line. Otherwise the bureau would cut off their allowances (which gave them a standard of living well above their British counterparts); they would not be able to finish their courses and their careers would suffer. Soon other pressures began to be brought to bear on Libyan students. On 6 November 1982 Sodani sent his closest ally in the people's bureau, cultural counsellor Abdul Hamid bin Moussa, to Manchester to address 150 students. Bin Moussa called on his audience to find the Manchester-based opposition leader Mohammed bin Ghalboun and eliminate him. Unless this happened, he threatened that all students in the city would be sent back to Libya.

Through an informer at the meeting, bin Ghalboun heard about the threat. He says, 'I reported it to the police because I thought such an incitement to kill was a crime. The police were not particularly interested. They said they knew about it anyway.' Bin Ghalboun thereafter decided to deal with the matter in his own way.

I was genuinely worried. This was the first time that this had happened and I wanted it to be the last. So I resolved to ring bin Moussa at his home. I got his number and I had something of a connection – his father had taught me in primary school.

187

When I rang he was out. I spoke to his wife. She thought I was some family friend from Benghazi. I left my name and asked him to ring me back. He never did, and I learned that two days later he had returned hurriedly to Tripoli. There he reported to the Foreign Liaison Bureau that I had come to kill him. He made a big story of it. The Libyans made an official protest to the Foreign Office which turned the matter over to the Home Office. The police came round to question me. I told them what had happened and they reported back that there was no truth in the allegations.

The whole bizarre episode cannot now be offically recalled by the Foreign Office. However, it illustrates a number of themes which were to crop up repeatedly in Britain's relationship with Libya over the next year and a half: a Libyan diplomat convening a student meeting and making threats against individuals lawfully domiciled in Britain; opposition groups infiltrating the gathering, the police knowing about it, but taking no effective action; the Libyans clearly continuing to be convinced of the possibility of counter-violence.

Bin Ghalboun observes, 'The police couldn't really do anything about [the threat on my life] because it was a political matter.' The police themselves are somewhat equivocal about this kind of comment. A senior officer who worked with Scotland Yard's anti-terrorist branch on Libyan cases throughout this period denies political pressure was ever put on him and his colleagues over their investigations. But he does say, 'There were a lot of things that might have been done if it had been the mood of the country at the time.'

Dr Omar Sodani realized this and cunningly prepared to capitalize on it. On 22 May 1983, after the razzmatazz surrounding Kenneth Clarke's visit was over, Sodani called seven of his closest revolutionary committee colleagues in Britain to a meeting in the education office of the people's bureau at 62 Ennismore Gardens in Knightsbridge.

Those present were Saleh Ibrahim, like Dr Sodani a former Gar Younis University activist from Benghazi who had served on the revolutionary tribunals which sentenced dozens of people to death in Libya's second city in 1980; Ali Musbah, a trained terrorist, now on a course at Oxford Air Training School; Abdul Ghadir Baghdadi, despite his thirty-seven years and his record as the man who purged Tripoli University of anti-Qaddafi elements as far back as 1976, an English student at Watford International College, a private language school twenty-five miles outside London; Ali Abu Jaziah, another Gar Younis graduate in his thirties with a reputation for brutality; Maatooq Mohammed Maatooq, a graduate engineer from Tripolil; Najib Hussein and Saleh Nahly.

Sodani explained that he was under renewed pressure from Tripoli to take resolute action to stem growing opposition among Libyan students in Britain. 'We've got to organize our people better,' Sodani told the seven. 'They've got to act more decisively against opponents of our revolution.' But how could they do this? As a first step Sodani and his colleagues decided to divide Britain into thirteen revolutionary committee cells, each with its appointed local co-ordinator.

Later that evening at a larger meeting of around sixty pro-Qaddafi students in the Libyan school in Chelsea, Sodani announced that all Libyan students in Britain must belong to one of these cells. Standing under a portrait of Colonel Qaddafi on a small dais in the room known as the theatre, he thumped the table in front of him, and told the students bluntly, 'I am determined to eliminate all opposition in Britain.'

Once again Qaddafi's opponents had a mole among the offical Libyan students. Twenty-three-year-old Khaled Lutfi (a pseudonym) was studying engineering at Newcastle Polytechnic. He had come to Britain directly from high school in Tripoli in 1980. Over the succeeding three years he had managed to keep his mouth shut enough for a friend in the revolutionary committees to believe he was a potential recruit to the student activists and to invite him along. This was his first attendance in these circles. Lutfi says,

> I had heard about Dr Sodani, but I was surprised at what I saw. He started off by telling us what was happening in Libya, what the Qaddafi leadership had been doing. He said he wanted all students to be updated on the successes of the revolution in Libya.
>
> As the meeting went on, he got increasingly warmed up. He started shouting about the need to eliminate anyone against the revolution. He clearly believed strongly in Qaddafi's philosophy. He also came across as a very violent personality, who would not stop at killing for his beliefs.

At the end of his speech Sodani asked for volunteers. 'You may be asked to do anything in the future,' he said. 'But for the time being your job is to identify who is for and who against the revolution.' He dismissed suggestions that this type of surveillance work would run foul of the British authorities. 'The British are arrogant,' he said. 'We must know how to penetrate their minds.' He then demanded that each revolutionary committee cell should open files on possible dissidents. Lutfi was told how to mix with and befriend other students. Revolutionary committee membership had to be kept secret. In true conspiratorial style, Sodani concluded the meeting by demanding that all present meet regularly once a month.

Sodani's revolutionary student cells were stirred into action towards the end of the summer. On 1 September forty-five supporters of Qaddafi met in a house in north Oxford to celebrate the fourteenth anniversary of his accession to power. While they were inside, a group of anti-Qaddafi students came along and smashed some of their car windows. Lutfi, who happened to be there, remembers the revolutionaries' meeting breaking up in panic. 'We spent the next hour bandying around the names of possible assailants and discussing how we could get back at them. Whenever I attended a meeting after that, a couple of committee members always remained outside guarding the cars and doors.'

Then on 3 September the National Front for the Salvation of Libya (NFSL) held its first ever demonstration in London. The revolutionary committees responded with their own counter-demonstration. Using their cell structure, over 2,000 students were bused into London from all over Britain. Shouting pro-Qadaffi slogans, they then marched from the capital's South Bank, across Westminster Bridge and past the Houses of Parliament, down Whitehall (dropping off a petition at the Prime Minister's official residence in Downing Street) to the Libyan people's bureau in St James's Square. A dangerous pattern of baiting and counter-baiting was developing between supporters and opponents of Qaddafi. In November, after graffiti – 'Down, down, down with Gadafi' and 'Long Live Libya' – had appeared on the walls of the bureau and its outlying offices, Sodani ordered students down to London to patrol official Libyan buildings.

Once again pressure was building up for some kind of decisive action. On 28 December, at a Libyan official residence at 31 Phillimore Gardens, the same eight who had met back in May (swelled by one additional figure, Fatima al Magarmad, sister of Ali Musbah's fiancée) reviewed the situation. They acknowledged that there had been leaks from their gatherings. They said they must check the loyalty of everyone working with them. A two-tiered leadership, with a think-tank under Dr Sodani and a more activist wing headed by Saleh Ibrahim, was formed. A week later on 4 January 1984 the revolutionary committees met again at 62 Ennismore Gardens. The agenda was as before – how to deal with the opposition. They decided that their patrols must be armed. The opposition had to be infiltrated and its members assaulted physically if need be. Present at this meeting was Abdul Hamid bin Moussa, the Libyan cultural counsellor, now back from Tripoli, and Mustafa Alem Gherbi, head of security at the bureau. Gherbi promised the revolutionary students not only an unlimited budget but also any weapons they might need.

By this time the Libyan opposition in Britain was well aware of the increasingly virulent and activist tone of these meetings, as was Scotland Yard's C13 or anti-terrorist branch. But if the police had wanted to act, it was difficult. Their reports on these meetings were sketchy. 'We're a police force, not an intelligence service,' says a senior C13 officer, adding, 'It's all very well having reports of these meetings and reading about hit squads. But we have got to have evidence of hit squads having done something before we can act. Most of these meetings took place on diplomatic premises where diplomatic privilege operated. It was easy for them to put a three-line whip on their students to attend, but there was no way we could march into these places.'

Dr Sodani chaired another meeting in London over the weekend of 14–15 January. The 14th was a university holiday in Libya – the anniversary of a student revolt against King Idris's regime in January 1964. This time around seventy revolutionary committee members from across the country were briefed on developments. No action was taken because Saleh Ibrahim, leader of the activist wing, was away in Libya getting directions from Abdul Salam Zadmeh, his revolutionary committee commander who liaised directly with Qaddafi.

While Ibrahim was out of Britain, on 21 January, two highly professional killers assassinated the Libyan ambassador in Rome, Amar al Tagazi. The murder was claimed by Borkan, and the incident was blamed by the Libyans on Qaddafi's opponents. This interpretation gave the revolutionary committees in London and ideal excuse for escalating its activities against dissidents. By the weekend of 11–12 February Ibrahim was back in London. At a specially convened meeting twenty top revolutionary committee members gathered to hear him reveal how he and his colleagues Baghdadi, Jaziah and Maatooq intended to take over the people's bureau the following week. Lutfi had now infiltrated the revolutionary committee set-up deeply enough to be present at this meeting. He was sitting close to Saleh Ibrahim. 'I was astonished. His eyes were red. I thought he was drunk. He harangued us in a very emotional manner.' Towards the end of his speech Ibrahim announced that he had been telephoned by Qaddafi himself, and had been told explicitly, 'You must do something to force Britain either to expel the opposition or to close the bureau and send back yourselves.'

On 17 February Ibrahim and his three colleagues duly took over the bureau. Adam Kwiri and Abdul Hamid bin Moussa were sent packing to Tripoli – ostensibly because their diplomacy had not been 'revolutionary' enough. The following day, a Saturday, the four revolutionary committee men held a hastily convened press conference in St James's Square. With Sodani in the background acting as interpreter, they accused Britain of harbouring people bent on undermining the Libyan revolution and pledged to eliminate all Qaddafi's opponents in the country. Though no one in Britian appeared to take them at their word or even to understand what they were driving at, the quartet stated uncompromisingly that the 'sole purpose of the takeover' was to escalate revolutionary activities in Britain.

Ibrahim, Baghdadi, Jaziah and Maatooq, all members of Sodani's inner circle of eight, had entered Britain at various times in the preceding two years and had signed on for courses at language schools within easy distance of London. But nothing much was known about them. Baghdadi appeared to take the lead in organizing the affairs of the bureau. But all the Foreign Office had on him were the briefest details – 'Baghdadi: studied business administration in the United States; lives in Coventry, but not registered at school or college.'

Even this gave an entirely false impression of one of Qaddafi's most trusted sidekicks. Baghdadi had been one of the Libyan leader's early recruits in 1973. After proving his revolutionary credentials against his leader's opponents at Tripoli University in 1976, he was sent in 1978 to the United States for a couple of years to study business administration. Then after further training which is said to have included a period in a terrorist school outside Tripoli, Baghdadi came to Britain in 1983 to take up a seemingly innocuous English language course in Watford. A Libyan who knows him describes him as 'cool, calculating, cold-blooded and quite brainy; if Qaddafi had ten or fifteen of his calibre among the revolutionary committees, he'd actually be quite successful. If he wasn't doing this kind of work, he might well be a Minister.'

While the revolutionary committees were taking over the people's bureau in London, that very same week, during a meeting of the General People's Congress, Qaddafi was announcing a number of changes in his 'cabinet'. In a further effort to cow opposition, Colonel Younis Bilgasim, the shadowy intelligence chief on whom he had relied for earlier clandestine activities against his opponents, now (in February 1984) took on a more public and threatening persona as Minister for External Security. Officially ranged under Bilgasim as his assistants in the newly formed Bureau for External Security were four of the top revolutionary committee gang chiefs – Ahmed Qaddafadam, Qaddafi's cousin and international fixer, Abdullah Senussi, who headed internal security in 1980–1, Sayed Rashid, a fellow tribesman of Major Jalloud, and Musa Koussa, former head of the Libyan people's bureau in London, who had been asked to leave Britain in 1980.

As well as making these changes, Qaddafi announced he was stepping up his campaign against stray dogs. As far as Britain was concerned, this meant sending the revolutionary committee security co-ordinator, Captain Abdul Salem Zadmeh, to London to take charge of operations. Only a few days earlier Swiss police had detected Zadmeh in Geneva. Paying for everything with an American Express card in the name of Abdul Salam Sherif, Zadmeh was staying at Geneva's Intercontinental Hotel after arriving from Vienna. His rough appearance was such that Switzerland's vigilant police wanted to know more about him. A former Libyan passport official living in Geneva confirmed that Sherif was in fact Zadmeh. According to one source, the revolutionary committee commander had been in Vienna to buy Czech explosive which was sent to London by the diplomatic bag. Towards the end of February Zadmeh slipped into London on a diplomatic passport claiming that he was a teacher.

Two days later another Libyan, forty-five-year-old Ali Jiahour, flew in from Tripoli. Well known in the British capital as a wheeler-dealer and bon viveur, he checked into his usual hotel, the Hilton on Park Lane, and began to visit haunts like the El Auberge night-club in Mayfair. Jiahour was a weak and complicated character. He made a large amount of money importing and exporting, mainly arms, during Qaddafi's first decade in power. However, when the Libyan leader first started attacking the business community and accusing it of corruption in 1978, Jiahour took fright and fled Libya for Switzerland where he made approaches to the embryonic opposition movement. His business career did not prosper in a foreign environment. Within eighteen months he had stitched up a deal with Qaddafi's roving envoys (at that time very keen to entice back any vaguely opposition figures). Jiahour could have his old job back as long as he co-operated with and did jobs for the Libyan intelligence service.

During the first weeks of March Jiahour remained in London while Zadmeh and Ali Musbah travelled to Bristol and other British cities to inform activist students that something was 'going to happen soon.' With the involvement of Baghdadi, Ibrahim, Jaziah and Maatooq, along with Sodani, in the people's bureau, Musbah was now the senior revolutionary committee member at large in Britain. A nephew of Qaddafi's trusted henchman, Abdullah Senussi, he, with Najib Hussein and Awad Hamza, had been part of the first team sent to Britain in 1980 specifically to establish revolutionary committees.

Whether Jiahour really knew what he was letting himself in for on the night of 10 March is uncertain. He was met at the Hilton that evening by Zadmeh, together with Musbah and Salhin Saleem, another dedicated Qaddafi zealot who acted as secretary of the revolutionary committee cell in Bristol. The four climbed into a Fiat Ritmo owned by the Libyan people's bureau. With Musbah driving, they travelled to four locations – two newsagents which stocked a wide range of Arabic periodicals, including anti-Qaddafi magazines, in Prince's Gate, Kensington, and Queensway, and the Omar Khayyam restaurant in Regent Street and the El Auberge night-club off Berkeley Square, Mayfair. At each stop Saleem planted crude but effective 1.1 pound bombs he had made with Czechoslovakian Semex explosive smuggled into Britain via the Libyan diplomatic bag.

During the night there was a series of explosions at these four sites. The worst and potentially most dangerous was at the El Auberge night-club where six bombs were placed and two exploded. Twenty-three people were injured, three seriously, but miraculously no one was killed.

Within hours Qaddafi's cohorts had struck again, this time in Manchester, where early the following morning a Syrian couple and their young child were slightly injured when three bombs went off outside their flat. Coincidentally their block was across the road from where Hasim bin Ghalboun (founder, with his brother Mohammed, of the Libyan Constitutional Union) had lived when he first came to Britain in the late 1970s. The main perpetrators of the bombing were two young Libyans who, after military training, had studied in Britain since early 1982.

In both London and Manchester the police quickly arrested all the bombers except Saleem, who was at large until August. But they quickly found they were confronted with a problem. In their custody was Zadmeh who was claiming diplomatic immunity, though Britain did not accept this. The Libyans were already protesting at his detention.

At the time the anti-terrorist branch had never heard of Zadmeh, which suggests a serious breakdown in communication between the security services and the police. The branch wanted to question him, but that needed time, and time was not available. One of its senior officers says, 'I well remember I had all these suspects but no time to make the necessary inquiries.' The Prevention of Terrorism Act, which allows detention of a suspect for forty-eight hours, extendable in certain circumstances to five days, then applied only to Ireland. The Act was extended to cover terrorism worldwide at the end of

March 1984. But 'when we detained Zadmeh under the then current law, we could only hold him for twenty-four hours. There was no evidence on which we could get him [in that time]. We had to chuck him out of the country. If we had had the powers we now have then it is likely many more people might have been remanded in custody.

Home Secretary Leon Brittan chose the easy way out. He decided to expel Zadmeh, along with five others who had played only minor roles in the bombings. However, the Home Office refused to admit that anyone called Zadmeh had been detained and asked to leave the country. As late as 1 May, British Foreign Secretary Sir Geoffrey Howe was telling the House of Commons, 'I must emphasize that none of these [six] had any form of diplomatic immunity, and that there was no firm evidence linking the people's bureau with these incidents.' The subsequent trial of Musbah and Jiahour suggested that indeed there was.

On its failure to take action over the links between the people's bureau and the revolutionary committees, the Foreign Office passes the buck. 'Essentially that would be in the province of the Home Office,' it says. 'If they were informed that specific leaders were revolutionary committees and it was regarded as being a potential security problem, then that would be entirely in their province. The Foreign Office would not get involved unless the Home Office tried to deport people or prevent them entering the country.' This same Foreign Office source adds, 'If we were to start, without any firm evidence, putting restrictions on who we would or wouldn't allow to come here, then that would be reciprocated at the other end.' British businessmen might have problems entering Libya to win precious export orders. 'This is one of the constraints one faces in trying to conduct diplomacy in a civilized way.'

To give the Foreign Office its due, Britain's attitude to Colonel Qaddafi's close associates was not nearly as craven as that of some of its European allies, who relied on Libya not only as an export market but also a major source of oil. Britain, with its North Sea oil, was not in the position of, for example, Italy, which relies on foreign suppliers for 85 per cent of its oil, about a third of that from Libya, where are found nearly half the worldwide reserves of the Italian state oil company ENI.

In 1983 senior revolutionary committee commander, Sayed Rashid, managed to put Libya's relations with both Italy and France in jeopardy when he was arrested in the South of France concerning the murder of Libyan businessman Ezzedin al Hodeiri in Milan in June 1980. Unusually for him, Qaddafi was so incensed at this that he personally sprang into action and refused thirty-seven French citizens (including women and children) permission to board a flight to Paris until Rashid was released. Qaddafi also appears to have squeezed the Italians on the issue. Although Milan police had been quite clear that Rashid was their man, their expected extradition warrant failed to appear within the statutory twenty days required by French law. Qaddafi sent his personal plane to pick up the freed Rashid from Nice airport.

Qaddafi's strategy over Rashid was a repeat performance of his successful blackmail of West Germany earlier in the year. In November 1982 the Germans arrested Dr Mustafa Zaidi and Abdullah Yahia, revolutionary committee members attached to the Libyan people's bureau in Bonn. The two were charged with enticing Al Hadi al Griani and Ahmed Shaladi, both students, to the Libyan diplomatic residence in the Bonn suburb of Bad Godesburg (on the pretext of holding a 'special congress' for students) and torturing them there.

Qaddafi responded by rounding up eight of the 3,000 or so West Germans working in Libya and charging them with sabotage and working for the CIA. He then called upon Colonel Younis Bilgasim, with his excellent contacts, to travel to Bonn and convince the German authorities to release Libya's diplomats. When the mission eventually proved successful, the eight Germans were given their freedom.

Britain clearly wanted no repeat performances with its citizens being held hostage in Libya over Zadmeh's detention. But as far as Abu Abdullah London leader of the National Front for the Salvation of Libya, was concerned, the British attitude was pure appeasement. 'The British authorities felt that if they kept him here it would increase Qaddafi's wrath further. That was a big mistake on their part.' How big a mistake became clear very soon. The revolutionary committees in Britain were in no mood to let reverses halt their activities. Tripoli would not have allowed them.

A major opposition demonstration was expected in London on 7 April, the anniversary of the campus rising against Qaddafi in 1976. Each year opponents of the Libyan leader commemorate the day. Characteristically Qaddafi had tried to appropriate the day, using it regularly for public hangings of detainees. Dr Sodani called a meeting of the revolutionary committees in London for 7 April. Around eighty people attended. He declared that the committees had to face up to any opposition to Qaddafi. He said members must 'not be afraid to be arrested or even killed'. Although he did not spell out his intention, once again he asked for volunteers 'to do what was required'.

Participants at that meeting composed a letter to Qaddafi which was sent in the diplomatic pouch the following day. It read:

Brother, Leader of the great Al Fateh Revolution, greetings,

report from the London Bureau

In response to our revolutionary call we have carried out disruptive activities in London according to your instructions in the confidential memo we received on 20 March 1984. We have carried out your instructions to the letter but the only obstacle we find in our way is not the British government but the Libyan opposition and their collaborators in London. If the British government collaborates with the opposition, giving them facilities, our revolutionary work would be impossible to carry out. We have some information regarding a proposed demo against us and we pledge if it takes place we will meet it with the strongest possible means. We would also like to inform you that our prisoners in London are held with no reason except that Libyan dissidents follow our activities and work as informers to the British authorities which has made them part and parcel of the British secret services

Greetings of the great Al Fateh
Forward we go
members of the People's Bureau London 8/4/1984

The revolutionary committees were right that the opposition planned a demonstration against Qaddafi. However, they had thought it would take place on 7 April, and they were now uncertain of the revised date.

After hearing that on 15 April two students had been publicly hanged on Tripoli University campus, the National Front for the Salvation of Libya, working closely with the Libyan Constitutional Union in Manchester, decided that the demonstration should now be held on Tuesday the 17th. Abu Abdullah of the National Front says, 'We chose 17 April mainly because it was an unlikely date, it had no significance. It wasn't even on a weekend, as had been the tradition for Libyan demonstrations in Britain.'

On Monday the 16th Abu Abdullah gave an interview to the African service of the BBC. Libyan bombing and hit squads were still in the news. Abu Abdullah informed listeners that twelve people had been dispatched from Cyprus the previous Friday to act as two roving hit squads in Europe. He said many of them were travelling on

United Arab Emirates passports. They had been trained in Syria. Some were Libyans, some not.

That evening Abu Abdullah informed selected correspondents that a demonstration was to take place outside the Libyan people's bureau the following morning at 10 o'clock. The first Baghdadi and those in the bureau itself knew about it, however, was the sight of police covering the meters in St James's Square on Monday afternoon. The police confirmed the imminence of the demonstration. Immediately there was a flurry of telexes to Tripoli inquiring what action should be taken. There were two sets of replies: one for the accredited diplomats – that they should protest vehemently to the Foreign Office, the other for the revolutionary committees in the bureau that they should resist the demonstration by any means, including force. These sort of messages are routinely intercepted by the government's General Communications Headquarters (GCHQ) in Cheltenham. But as there had been no order to decode and check all traffic between the bureau and Tripoli, these particular ones went unread until many hours later.

Baghdadi, leader of the revolutionary committee 'four' in the bureau, and Sodani immediately began activating their cells throughout Britain. Students were ordered to drop everything, hire a car if need be, and turn up in St James's Square before the day was up. Already that evening Qaddafi sympathizers began assembling at the bureau. Baghdadi told them a dissident demonstration was going to take place the following morning and they must counter it in any way possible, using force if necessary.

The two senior diplomats in the bureau, Muftah Fitouri and Hamed Zlitni (the political counsellor who had accompanied Health Minister Kenneth Clarke to Tripoli the previous year), were alarmed at this turn of events. Around midnight they roused the duty clerk at the Foreign Office and told him in no uncertain terms that the Libyan opposition demonstration should be halted, 'otherwise there would be trouble'. The clerk contacted the desk officer for North Africa who told him to warn the Home Office's F4 section, responsible for anti-terrorism and public order. F4 duly passed the message on to Scotland Yard's A8 section, which would be in charge of controlling the demonstration. Once again the chain of communication appears to have broken down. For A8's commander Bob Inness denies ever receiving this information. Nevertheless he resolved to do something to keep Qaddafi's opponents from his supporters. This meant erecting a barrier between the demonstrators' route and the bureau.

When John Sullivan, from Tubular Barriers, the firm subcontracted for this job, arrived at seven in the morning, he found Baghdadi addressing a group of his counter-demonstrators outside the bureau. Seeing the barriers go up, Baghdadi became alarmed. His plan was simply to snatch as many anti-Qaddafi demonstrators as possible and drag them into the bureau. The barriers seemed to pre-empt this. Baghdadi retreated into the building and told Sodani and Ibrahim to go out and protest against the erection of the barriers. Sullivan recalled Ibrahim threatening, 'We've got guns here and there's going to be fighting here today.' Seeing an argument developing between the two Libyans and Sullivan and his associates, the police intervened and arrested Sodani and Ibrahim.

At this stage Baghdadi revised his plans. He ordered his supporters to stay away from the front of the bureau. What he did not tell them was that he had decided to shoot at the demonstrators. Fearing if not actually knowing this, Fitouri and Zlitni scurried back to the Foreign Office to make a last-minute plea that the demonstration be cancelled. It was too late. While they were still at the Foreign Office, at around 10.20 a.m., seventy opponents of Qaddafi marched into St James's Square carrying slogans in English like 'Gaddafi poisons children' (a reference to the Ghesuda case in Portsmouth) and shouting in Arabic 'God Is Great' and 'Long Live Libya'.

A marcher recalls noting a counter-demonstration taking place, not outside the bureau, as might have been expected, but well to the side of it. He thinks this was a ploy to allow participants the possibility of easy flight. He was also aware that loudspeakers had not been put out to broadcast Qaddafi speeches from the first-floor window ledges, as had been the practice at all demonstrations in the past.

The anti-Qaddafi demonstrators had reached the corner of the square in front of the bureau and were trading insults and slogans with their opponents on the other side of the street when a series of shots rang out from a first floor window. The shots – a burst of continuous machine-gun fire – lasted nearly ten seconds. During that time twenty-five-year-old Woman Police Constable Yvonne Fletcher, on duty in front of Qaddafi's opponents, was felled to the ground and killed. At 5 foot 2½ inches, she is believed to have been the smallest police officer in Britain. An exception had been made to the rules to allow her to join the police force. As her fiancé, fellow Constable Michael Liddell, struggled to reach her, eleven anti-Qaddafi demonstrators behind him fell wounded. One shot travelled 300 yards across the square and through a first-floor window in an office building on the other side.

One of the leaders of the demonstrators was, and remains, certain that there were two people firing from the bureau – one from the first floor, and other from the second. He says, 'We learned from someone within the revolutionary committees that they were expecting a large number of us would be hit and killed. People inside the bureau were told, "If this leads to the closure of the bureau, so be it. The more violent we are, the better. It will prevent the opposition from fighting back." This plan was thrown into disarray when the policewoman was shot.'

The pro-Qaddafi demonstrators scuttled away out of the square. According to some sources, a number of people also escaped out of the back of the bureau. Thirty were left inside the building to endure a ten-day siege. High blue plastic barricades were erected at all entrances to St James's Square. British television viewers got used to the sight of police marksmen from Scotland Yard's D11 branch, jauntily walking through these barricades going on or coming off duty, carrying their rifles in special-issue bags.

Within an hour and a half of the shooting Edgar Maybanks, Deputy Assistant Commissioner (DAC) of Scotland Yard, had set up an operations room, known as Zulu (or Forward) Control, on the first floor of the advertising agency D'Arcy-Macmanus and Masius, adjoining the bureau. In front of him television monitors showed him what was happening at the front and back of the bureau. Telephones linked him to the bureau and to the special Cabinet Office Briefing Room (COBRA) in Whitehall where, in the absence of Margaret Thatcher who was abroad at the start of the siege, Home Secretary Leon Brittan took charge.

Upstairs from DAC Maybanks, on the second floor, Scotland Yard's elite C7 or technical support branch had a room where its boss Detective Chief Superintendent Mike Marshall also had a battery of monitors where he could keep an eye on pictures from tiny visual probes planted into the outside of the bureau. Officers had planted auditory bugs in all outside walls of the bureau. For the first time it was using infra-red detectors which pinpointed where everyone in the bureau was – from his bodyheat. Among the many other gadgets used by C7 was a television aerial which was attached to the bureau's own aerial and allowed Scotland Yard, if it wanted, to pipe in false television programmes.

However, the latent tension between police and diplomats could not be set aside, even at this stage. As a policeman DAC Maybanks wanted to go into the bureau and find the perpetrators of the shooting. Leon Brittan chairing the COBRA (and as Home Secretary representing the police on it) tried to convey this viewpoint. But he was held back by Foreign Office officials who claimed to be astonished that the police should even presume to control operations against representatives of a foreign power. The police persevered. Telephone lines to the bureau were still in operation. On one of these Zulu issued an ultimatum: 'Everyone of you must come out and assist the police – and we are going to search the entire building for explosives and weapons.'

But those in the bureau had been ordered by Tripoli to sit tight. On day six of the siege Colonel Rahman Shaibi, a respected ex-policeman who was Colonel Bilgasim's deputy at the Jamahiriya security agency, came to London to negotiate conditions for its end. When Commander Bob Inness demanded that the Libyans inside the bureau should come out of the building with their hands above their heads and then be questioned, Shaibi, quickly sensing conflict between police and diplomats at COBRA, played to the Foreign Office gallery with his reply that in that case British diplomats in Tripoli would have to crawl from their embassy.

Eventually Shaibi agreed that the Libyans should go to the Civil Service College at Sunningdale in Berkshire, close to Heathrow airport, for 'immigration procedures and protective care'. There police officers learned little more than they had in the course of the siege, during which the Libyans in the bureau, when they wished to discuss their predicament, used to huddle in the safe room in the middle of the seventy-room complex, out of range of police bugging devices.

According to the BBC television programme *Panorama*, reviewing the incident a year later, the main police suspect among the thirty was Abdulgadar Tuhami, a non-diplomat with proven revolutionary credentials, who had arrived in Britain a few weeks before the shooting.

Libyan television viewers had their own version of the event. At the start of the siege they were shown a British police helicopter circling over a sunny square. In a corner the Libyan people's bureau was under siege after attack by British forces who had killed one of their own colleagues in the process. As Colonel Qaddafi told the US televison network NBC on 19 April, '[The bureau] faced there an armed British attack by air and ground, by weapons. I heard that the British police used bullets and shot [the] bureau and they are supported by helicopters and some group from [the] Middle East. . . . I think the British policemen killed themselves because they shot our bureau during the attack.'

Nine days later the siege was over and Libyan television showed the triumphant return of the thirty heroes who had been holed up in the London bureau. Britain had cut diplomatic relations, but the

Colonel was undeterred. He told his audience, 'Now the time has come to treat Britain in a reciprocal manner, after it has been confirmed British protects terrorists and enemies of the the Libyan people.'

Two weeks on and Libyan television had further remarkable pictures to show. The National Front, in conjunction with the Muslim Brotherhood (and, the Libyans said, the CIA), had mounted a putsch against Qaddafi. But the effort had been precipitate. The opposition had clearly hoped to cash in on the aftermath of the London bureau siege. As they began to learn from foreign radio stations what had really happened, ordinary Libyans were genuinely sorry about the murder of the British policewoman. They were angry at the uncivilized antics of Qaddafi's henchmen. The eyes of the world were still on Libya. The National Front was encouraged to try to stage a coup. But a hasty operation had to be speeded up further when Ahmed Ahwas, commander of the National Front's military wing, was killed in a gun battle entering Libya from Tunisia. His colleagues were forced to make their attack on the Aziziya barracks two days later, on 8 May, rather earlier than they had wished. A bitter battle ensued in which nine commandos and up to eighty regular Libyan troops were killed.

An estimated 5,000 opponents of Qaddafi inside Libya were arrested. Among them were the half-dozen commandos who survived the attack on Aziziya. Libyan television left no doubt about their fate. Every night it showed the bullet-ridden bodies of their colleagues. Its cameras lingered over their wounds and blood-stained clothes, as an announcer warned, 'This is the fate of stray dogs who conspire against the state of the masses.' There was also footage of the few survivors of the raid in their cells. They appeared contrite as an interviewer asked them, 'You do know your fate, of course?' Within days they were marched off to the public gallows.

By the weekend of 12 May, Libyan television was back to its usual programming. It showed crowds chanting pro-Qaddafi slogans and celebrating the deaths of the traitorous insurgents. 'The masses have decided to turn the thousands of sons of the Libyan Arab people into suicide squads to liquidate the enemies of the revolution,' ran a commentary, 'and to pursue them anywhere in the world and eliminate them physically.' It added, 'American imperialism and the British administration are held completely responsible for protecting the stray dogs and helping them. The revolution must pursue them.'

13 Foreign Adventures

Cowing opposition to Colonel Qaddafi at home and abroad is one aim of Libya's terrorist network. Another is to bully or subvert neighbouring African and Arab states into adopting the precepts of the Green Book. In the Middle East context this means backing Palestinian groups, and their supporters, opposed to any peace settlement with Israel. As far as Major Jalloud was concerned, however, much of the funding of obscure factions was amateur stuff. He was more interested in acquiring the hardware which would really make Libya a force to be reckoned with, not only in the region but in the wider world. He was particularly keen to obtain the nuclear bomb. He began his search for the ultimate weapon in China in the first months of the revolution. When he was told, politely, by the Chinese that atomic weapons were not for sale he did not give up. According to Dr L. B. Ware, associate professor of Middle Eastern history at the Air University in Alabama, Libya deposited $1 million in gold in a Swiss bank vault as a reward for the delivery of the weapon. Ware said that the million dollars were collected by a Lebanese who sold the Libyans a fake nuclear warhead but did not live to spend the money: he was executed when the fraud was discovered.

Suggestions that Libya subsequently succeeded in making or buying a nuclear weapon terrify its neighbours. President Hissein Habré of Chad told the authors in 1985, 'That disease called Qaddafi had the raw materials and it will not be long before he has the bomb. The West should beware.' Habré is almost certainly wrong. Libya had one research reactor under construction but no power reactors either in operation or under construction, according to evidence before the US Senate foreign relations committee in 1982. Although the Soviet Union and Libya signed an agreement in 1975 to establish a nuclear centre, including a research reactor, the Russians have failed to provide one, despite repeated requests by the Libyans, most recently by Qaddafi himself during his visit to Moscow in 1985.

In anticipation of its new Soviet reactor Libya signed the Non-

Proliferation Treaty, but has spent the past sixteen years in a vigorous effort to proliferate. In the late 1970s Qaddafi asked Yasser Arafat to assemble a group of Arab scientists with the technical expertise to make a bomb and although Arafat is said to have scoured the universities in the Arab world, he failed to come up with a nuclear team for Libya. Even the creation of a Secretariat for Atomic Energy headed by Qaddafi's close associate Abdul Magid al Mabruk brought Libya no nearer to its goal.

In 1976 Jalloud looked for help from the French, who talked about providing a nuclear power plant but refused to provide nuclear research facilities or the means to produce heavy water, an essential ingredient in the building of the bomb. He also approached the US General Atomics Corporation for help in building a nuclear plant for peaceful purposes, but the deal was promptly rejected by the US State Department. Nevertheless, according to the evidence before the foreign relations committee, there were 200 Libyan students studying nuclear science at universities in the United States in 1978. Twenty-five Libyan students were also studying nuclear power at Finlands's National Technical Research Centre.

Libya then applied to India and offered to exchange oil for nuclear expertise. During a visit to Delhi in July 1978 Jalloud pushed hard for an Indian commitment to help Libya acquire an independent nuclear capability. The Indians offered assistance only with nuclear training in the peaceful uses of the atom; the Libyans were so dissatisfied that they suspended oil deliveries to India in 1979.

Jalloud left no stone unturned. After China, the USSR, the United States, India, France and the PLO he persuaded Argentina to provide Libya with scientific equipment to prospect for radioactive materials and to train Libyan chemists in uranium extraction and purification. However, Libya has little if any raw materials for its students to work on. This helps explain why Libya annexed the Aouzou strip in northern Chad in 1973. This barren stretch of rocks and deserts is widely believed to contain uranium deposits. Neighbouring Niger also mines uranium and is reported to have sold 450 metric tons of uranium to Libya on condition, the government of Niger said lamely, that it would not be used for bombs.

By 1980 Qaddafi was getting impatient. He called the refusal of nations with nuclear technology to make it available to others 'reactionary' and said that it 'hindered world development'. The conclusion of the US foreign relations committee was that:

Libya has little potential to attain nuclear weapons through its own efforts. While it could come somewhat closer to nuclear

204

weapons capability by 1990, even then it would still have far to go unless it were able to obtain extensive technical assistance and supplies from abroad. It probably would not have enough weapons-grade material to conduct a test and certainly would be far from any capability to produce enough for a nuclear arsenal.

The picture looks rosier for Jalloud in the 1990s when, the committee concludes,

Libya could somewhat increase its supply of nuclear scientists, engineers and technicians although most likely with extensive foreign assistance. It might also find a supply of uranium in Chad. Libya could have a small research reactor in operation and possibly a nuclear powerplant if the Soviet Union moves quickly to supply it. The spent fuel from such a plant could be a potential source of low-quality plutonium if the Soviet Union does not require its return after use. However, it seems unlikely that Libya could by then have a working reprocessing plant for this kind of spent fuel, or an enrichment capability, or the industrial base to build either without extensive external assistance.

Despite the foreign relations committee's apparent lack of concern at the prospect of Libya gaining nuclear capability, in 1985 the US State Department put considerable pressure on Belgium's Belgonucléaire to withdraw from a lucrative contract for which it was widely tipped to build two 440 MW reactors in the Gulf of Sirte. The irony of the US position, which was confirmed by the Belgian government, was that it meant that Libya was more likely to turn to the Soviet Union for its eventual nuclear plant.

Qaddafi and Jalloud are fascinated by sophisticated weaponry. They did not get the bomb, but they built up an arsenal of military hardware almost ludicrously out of proportion to their needs and they were not choosy about where they bought it. Soon after coming to power Qaddafi found that, with oil money, he could buy weapons wherever he wished, without respect for ideological niceties. The French sold them Mirage fighter bombers, missiles, helicopters and tanks. Britain sold them ships, troop transports came from the US and armoured personnel vehicles from the Italians.

In the early 1970s Qaddafi did seem to be the malleable material the Americans had hoped for. He could, in their view, be forged into a friend of the West, despite the closure of Western bases and the massive increase in oil prices. Indeed, in 1971 he came to the aid of his then friend, President Numeiri of Sudan, when he forced down a

British passenger plane over Libya carrying two leaders of a coup against the Sudanese head of state. The two rebels, both Marxists and, therefore, anathema to Qaddafi, were handed over to Numeiri and promptly executed. The same year, in an essentially pro-Western move, he sent Pakistan F5 fighter bombers to assist in its war against India.

By then he was already involved in arms deals with the Soviet Union. Two shiploads of T54 and T55 tanks, with armoured personnel carriers and trucks, arrived from Russia at Tripoli harbour in July 1970. At first this relationship was a shaky one. Qaddafi criticized the Russians for not giving the Arabs more support in their conflict with Israel and for fomenting anti-Sadat rallies in Cairo. The Soviet Union charged him in its state-controlled press with 'extremism and adventurism'.

However, both Libyan and Soviet relations with Cairo chilled and the West grew increasingly suspicious about Qaddafi's 'adventurism', so the Muslim fundamentalist and the atheist Marxists found they had a good deal of common ground. The Russians wooed him carefully. After their expulsion from Cairo they needed an ally in the Middle East – a place where their Mediterranean fleet could dock and where intelligence could be gathered. Most of all they needed hard currency. The breakthrough in Libyan/Soviet relations can be pinpointed to Jalloud's visit to Moscow in May 1974 when he was given the red-carpet treatment and paraded before the Politburo. The statement issued at the end of the meetings announced 'the identity or closeness of the positions of the Soviet Union and the Libyan Arab Republic on the most important international problems'. That was a lie. Moscow and Tripoli viewed most important issues differently. The only thing they could agree on was their mutual dislike of 'Western imperialism' and even here they were poles apart. Qaddafi's present-day anti-Americanism is greeted with derision by Eastern-bloc diplomats in Libya. They think, quite simply, that he is a fool and a dangerous one at that. Qaddafi's meddling in Africa and the Islamic world upsets Moscow's carefully laid plans, as does his attitude to Israel and the Palestinian issue.

In the 1980s, as the Soviet Union attempted to repair its relations with Israel through a series of intensive secret talks, Qaddafi's hysterical anti-Zionism became even more embarrassing. When he visited Moscow in April 1981, there was bickering over whether he could pray in the shuttered Grand Mosque in Moscow, whether the prayers would be broadcast from the minaret and, after the Russians agreed, whether he would reciprocate by laying a wreath at Lenin's mausoleum. Jana, the Libyan press agency, celebrated his visit as a triumph of the faithful over the non-believers. During another visit, in 1985, Qaddafi objected to vodka being served at the official reception and then complained that he was not being treated with the honour due to a Libyan head of state.

Publicly both capitals talked only of their solidarity and friendship as Soviet arms poured into Libya and the dollars flowed into the Kremlin. In the years 1974–8, according to Edward Haley in *Qaddafi and the US since 1969*, Libya increased its arms imports by 50 per cent a year. Soon ground-to-ground Scud missiles were being paraded through Green Square in Tripoli. By the end of 1985 it is estimated that Libya had spent $20 billion on military supplies from the Soviet Union alone. It is a strictly cash relationship, as Aziz Shenib discovered when he was a Libyan ambassador to the East bloc. 'You would not believe the angry notes from Moscow when any payments were delayed. They wanted cash money, on the dot,' he said.

The Libyans collected weapons as small boys collect stamps, until military expenditure became a burden even for Libya's oil-rich economy. Brand new tanks still lie in warehouses in Tripoli, lines of armoured troop transports trundle along the Libyan highways from one base to another. The jet fighters are mostly under wraps because the Libyans simply do not have the pilots to fly or the technicians to service them. Quite why Libya needed so much hardware has always puzzled observers.

Generally speaking, Libya is much happier using its oil wealth as a weapon in itself – to bolster its friends or undermine its enemies. However, even here much of the funding is so inept that, according to Qaddafi's fellow revolutionary Fidel Castro, it can even rebound on his allies. Since winning its independence in 1978, Nicaragua has received around $400 million of Libyan aid. Maria Laura Avignolo wrote about the antics of Libyan advisers in Nicaragua in the *Sunday Times*. She reported how, in a conversation with an Eastern-bloc ambassador in the Nicaraguan capital, Managua, Castro called Qaddafi 'a reckless adventurer who could endanger the Sandinista revolution'. In his view the presence of Libyans there was an unnecessary irritant to the Americans and provided a pretext for a US invasion. Castro's view, expressed privately to the ambassador, would fit more logically into the mouth of a US State Department official: 'Insurrection against a dictator is the right of all people, but terrorism can never win power,' said Castro. 'We, the Cubans, were never terrorists. Those Arabs are very violent and only want to provoke the United States, They don't know what prudence is.'

The Libyans began to arrive in Nicaragua in 1981 following a visit by the Sandinista Minister of the Interior, Tomas Borge, to Tripoli. The heavily fortified Libyan embassy in Managua established a Libyan cultural centre which gives Arabic classes and shows films.

Libyan 'diplomatic' personnel formed attachments with local ladies, attracted more, perhaps, by their dollars than their charm. A hotel receptionist told Maria Laura Avignolo: 'We only earn the equivalent of twenty US dollars a month. The Libyans have a great deal of money and they flash it around. Several young women have left their jobs to go and live with them. I had a Libyan boyfriend and can tell you that apart from the ambassador, Ibrahim Farhat, who is a civil engineer, all the others are either security police or soldiers.' The Nicaraguan government was, like the ladies of Managua, pleased to get the Libyan money. 'Our relationship with Libya is eternal,' said Borge.

Other governments were often less happy when Libya began setting up cultural centres and flashing its wealth. Nigeria, Senegal, Gambia, Mauritania, Mali, Malaysia, Indonesia, Thailand and the Philippines are among literally dozens of countries which at one time or another have accused Qaddafi of funding Marxist, Muslim or tribal opposition groups in their countries.

Initially Qaddafi supported the Eritrean rebels against the Ethiopian government of Haile Selassie, but, when President Mengistu came to power in Ethiopia after a military coup in 1974, he switched allegiance. The Libyan leader suddenly and mistakenly discovered to his satisfaction that the long-time Christian country of Ethiopia was predominantly Muslim. The Eritreans were out in the cold. Libya supported the Polisario guerrillas in their battle against King Hassan of Morocco for a huge chunk of the Western Sahara. But when, in 1984, Qaddafi forged a treaty of unity with Hassan, Polisario was unceremoniously dumped, only to be taken up again when his liaison with Morocco faltered in 1986. In 1984–5 he backed the Sudanese People's Liberation Army (SPLA) in its battle against the Numeiri regime in Sudan. Libyan security officials went to Addis Ababa, the capital of Ethiopia, to organize the funds and arms deliveries. They had problems with the local women which were more tragic than their colleagues' experiences in Managua. When a bomb exploded in the house in Addis where the Libyans were preparing explosives for delivery to the SPLA, the bodies of a number of prostitutes were found in the rubble. When Numeiri was deposed in a military coup in April 1985, Libya thought it could enjoy a better diplomatic relationship with his successor. There were reports in the summer of 1986 that

Libyan planes were flying sorties for their former enemies, the Sudanese government, against the SPLA.

Qaddafi's over-equipped army has never seen action against Israel. However, in July 1977 its effectiveness was put to the test during a four-day border war against Egypt. Libya did not acquit itself well. Egyptian armour crossed into Cyrenaica at Musaad, while Egyptian planes struck at Al Adem airbase near Tobruk and at border villages. A cease-fire was only reached after Algerian and Kuwaiti intervention.

Two years later Libya was flexing its military muscle in Uganda. Qaddafi had supported the sanguinary dictator Idi Amin since 1972 on the grounds that he was a Muslim and had expelled his Israeli military advisers. As he told the Italian journalist Oriana Fallaci in an interview in 1979:

> Amin's internal policies do not interest me; what I am interested in is Amin's position in the field of international relations. That is, the private personality of Bokassa [the former President of the Central African Republic] and Amin might not be to my liking. I might even disagree with their internal policies, but I dislike even more the interference of France and Tanzania and worst of all I dislike the support provided by the Westerners to Israel.

At the end of 1978, when the Tanzanian army, supported by Ugandan exiles, invaded Uganda with up to 6,000 men, Libya flew a reported 2,500 troops equipped with tanks and armoured transport to the aid of Amin. The Ugandan army, which was 20,000 strong, disintegrated and the Libyan forces were left to defend the capital, Kampala. The Tanzanian assault on Kampala began on 29 March but the Libyans were defeated and expelled, with more than 400 dead, within six days. It was a humiliating *débâcle*.

It is difficult to see from this succession of diplomatic and military failures why anyone should take Qaddafi seriously, least of all should consider him a threat. His scattershot approach to foreign policy, the random peddling of funds, give the impression of a muddled dilettante rather than a serious empire-builder. A case in point has been his adventures in Chad, Libya's vast impoverished Southern neighbour. It has not traditionally been a country that concentrates the minds of the US State Department. As one American official said: 'Why should the United States care? Chad is a fly-blown piece of real estate. Only 8 per cent of the United States knows what's going on in Central America so I should think only 1 per cent of them would know where Chad is and only 1 per cent of them would care.'

Libya's interest in Chad, fly-blown as it is, dates back a long way. There has always been a strong trading partnership between the two countries and the Senussi order set up military, commercial and religious centres in northern and central Chad in the nineteenth century. Qaddafi's nomadic ancestors would have moved their herds across its northern deserts. Chad had a tradition of fierce independence. The Senussi and their Muslim allies had bravely resisted French colonial expansion there. It had been one of the first African countries to win its independence in 1960. yet when Qaddafi came to power nine years later, French influence was still strong in its capital, Ndjamena. Qaddafi, the anti-Western revolutionary, resented this. He believed he could use Libya's traditional ties in Chad to strike a blow against Western neo-colonialism and establish the first link in what he hoped would be a Libyan dominated Islamic empire in Africa.

Qaddafi's tactics in the labyrinth of Chadian coups and counter-coups are a lesson in Machiavellian politics. He began meddling in Chad immediately after his accession to power. From 1970 he provided increasing military support for Muslim insurgents from the north of the country. His primary objective was to obtain control of the Aouzou strip, a small band of desert (3,700 square miles) in northern Chad which is thought to contain valuable minerals and large deposits of uranium. The strip was ceded to Italian-governed Libya by France in the 1930s, although the agreement was never ratified by the French government; legally, therefore, it still belongs to Chad. Qaddafi, the arch-opponent of imperialism, uses the French/ Italian deal as proof of his inalienable right to the territory.

Before and after Chad's independence, France had a strictly utilitarian view of the country. It was primarily interested in what they called 'Tchad utile' – useful Chad – and that meant the cotton-growing south. Only black southerners, or Sahrans, received education, and they happened to be animist and later Christian rather than Muslim. It was these Sahrans who ruled the country under President François Tombalbaye after independence.

The northern Muslims who made up over half Chad's inhabitants were excluded from power. This iniquity, involving usurpation of Muslims rights by Christianized blacks dependent on neo-colonial Western power, was like a red rag to Qaddafi's bull.

Slowly Qaddafi began building up support for Chad's northern rebels, who grouped themselves in the liberation front, Frolinat. As Qaddafi moved into Aouzou, Frolinat started sporting Libyan uniforms and gradually becoming a semi-regular army. Initially Qaddafi was cautious about giving Frolinat his total support, particularly as he was still trying to convince France that he could be trusted to buy its latest jet fighters. However, his support for the rebels was enough to shake Tombalbaye.

Qaddafi worked to capitalize on this. In 1972 he told Tombalbaye that if he agreed to break off diplomatic relations with Israel and formally hand over the Aouzou strip, which had already been occupied by Libyan troops, Libya would give Chad money and reduce its support for the Frolinat rebels. Tombalbaye had little choice and signed a treaty of friendship with Libya in December 1972. However, the promised financial aid never materialized and Libyan support for Frolinat continued.

When Tombalbaye was deposed by his former chief of staff General Felix Malloum in 1975 Qaddafi promptly recognized the new regime, hoping it at least would recognize the realities of the Libyan presence in Aouzou.

When Malloum showed little inclination to do this, Qaddafi stepped up his support for Frolinat and, in 1976, tried to oust the President in a Libyan inspired *coup d'état* which failed. By 1978 Libyan fire power and funds were beginning to have an effect in a growing civil war between north and south Chad. That year Faya Largeau, the largest town in northern Chad, fell to Frolinat. After almost half the Chadian army had been lost in fighting, Malloum was forced to the conference table in Sebha in southern Libya. There he agreed to sweeping concessions which institutionalized Libyan intervention in his country. In July 1978 Qaddafi decided to divide Chad across the 14th parallel into Libyan and French spheres of influence. As Qaddafi put it, crudely, to the French, 'If you give me the Muslims [in the north], I will leave you the blacks [in the south].' This, of course, was the sphere of influence Paris had always coveted.

Qaddafi's problem in this neat slicing of the Chadian cake was that many of the rebels did not like him or Libya. A rebel leader, Hissein Habré, broke away from Frolinat (then headed by Goukouni Woddeye). He started a new faction called FAN (Forces Armées du Nord), accusing Libya, in a document published in 1977, of racism against blacks.

The next twist in Chad's complex internal politics was a coalition between President Malloum and Habré's FAN. Now Qaddafi sent Malloum a telegram congratulating him on his new coalition, while privately calling his regime 'colonial and Fascist' and making plans to depose him.

As Malloum and his new ally Habré quickly fell out, Frolinat, with substantial Libyan financial and logistical support, marched southwards and in March 1979 entered and took control of Ndjamena. Frolinat's leader Woddeye became the provisional President of Chad. Initially he tried to rule in coalition with his former colleague Habré. But their ad hoc alliance soon fell apart. The country was again convulsed by a bloody civil war. With Habré's rebels attacking in the south, and another faction led by the anti-Libyan southerner Colonel Kamougue pressing the capital, Woddeye formally asked the Libyans to intervene. It was the kind of request Qaddafi had always longed for. He sent a massive force. An estimated 7,000 Libyan troops, with air support, attacked Habré's forces in the south. Then his armoured divisions, spearheaded by the latest Russian tanks, crossed 700 miles of desert to mop up the opposition in Ndjamena. Habré was forced to flee across the Chari River to Cameroon. Qaddafi had won his first decisive military victory. The French, who had given tacit support to Habré, had been humiliated. Qaddafi was the virtual ruler of Chad and he could defend himself against criticisms of expansionism because he had only entered Chad at the request of the provisional President.

Qaddafi's victory in the Chadian quagmire was shortlived. In 1981 he made his first major mistake when there were reports from Tripoli of a Chad/Libyan merger, with the strong suggestion that Qaddafi had threatened to execute Woddeye if he refused to comply. The reaction in Chad was a mixture of horror and dismay and a Libyan merchant was quoted by the magazine *Jeune Afrique* as saying: 'Even the dogs in Chad oppose unification.'

If the dogs did not, almost the whole of Africa did. Libyan diplomats were expelled from countries across the continent and the Organization of African Unity (OAU) roundly condemned the merger. Its members saw it as evidence of unwanted Arab penetration of Africa, and Qaddafi, who hoped to chair the Organization in 1982, had to retract, making vague and ambivalent statements that the Libya/Chad union was 'a unity of people' and not 'a political unity as constitutionally known'. Chad began a gradual extrication from Libyan influence. Within a week Woddeye was declaring on the radio in Paris, safe from Qaddafi's wrath, that Chad and Libya were two separate countries. Woddeye, who had asked Libyan troops into Chad, then asked them to leave. Bowing to pressure mainly from the OAU, the Libyans retreated.

Although an African peace-keeping force moved in to take their place, it was not long before Chad was back at war. In 1982 Habré, backed by US and French funds and operating from Sudan, returned and drove Woddeye out of Ndjamena. Habré became the new President of Chad.

By 1983 Woddeye, backed by Libya, was on the offensive once again in the north, recapturing Faya Largeau. From June to August the town changed hands three times and the fate of this 'fly-blown piece of real estate' became for the first time, an international issue. As René Lemarchand of the University of Florida wrote: 'Not since the Congo crisis has an African conflict figured so prominently in the calculations of cold war strategists'.

The reason, as Qaddafi clearly realized – and relished – was a latter-day version of the domino theory. In a curious way Western foreign ministries, particularly in France and the United States, saw Chad as a bastion of Western influence in Africa. Even under Habré in the mid-1980s, French culture remained dominant in Ndjamena. It was feared that if Woddeye, with Qaddafi behind him, took Chad, neighbouring states like Niger and Upper Volta might fall out of the Western sphere of influence and take up Libya's strange brand of Islamic radicalism. (In 1984 Upper Volta did. It became Burkina Faso and enjoyed a brief but unproductive flirtation with Libya.) Worse still, it was feared that Qaddafi's ideas might penetrate the volatile but successful quasi-capitalist economies of West African states like Senegal, Gambia, Sierra Leone and Ivory Coast. Nigeria could generally be relied on to take care of itself. But to the east of Chad there was another danger. Qaddafi could use influence in Chad to stir up trouble in southern Sudan, making life difficult for the generally pro-Western government in Khartoum and, through it, for Egypt.

This time in 1983, Qaddafi did not have the moral cover of coming to the aid of a president: he was fighting on the side of a rebel army and he consistently denied that his troops were in Chad, despite overwhelming eyewitness and photographic evidence that they were. Habré appealed for military support from France, which at first refused. But the US administration, fearing a Libyan victory, supplied arms to Zaire, which dispatched a force to help Habré. The US aircraft carrier *Coral Sea* was sent to join the *Eisenhower* off the Libyan coast, and two AWACS radar planes and eight F15 fighters were sent to Sudan, ready to fly to Habré's support. Qaddafi's actions created a rift between the United States and France, which accused Reagan of being 'obsessed' by Qaddafi. Reagan sent his special envoy General Vernon Walters to Paris to put pressure on President Mitterand to take military action on Habré's behalf.

With more than 2,000 Libyan troops on the ground in Chad backing a 3,000-strong rebel force trying to cut off government troops holding the town, and with Libyan bombers reportedly dropping 500-pound fragmentation bombs and napalm, France eventually agreed to come to Habré's rescue. It flew in over 3,000 troops, backed by eight jet fighters – four Jaguars and four Mirages – and an air tanker, thus outranging Qaddafi's aircraft, which had no refuelling capability. Woddeye's Frolinat was repulsed, but the battle turned into a military stalemate with Libyan-backed rebels holding the north and Habré hanging on to Ndjamena in the south.

For over two years Chad remained uneasily divided. Then in January 1987, spurred on by a green light now coming from Washington rather than Paris, Habré launched an offensive which drove the Libyans out of, first, Fada, and then Faya Largeau, some 170 miles to the west.

Qaddafi by this stage had abandoned any pretence of supporting Woddeye's claims. He had an army of 8,000 men in occupation in Northern Chad. Habré's attack forced him to pull them back to the disputed Aouzou strip. There was no stopping the Chadian President now. At the beginning of August his army captured Aouzou itself. Three weeks later the Libyans temporarily won it back again.

But in early September Habré delivered his coup de grace. Driving fast lightly-armoured Toyota trucks, ideal for desert warfare, his troops raided 100 miles inside Libya, where Qaddafi's base at Maaten es Saara, an important staging post en route to Aouzou and Chad, was overwhelmed. Nearly 2,000 Libyans were killed in the attack, led by Habré's daring young commander in chief, Hassan Djamous. In addition, twenty-six planes, including six Russian MiGs, and over one hundred tanks and armoured cars were destroyed on the ground at the Libyan base.

Qaddafi was not quite finished. Two days later he despatched two Russian-built Tupolev-22s on a bombing mission to Ndjamena. France still had its Sparrowhawk force of 1,300 men in place in the Chadian capital. Clearly wanting no part in what was going on, it had taken a back seat during Habré's expeditions in the North. French premier Jacques Chirac was reported to have told aides, 'It's the Americans who are pushing Hissen Habré into idiocies like the one at Aouzou. They push, and we pay the bill.'

But when the Tupolevs appeared across the 16th parallel, the 'red line' France had figuratively drawn as the northernmost limit of its influence, members of Sparrowhawk shot down one of the planes. The other quickly about-turned and fled home. Significantly the French used an American Hawk missile for the job. President

Mitterand sent his personal chief of staff, General Jacques Fleury, to Ndjamena to plead with Habré to treat with the Libyans.

The Chadian leader relented (he had to, for Paris was still paying around $60 million to keep the civilian side of his administration going). He agreed to send his foreign minister, Gouara Lassou, to meet his Libyan counterpart, Jaddallah al Talhi, at a special conference convened by the OAU in the Zambian capital of Lusaka.

The conference proved inconclusive. 'Aouzou is Libyan territory,' declared Mr al Talhi. 'We have proved the Aouzou is Chadian,' countered Mr Lassou.

One thing clear towards the end of 1987 was the United States' interest in developments in Chad. One can speculate on its motives. It did not trust France to keep the Libyans out. It wanted to secure the country for American interests. (Conoco, of the US, had been the major oil producer and explorer in the 1970s.) It still hoped to topple Qaddafi by hitting at him through his back door.

US relations with Qaddafi had started well. Washington had been happier to deal with a strong military dictator rather than a vacillating King. American oil companies had done well out of the nationalisation of foreign oil companies in the early 1970s.

But the honeymoon was soon over. The United States grew suspicious of the growing revolutionary rhetoric of Qaddafi's regime. By 1973, around the time when Libya was first shopping for arms in the Soviet Union, Washington reduced its diplomatic representation to the level of chargé d'affaires and, under the terms of its Arms Export Control Act, stopped sales to Libya of weapons and products which could add significantly to Libya's military capability. This action blocked the delivery of eight C130 Hercules transport planes, which had been ordered by Qaddafi.

Normal commercial transactions continued, notably the sales of nine Boeing 727s and one Boeing 707 aircraft. But in 1978 the State Department recommended that an application for a licence to export two 727s to Libya be turned down. Although Libya's military warehouses were overflowing with armaments from the Soviet Union these C130 aircraft took on what one US government official described as a 'mystical significance' for the Libyans. Efforts to persuade the US government through the normal channels were not working, so Qaddafi turned to what a US Senate judiciary committee described as 'the people to people approach'. Qaddafi maintained even during a period of overt hostility in 1986 that, although the US government was against him, the people, 'the masses', were not. He was shocked when he was told by an American reporter that many of the American people 'love' President Reagan. 'Love him, love him, how could they love him?' he exclaimed.

The 'people to people' policy began in 1977, with the idea that, by establishing good relations with US politicians, business and organizations, Libya would be able to get the weapons and technical systems it wanted. More than half a million dollars was pledged to Georgetown University to set up an Arab studies department. Links were forged with social and religious organizations, including black Muslim groups. The Libyan dialogue with the American people was extensive: two study courses on Arabic language and the Muslim civilization were set up at the University of Michigan; there were contacts with the Universities of Idaho, Georgia, Louisiana, Miami and Wyoming, with the National Council of American Indians and with the National Association of Arab Americans. The Libyans sent delegations to Washington, Louisiana, Florida, California, Georgia, Wyoming, Utah, New Mexico and South Dakota. The Libyans invited US delegations to Tripoli, and sixteen American groups including the farmers' union, the American women's union, and a delegation of black Americans, took them up on the offer.

The strangest contact was in 1978. Working on the principle that business in the Arab world is done through family and friends, the Libyans decided to win the heart and mind of the brother of President of the United States, Billy Carter, who at that time ran a gas station in Plains, Georgia. President Carter spoke often of 'brotherly love' and the Libyan hoped he loved his brother enough to release a few C130 transport planes.

This brilliant idea sprang from the mind of a Sicilian, Michele Papa, a lawyer and businessman from Catania, who cultivated his contacts with the Arab world as president of the Sicilian/Arab Association and founder of the first mosque in Sicily. He claimed to be a friend of Qaddafi and said that it was he who suggested Billy as a target for Libyan seduction. His first efforts to reach Billy were ludicrous. He contacted a friend, Mario Leanza, who had emigrated to America from Sicily about thirty years before and happened to live in Atlanta, the capital of Carters' home state, Georgia. Papa seemed to assume that anyone living in Atlanta would have easy access to Billy, who lived 200 miles away in Plains. On 9 April Papa wrote to Leanza: 'I have spoken with my Arab friends. I invite you to Libya with President Carter's brother at my expense. *Non sciuperare tempo* [Don't waste time].'

In fact Leanza had never met Billy, nor had any of his friends, and despite Papa's badgering phone calls, which cost the Sicilian some

$15,000, was getting nowhere. Then, in the summer of 1978, he met Tom Jordan, an Atlantic real-estate agent who, though he did not actually know the Carter entourage himself, knew someone who did, Georgia Senator Floyd Hudgins, and contact was made.

Libya's ambassador to Rome, Jibril Shalluf, visited the United States and drove down to Plains where he met Billy in the back room of his gas station. Shalluf promptly invited him on a trip to Libya, all expenses paid. Billy said he would love to but could some of his friends come too? Shalluf said that would be fine 'provided they were not Jewish'.

Billy did not find it difficult to recruit a party of 'friends' who had their own ideas about how Libyan money could be invested. One of them suggested selling the Libyans a patent for a machine that made bricks out of desert sand, another intended to ask the Libyans to deposit $5 billion in a Bahamian bank for an ambitious South American engineering project.

And so this rather untypical sample of the US masses, nine in all, arrived at the Rome Hilton on the first leg of their trip to Libya. They had flown across the Atlantic in the first-class lounge of an Alitalia jet, reserved just for them at a cost of $36,000 courtesy of the Libyan government. *En route* they had been entertained by a beautiful young woman who joined them at Kennedy airport in New York. 'She was smooching with the party, drinking and drunk all over the Atlantic,' said one member of the group. The fun continued in Rome in the floor reserved for them at the Hilton. One guest opened the door and found a Roman orgy in full swing, 'full of naked men and women and trashy prostitutes'.

Before leaving for Tripoli, they bought four cases of whisky for their stay in the dry Muslim country and concealed the bottles in brown paper bags. When they arrived there Billy was free with his promises to help the Libyans and one Libyan official suggested just how he might do that. 'If you really want to help, then you could get the aeroplanes that we have bought delivered.'

The 'Billygate' affair erupted in the American press while the Justice Department and a Senate judiciary committee examined, in massive detail, why the Libyans had paid $220,000 into Billy's bank account, whether the President discussed US policy towards Libya with his brother and whether he showed him classified documents. Billy emerged from these inquiries as a bumbling fool, greedy for Libyan money, and his brother Jimmy's only offences were naivety and an overabundance of brotherly love. The Libyans' concern was that they were a quarter of a million dollars poorer, and no closer to

217

the C130 aircraft. Even Michele Papa grew tired of Billy and reflected perhaps the unofficial view from Tripoli: 'Billy turned out to be no more than a fatso, poor thing.'

The eight C130 transport planes languished in a warehouse on a landing strip at Lockheed's plant in Marietta, Georgia. According to the judiciary committee of the US Senate, which, after the Billygate fiasco, conducted another investigation with the ponderous title 'The Undercover Investigations of Robert L. Vesco's Alleged Attempts to reverse a State Department Ban Preventing the Export of Planes to Libya', the Libyans made another attempt to recover their aircraft a variation on the 'people to people' technique. The allegation was that the Libyans attempted to bribe top officials in the administration of President Carter, including the chairman of the Democratic Party national committee, John White, to obtain the release of the C130s and Boeing 747s and 727s, which the Libyan government had bought, but which had not been delivered because of the State Department export ban. A slush fund of $7.5 million was supposed to have come through associates of the fugitive financier Robert Vesco, and the Libyan official at the centre of the scandal was said to be the ambassador to the United Nations, Mansur Kikhia.

Kikhia did indeed meet White at the Sky Top restaurant in Washington in June 1979, although there never was any question of a plot or of financial inducement from Kikhia to White to take action on the aircraft. Kikhia told one of the authors that he met White as he met many other American politicians and the only surprising thing about the meeting was that no one asked him for money. Kikhia has an extremely jaundiced view of American society. 'I remember talking to someone at the Waldorf Astoria [a New York hotel] who slipped me a piece of paper under the table and whispered 'that is the number of my Swiss bank account', said Kikhia. 'What does he think we Arabs are? Completely immoral and unintelligent? I met more Americans who were immoral and unintelligent while I was ambassador than I have Arabs.'

Immorality was a commodity which was not difficult for the Libyans to find in the United States, and two men who embodied it, both former members of the Central Intelligence Agency, were on the Libyan payroll providing a very special, and illegal, service.

Despite the billions of dollars the Libyans spent on their arsenal of Soviet equipment they were still disappointed. They complained, according to Joseph Goulden in his book *The Death Merchants*, that they only got 'second-generation items, decade-old designs of jet fighter planes, tanks, armoured personnel carriers and artillery pieces. But not even Qaddafi's billions could persuade the Soviets to turn loose their more advanced military gear. Perhaps the tightest restrictions were imposed on the sale of electronic gadgetry, advanced communications equipment, radar and sensory devices.' Even when the Soviet Union agreed to send Libya its Sam 5 long-range ground-to-air missile system in 1985, the electronic equipment that went with it was 'absolutely bloody hopeless' according to a British radar engineer working in Libya. 'The Libyans got most of their electronic equipment from Europe and, through middlemen, from the United States; the Russian stuff was completely out of date,' said the engineer.

America was the source for the gadgetry of modern warfare but, officially at least, the doors were closed. Qaddafi, working on the Kikhia principle that Americans were both greedy and immoral, decided to try the 'people to people' approach, and the man who knew best how to exploit it was his cousin, Sayed Qaddafadam. For a member of both the family and the ruling elite in Libya, Qaddafadam was allowed extraordinary license in the West. As an attaché to the Libyan embassy in London in the 1970s, he bought a chic apartment just off Kensington High Street where he liked to entertain in grand style. One of his guests recalled: 'There were no Muslim strictures on morality. The booze flowed all night. There were belly-dancers and always a bevy of young girls swooning around Qaddafadam, attracted by his charm and wealth. Some of the guests took advantage of his hospitality and left with their coat pockets stuffed with bottles of whisky and cigars.' Qaddafadam was not just a playboy, however; he was also Libya's chief buyer of sophisticated electronic equipment for the Libyan army. His shopping list included an array of devices from timing mechanisms and blasting caps to plastic explosives. The hardware ranged from small arms and material for making anti-personnel bombs to at least one US-made ground-to-air missile. The two men Qaddafadam found to fill this exotic gap in the Libyan armoury were both Americans who had learned their dirty tricks as members of the Central Intelligence Agency. For large amounts of cash they were more than willing to sell their skills to the Libyan government.

Edwin Wilson, 6 feet 4 inches tall and weighing in at almost 17 stone, and his sidekick Frank Terpil had operated on the murkier fringes of the CIA's covert operations – Terpil in the Middle East and Wilson in a range of operations from the Bay of Pigs to Vietnam. Both had a distinctly cavalier attitude to the rules which governed their profession. Terpil's CIA career came to a sudden end in 1971 when he was fired, 'terminated unfavourably' in the official phrase. Associates said his unpolished manner did not live up to his superiors' expectations. In other words his methods were a bit too rough even for that hard-bitten organization. His experience in the agency was helpful, however, in smoothing his move into the world of international business consulting.

Terpil's firm, Oceanic International Corporation, an export/import marketing concern, sent him all over the world to pick up seemingly innocent orders for fire engines, electrical generators and musical instruments. On the side, however, he became adept at arranging huge illegal arms deals for, amongst others, Idi Amin's secret police. These orders involved some highly specialized equipment, including attaché cases fitted with tape recorders, remote-control detonators and instruments of torture. One of these was an electronic collar; the torturer would strap this round the neck of his victim and, at the turn of a switch, pass a current through him.

Ed Wilson worked for the CIA's office of security in 1951 and became a full-time employee in 1955. He helped to organize a Washington firm called Consultants International Inc., which was a front for the CIA but which helped to build up Wilson's business acumen and his bank balance, since he took huge kickbacks from American manufacturers and foreign governments on his procurement contracts. In 1971 he left the CIA to join Task Force 157, a secret navy intelligence unit that employed fifty to seventy-five agents to monitor and collect information on Soviet shipping. He also built up a commercial empire and boasted of having a controlling interest in more than 100 companies in the United States and Europe. Physically he was suited to his role as agent. Apart from a formidable build he was a judo black belt and an expert in hand-to-hand combat. He liked to think of himself as a John Wayne figure and his bar-room exploits became something of a legend. One associate recalled Wilson flooring three longshoremen in a brawl, then strolling nonchalantly back to the bar to finish his beer.

Using their CIA connections and business contacts, Terpil and Wilson filled at least part of the gap in Qaddafi's shopping list, although it cost him dearly. Under cover of the export/import business which they had set up together, they helped Libya establish a manufacturing plant for the production of assassination weapons. They recruited former American soldiers to teach the Libyans the art of making bombs, while making themselves extremely rich. The export of restricted military equipment to Libya proved simple. For example, Terpil and Wilson bought a US army vehicle fitted with night surveillance gear for shipping to Libya in direct violation of all regulations. The vehicle was sent first to Canada and then transhipped to Libya. It cost $60,000 to buy and they charged the Libyan government $990,000.

They sold the Libyans 500,000 timers for $35 million. Their cost price was $2.5 million. The Libyans wanted explosives, and a particularly powerful one was RDX, or cyclotrimethylene trinitramine, so volatile that it was banned from being carried on passenger or even cargo aircraft. Wilson and Terpil contacted a California firm, J. S. Brower and Associates of Pomona, which agreed to supply the chemicals for the explosives. There remained the seemingly insuperable problem of how to get them halfway across the world to Libya. For the daring duo the answer was simple. They packed it in 55-gallon drums marked 'industrial solvent' and put it on a scheduled passenger flight to Dulles airport in Washington, although the material was so unstable that a severe air pocket could have caused it to explode. It was then flown to Europe, and carried on a Lufthansa passenger flight onward to Tripoli.

Wilson also had a $1.2 million a year contract to provide American military officers and NCOs to run an infantry training school at a military base near Benghazi. As Goulden reports, it was 'doomed from the start'. He tells the story of the Libyan request for training in dropping heavy loads by parachute, or 'heavy drops' as they are called in military jargon. 'One of the first tests went spectacularly awry,' Goulden writes. 'The parachute in a cargo drop is opened by an explosive time set to detonate at a given time after being shoved from the aircraft. As a test [a colleague] dropped a jeep from a C130 cargo plane with the Libyan-provided timer supposedly set to go off after three seconds. . . . It went off at 12 seconds, an instant before the jeep crashed into the desert. The jeep was smashed to bits. The Libyans didn't like this.'

Terpil and Wilson plied this lucrative trade throughout the 1970s despite the efforts of defectors from their illegal empire to tell the CIA and the FBI exactly what they were doing. In the end Wilson was caught, prosecuted and sentenced to twenty-five years at the US penitentiary in Marion, Illinois. Terpil disappeared. Rumours say that he is living in considerable discomfort in the Bekaa Valley region of Lebanon. The explosives and timing devices he and Wilson sold the Libyans, however, still blow up, periodically, around the world.

The Libyans were confused about US policy towards them and this is not surprising. The US government was hostile, yet senior,

221

albeit former, members of the US intelligence community conspired to help them. The Libyans were further bemused by the policy of the Carter administration. Under President Reagan the US attitude has been consistently hostile. Under Carter there were no clear messages. The United States banned the sale of the C130s at a time when other trade flourished. The export of Libyan oil grew from 4 per cent of US imports in September 1973 to 9 per cent in December and 10.8 per cent, or 700,000 barrels a day, in August 1980. This made Libya the third-largest oil supplier to the United States after Saudi Arabia and Nigeria, and the United States Libya's largest single customer, accounting for almost 40 per cent of Libya's total production each year. In 1978, however, because of the persistent reports of Libya's support of terrorism and its implacable hostility to the Camp David peace process, there was pressure building up in the United States that some trade should be curbed. Having banned the sale of two Boeing 727s, the US government recommended in March 1978 that the sale of 400 heavy trucks should also be stopped because they might be converted for use as tank transporters. The Libyans learned that they could rely on American businesses to find ways round such small matters as State Department bans.

They received their trucks, although slightly smaller versions, from the US company Oshkosh on the flimsy Libyan guarantee that they would not be converted for military purposes. Once in Libya, the trucks were altered at a cost of $15 million into tank transporters by Canadian mechanics using Austrian parts. By the end of the year the State Department had changed its mind on the two Boeing 727s and they were delivered to Libya.

According to the former US ambassador David Newsom in his evidence to the Senate judiciary committee, the US government was also puzzled about the different signs, some friendly, some hostile, coming out of Tripoli:

The attitude of Gadafy and his followers toward the United States has been ambivalent and often self-contradictory. They have seen the value of co-operation with American companies in the production and marketing of their oil and have recognized the role American citizens have played in keeping production high. At the same time, in Gadafy's revolutionary philosophy the American government and all it stands for is, to quote one of his statements, 'the embodiment of evil'. It is both in the latter connection and consistent with Gadafy's general political theory that government and people can be separated, that Libya has made efforts over the past two years to improve its ties with non-official Americans. For

222

example, in October 1978, the Libyans sponsored an 'Arab–American dialogue' which took the form of bringing to Libya a large group of private Americans for meetings and discussions with senior Libyan officials. Ahmed Shahati, head of the Foreign Liaison Office, came to this country with a good-will delegation in January 1979 and visited several American cities. . . . A Libyan women's delegation in March of 1979 made a good-will visit.

In the last public attempts by a US administration to improve relations with Libya, Newsom had talks with Major Jalloud in Tripoli in June 1979 and the Secretary of State Cyrus Vance met the Libyan Foreign Secretary in October. 'All these talks confirmed that wide differences still divided our two governments, but also suggested that Libya wanted to find a way to contain those differences and agree to disagree.' Newsom continued his mission in November by meeting Kikhia in New York, four days after the US hostages had been taken at the embassy in Teheran. He urged that Libya should take a stand against the seizure of the hostages:

> While Ambassador Kikhya showed understanding and a helpful attitude, other official Libyan statements, including a public call at the Arab Foreign Ministers' meeting in Tunis by the Libyan foreign secretary for a concerted Arab boycott action against the US following our freezing of Iranian assets, all of this prompted us to weigh in strongly with the Libyan officials to make the point that Libya could not have it both ways.

If Qaddafi had hoped to open up a direct channel of communication to the American masses, his own masses had a different idea. On 2 December 1979 a Libyan mob attacked the US embassy in Tripoli, in support of the Iranian revolution, and burned it. The last two American diplomats were withdrawn from Tripoli on 2 May 1980.

14 Financial Empire

The world has concentrated on Qaddafi as the managing director of the mythical company Terror Inc. but has ignored the Libyan financial empire abroad which stretches through more than 100 companies and twenty-five banks. While expenditure on development at home has often been haphazard and wasteful, Libya's foreign investments, indeed its whole handling of financial transactions overseas, have been canny and successful.

Until recently, tourists who, say, hire a Fiat Ritmo while staying in the Jerma Palace Hotel in Malta and pay with dollar travellers' cheques issued by Arab Financial Services in Bahrain would, indirectly, be contributing to the Libyan economy in three different ways.

Qaddafi has been advised by experienced financiers like Abdullah Saudi, a former Libyan national basketball player who learned his skills with the Midland Bank in London, became the first head of the Libyan Arab Foreign Bank and now heads the highly successful Arab Banking Corporation in Bahrain, and his colleague Rajib Misellati, former governor of the Central Bank of Libya. Men like these have helped Qaddafi build up a complex network of foreign investments. They began in the mid-1970s when, following the oil-prices rises of 1973–4, revenues began to take off, jumping from $2.3 billion in 1973 to $6 billion in 1974 and $8.6 billion in 1978. Expenditure on development projects was stepped up but there was still plenty of cash floating around for other enterprises.

Libya's stake in banks like the Union de Banques Arabes et Françaises (UBAF) in Paris was acquired without recourse to foreign borrowings. When oil earnings began to dip precariously in the mid-1980s, such holdings provided Libya with useful additional income.

Saudi and Misellati's key investment was made in 1976 when, on 1 December, the chairman of the Italian car company, Fiat, announced that Libya had bought a 10 per cent share in Fiat for the bargain price of $415 million. This liaison prospered and the Libyan Arab Foreign Bank's stake in the Italian motor company, which was transferred to a new holding company, the Libyan Arab Foreign Investment Company (LAFICO), in 1981, became the centrepiece of Libya's commercial empire.

One of Qaddafi's first acts after coming to power was to expel thousands of Italian farmers and small businessmen, most of whom had been in Libya since Fascist times. But this did not mean that he rejected Italian expertise to help him develop the country. He simply wanted it on his own terms and that meant establishing an intricate commercial network based on the love/hate relationship between Libya and its former imperial ruler. The Italians in turn were eager to get a slice of the action when Libya's oil money began to pour into massive development projects. Qaddafi's first development plan covering the years 1972–5 had projected an annual growth rate of 10.7 per cent. Fifteen per cent of oil royalties was reserved for a special account, used largely for defence purposes.

Of the remaining 85 per cent, around two-thirds was scheduled specifically for development projects, although it is possible that as much as half the oil revenues were used directly and indirectly to build up the weapons arsenal mostly from the Soviet Union. According to Dr Mohammed al Magharief, auditor-general in Libya from 1972 to 1977, and now leader of the opposition National Front for the Salvation of Libya, an arms deal worth more than $1 billion in cash with the Russians in December 1974 was followed in May 1975 by a $1.5 billion deal for submarines and other weaponry.

At first, when the US oil companies began dealing with the revolutionary government in Tripoli, they were astonished at its honesty. There were none of the backhanders which normally accompany such multimillion-dollar deals and which were so rampant in King Idris's reign. It did not take long for things to revert to their bad old ways. According to Magharief, 'most of these amounts were not correctly spent'; even the money earmarked for development was not necessarily spent on it. He maintains that corruption went on at an astonishing level. 'There is no doubt that a figure varying from between two and three billion dollars found its way into the pockets and foreign bank accounts of a large number of the political leaders and high-ranking administrative and technical personnel during the five-year period 1972 to 1977,' said Magharief, who recites a litany of the misappropriation of finances:

> Funds were withdrawn from development budgets for use as general budget support loans and other credits; money from the

225

reserve account was diverted and loans were contracted from the central bank. The treasury also issued treasury bonds, some of which were only repaid by income from the issue of new bonds. Loans were taken from the Public Corporation for Social Security at an interest of five per cent; funds were taken from the Committee for the Prosecution of Recoverable Funds set up by the Italians and used in illegal ways.

There was enough money around in Libya in the 1970s to ensure that such large-scale fiddling went almost unnoticed. There was still cash to buy arms, to fund the revolution at home and abroad and to start the huge development schemes. Western salesmen and consultants rushed into Tripoli to stake claims on two new oil refineries, a gas-processing plant, a large-scale agricultural project, a desalination scheme, eleven new hospitals and a variety of light industrial plants.

When dealing with economic matters, Qaddafi seemed to have forgiven and forgotten the West's imperialist role. In 1972 he told the Lebanese magazine *Al Hawadeth*: 'Western Europe has got rid of its imperialist trend and it is looking for free economic and commercial relations with countries like Libya.' Most of the important contracts went to Western firms. In 1974 Ruth First wrote in her book *Libya: The Elusive Revolution*: 'Relations with France have never been better; West Germany is now the largest importer of Libyan oil; Britain's trade with Libya, despite its running battle over the BAC contract monies, is the largest in the Middle East.'

First could have added Italy, which was well ensconced in the oil sector. Its state oil company ENI was happy to take crude which would otherwise have been marketed by recently nationalized multinationals; an ENI subsidiary quickly found work on the new Zawiya refinery. Italy also provided most of Libya's day-to-day consumer needs, particularly food. In 1974 Italy was Libya's main trading partner, providing a quarter of its imports and taking 34 per cent of its exports.

As one incident neatly reveals, the Europeans, and the Americans, turned a blind eye to the fact that Libya was pouring a good chunk of its revenue into revolution and terror. In 1974 the Paris right-wing newspaper *Minute* reported its exclusive evidence that Qaddafi was supporting Palestinian terrorism. It reproduced a draft for $250,000 on a bank in Zurich, signed by Abnagela Mohammed Huegi, first secretary of the Libyan embassy in Rome, and payable to Amin al Hindi, a former secretary-general of the Union of Palestinian Students. He was described as the head of the Al Wiqab Palestinian guerrillas recruited and financed by Qaddafi. *Minute* reported: 'A few days after the transfer in August 1973 two events occurred which justified the use of such a sum: the attack on 5 September in Paris by a Palestinian commando on the Saudi Arabian embassy, and the discovery the same day at a villa in Ostia, near Rome, of two Russian Sam 7 missiles.'

Thirteen years later, in May 1986, General Ambrogio Viviani, the former head of Italy's military counter-intelligence in the Servizio Informazione Difesa, the Italian secret service, threw new light on the Ostia incident. Viviani says that five Libyans were arrested in October 1973 at Fiumicino, close to Ostia. These Libyans had two Strela anti-aircraft missiles which they intended to fire at an El Al passenger plane. The Libyans were not held in Italy, according to Viviani. The Italian Prime Minister, Aldo Moro, told the secret service that he did not want Italy to get involved in a terrorist dispute. He ordered that the five Libyans should be flown back to Tripoli. Three days later the aircraft used to fly the three Libyan terrorist home mysteriously blew up in the skies above Venice. Viviani believes that it was a warning from the Israeli secret service not to appease Qaddafi.

Appeasement was exactly the game the Italians were playing. On the wider stage Christian Democrat leader Aldo Moro was following a pro-Arab foreign policy with the aim of not only securing Italy's oil supplies (98 per cent dependent on foreign, mostly Arab, sources), but also easing himself towards his 'historic compromise' with the Italian Communist Party. General Viviani says that throughout the early and mid-1970s Italian intelligence services were engaged in a systematic effort to shore up the relations between Rome and Tripoli. He says that his superiors told him that Italian economic interests, particularly those of the Italian state energy company, should be paramount in everything he did. He himself was sent to Tripoli to assist in organizing the Libyan secret service. 'We helped the Libyan leader defeat enemies of his regime,' says Viviani. 'We supplied him with arms, organized his intelligence service and gave him advisers to deal with the modernization of his armed forces.'

This type of initiative is confirmed at a senior level in the Palazzo Farinese, the Italian Foreign Ministry. It was a matter of Italy fighting for its rightful place in the economic development of Libya. A top Italian diplomat explains, 'Because of the leverage US oil companies had gained in Libya, there was a distinct danger that, between 1969 and 1972, ENI, our Italian oil company, would lose the very slight position it had in Libya. Our interest in saving ENI's position in Libya was enormous. It was ENI's first discovery abroad. This explains why we had to do some rather curious things in order to keep Qaddafi's goodwill towards Italy.' Arms and gadgets were supplied by Italy 'to induce the Libyans to be more responsive'.

Qaddafi was delighted to respond, but in his way. Italy, like other European countries, clearly needed his oil and his custom. He calculated that he had to do little more than supply their oil requirements and offer them assured markets for their goods and they were hooked. From 1975 he began tightening the knot of Italo-Libyan economic interdependence. With his Treasury over-flowing, he began making acquisitions, mainly property and land, first in the strategic island of Pantelleria between Libya and Sicily, and then in Sicily itself. He opened a hotel in Pantelleria and began to build a holiday village in Sicily. In November 1975 a Libyan interests office was opened in a plush ten-room apartment in a palace in Via Liberta in the centre of Palermo. One of Libya's earliest propagandists was the Sicilian lawyer Michele Papa. An Institute for the Promotion of Arab and Sicilian Culture and later a Sicilio-Libyan Chamber of Commerce were set up with Libyan backing.

Then Qaddafi turned his attentions northwards to the mainland. In December 1976 he took his substantial interest in Fiat. Subsequently Libya's commercial interests in Italy spread fast – a printing company in Rome, a tape cassette manufacturer in Pescara, a publisher in Cagliari (Sardinia).

Although none of these companies were involved, Libyans in Italy did peddle drugs, mainly through the Mafia, in return for arms, and provided various terrorist groups of both the left and right with funds and weapons. Qaddafi became adept at playing off the pro-Arab and pro-Israeli factions of the Italian secret service. In June 1980 a Florentine magistrate, Giovanni Tricomi, who was investigating the drugs link between Libya and Sicily, was flying from Bologna to Palermo *en route* to Pantelleria when his plane, an Alitalia DC9, suddenly exploded, killing all eighty-seven passengers on board. The cause of the explosion was never discovered, but the officially primed rumour-mill put it down to a Libyan-inspired bomb (in the more outrageous versions to an air-to-air missile fired from a Libyan Mig 23 fighter aircraft).

Italian businessmen and politicians chose to ignore these signs. To them, Libyan commercial interests in Italy simply showed Qaddafi's desire for closer economic co-operation. Realizing their dependence on Qaddafi's oil, they redoubled their efforts to win new markets in Libya. As well as construction equipment, cars and food, the Italians were happy to provide weapons. Press reports, denied by the Italian authorities, suggested that in February 1976 five West German Leopard tanks assembled in Italy (but banned under West German regulations from sale to all but NATO armies) had found their way to Libya via the Italian port of La Spezia and Marseilles.

In May 1978 the Italian company Siai-Marchetti announced that it had won an order to supply 200 SF260 light military training aircraft to Libya. In June that year four Wadi-class corvettes built for the Libyan navy by Cartiere de Muggiara underwent their preliminary sea trials. However, when Aeritalia sought to export G222 military transport planes to Libya, the US firm, General Electric, from whom the licence to assemble the aircrafts' T64-PD4 engines was held, banned their sale.

By 1980 Italy had lost its position as Libya's main export market. Remarkably, as it sought to diversify its sources of oil in the wake of the Arab/Israeli October War of 1973, the United States had taken the lead. Its share of Libyan oil sales jumped from 0.1 per cent in 1974 to 25 per cent in 1976, and stood at over 30 per cent in every subsequent year until 1980. However, in 1980 Italy was still by far and away Libya's main supplier, with 29 per cent of the market, more than double its nearest challenger, West Germany, which in turn sold nearly twice as much as Britain and France. OECD countries were providing Libya with more than 85 per cent of imports worth $9.2 billion (up 27.5 per cent from the year before).

With the oil-price rises of 1978, Libya was a more attractive customer than ever. In 1980 it started discussing projects for its socio-economic transformation plan 1981–5, which envisaged the mouth-watering expenditure of 18.5 billion dinars ($62.5 billion). Italy, particularly, needed Libya more than ever. In 1979 the Rome press got hold of a story that Italy, in its hunger for guaranteed oil supplies, had been paying commissions to Saudi royalty. The Saudis were so enraged to see these details paraded in the newspapers that they stopped oil shipments to Italy completely.

Italy was desperate. It set up a bilateral economic commission with Libya and, in return for Italian government involvement in Libyan development projects, agreed to take 20 million tons of Libyan oil over the next three years. It seemed an ideal solution for both sides. ENI was again at the forefront of Italian commercial activity in Libya. Already drawing crude from the vast Bu Attifel on-shore field, during 1980 it discovered a new off-shore field at Bouri, with a capacity of 150,000 barrels per day, the largest in the Mediterranean basin. As in its deals with other oil companies, Libya's National Oil Company cleverly allowed ENI a guaranteed equity share in the output of these fields. As a result by the mid-1980s ENI depended for 45 per cent of its much needed reserves on Libya.

But by that time, 1985–6, the Italo-Libyan commercial connection had become a mixed blessing. The attractions of the Libyan market had begun to dwindle as Libyan oil revenues fell from $20 billion in 1980 to around $8 billion in 1986. Libya found itself cancelling projects and cutting budgets. It failed to get round to issuing a new five-year plan to follow its ambitious 1981–5 socio-economic transformation plan. For Italy, guaranteed supplies of Libyan crude were no longer an attraction. Oil prices had fallen dramatically and not only was ENI able to secure its oil needs cheaply on the world spot markets, but Italian companies were beginning to find that, because of Libya's growing indebtedness, their regular bills were not being paid.

Italian companies quickly got the message. Italian exports to Libya fell from $2 billion in 1980 to $1.26 billion in 1985. But Italian businesses found they could not easily break loose from their Qaddafi connection. In 1985 Libya owed Italian firms around $1.5 billion in outstanding payments. In addition they were still working on contracts in Libya worth $1.25 billion. As the United States began to apply pressure on European countries to cut their business links with Libya, Qaddafi simply made it clear to the authorities in Rome that Italian firms would only get paid if they continued to supply him with goods. As if to emphasize his hold, he negotiated a barter deal whereby ENI took an extra 40,000 barrels of oil a day in lieu of payments to Italian exporters. The arrangement soon broke down because of disputes over the price of the crude.

Finally Qaddafi demonstrated the unbreakable nature of his relationship with Italy by contributing to a large-scale restructuring of the capital of Fiat and upping his take in the company to 15 per cent. Subsequently the price of Fiat shares rose dramatically. In 1986 the *Economist* estimated that Libya's holding in the company was worth $2.5 billion; its dividend income in 1985 was $28 million. With this success LAFICO turned acquisitive again, paying an undisclosed sum in December 1985 to buy Tamoil, formerly Amoco's Italian subsidiary, with its 900 petrol service stations throughout Italy and its refinery in Cremona producing 105,000 barrels a day.

As Italy's businessmen began to fight shy of their Libyan commitments, so did its politicians. With Italian sales to the Arab world down from nearly 20 per cent of world exports in 1981 to 10 per cent in 1985, the Palazzo Farinese no longer needed the demonstrably pro-Arab foreign policy with which it had been associated in the

1970s under the Christian Democrats. If one needs to pinpoint a moment when Italy's attitude to the Arab world changed, one can look to October 1985 when the notably Atlanticist Defence Minister Giovanni Spadolini resigned from Socialist Prime Minister Bettino Craxi's government in protest against its decision to deport Abu Abbas, the Palestinian believed to have masterminded the hijack of the *Achille Lauro* cruise-liner in the eastern Mediterranean. The powerful Spadolini agreed to return to the coalition only if it took a tougher line on terrorism and moderated its pro-Arab policy.

Spurred again by the United States, Italy's relations with the Arab world, and with Libya in particular, hardened following the bomb attacks at Rome and Vienna airports in December 1985, and deteriorated further after Libya's missile attack on the Italian Mediterranean island of Lampedusa in April 1986, following the US air raids on Tripoli and Benghazi.

During April and May 1986 over twenty Libyan diplomats and officials were expelled from Italy. Among them were thirty-year-old Mohammed al Akresh, an official at the Libyan consulate in Palermo, who was accused of recruiting Arab immigrants to spy on NATO bases at Comiso and Sigonella in Sicily, and Mohammed Naas, head of the LAFICO office in Rome. Naas later appealed against the expulsion order and was allowed to stay. Arabi Mohammed Fituri, another LAFICO employee, was not so lucky. He was charged with plotting to kill the US, Egyptian and Saudi Arabian ambassadors in Rome in 1985.

This was only the start of a growing campaign against Libyan commercial interests in Italy. Fiat wanted to participate in the United States Star Wars programme. Washington made clear that this would be impossible as long as LAFICO remained one of its shareholders. Then Les Aspin, Democratic chairman of the US House of Representatives armed forces committee, argued that the US Defence Department should cancel a proposed $7.9 million purchase of 178 Fiat-Allis trucks for the American armed forces because this could indirectly constitute 'financial sustenance for Libya's support of international terrorism'. Giovanni Agnelli, who earlier said that the Libyans on his board behaved like 'Swiss bankers', was again reported as wanting to cut his links with Libya. Eventually a fudge was worked out, with the Pentagon declaring, 'Fiat has agreed to take the steps necessary to prevent profits earned from contracts with the Defence Department from being paid to the Libyan Arab Foreign Investment Company (LAFICO).' Within a few months, in September 1986, Fiat surprised the world with its announcement that, in conjunction with two banks, it was repurchasing Libya's 15 per cent stake in its stock. Mohammed Siala and Ali Mohammed Algheriani, both directors of LAFICO, immediately left the Fiat main board. However, Libya walked away from the deal with a sum variously estimated at between $2 billion and $3 billion.

If Italy's attitude to Libya seemed clear in the summer of 1986, it became ambivalent again in October when Rome arranged a swap of prisoners with Libya. In return for the release of four Italians from Libya, Signor Craxi's government freed three Libyans serving sentences for murdering or attempting to assassinate anti-Qaddafi dissidents.

Libya's commercial relationship with Italy was mirrored in its dealings with most other countries. Libya remained a large supplier of oil to Western Europe, particularly West Germany. In 1985 its trade with the European Community still ran at $11.5 billion (approximately two-thirds in exports of oil, one-third in imports of goods and services), with Italy and West Germany remaining Libya's best customers and suppliers.

Despite falling oil prices, easily transportable Libyan crude and Libyan markets were still attractive to both Western governments and businessmen – certainly until early 1986 when the spot market provided alternative sources of oil. Qaddafi knew this, and was never slow to use his economic clout in Europe. On the one hand, he would pressure the West German government to release Libyan gunmen accused of murdering dissidents; on the other, he would call on British businessmen to lobby Whitehall for a resumption of diplomatic relations with Libya. When they came under pressure from the United States to cut their economic ties with Libya and adopt sanctions against it, European countries were discreetly reminded by Qaddafi's aides that their still lucrative Libyan business was at stake.

As Washington began to call upon its allies to adopt sanctions, it was forced to take stock of its own close economic ties with Tripoli. When Reagan came to power in 1981 (shortly after the conclusion of the hostage fiasco in Iran), he was under considerable pressure to make a quick military strike against Libya. In January the Libyan people's bureau in Washington was closed in retaliation for the sacking of the US embassy in Tripoli the previous year. Everything looked set for an escalation of rhetoric or even hostilities between Washington and Tripoli. However, wiser counsels prevailed. Taking note of the falling oil markets, the United States opted to wear Libya down economically.

Pressure to take more direct action mounted again following the skirmish in the Gulf of Sirte in August 1981 when two Libyan planes were shot down by US fighters. A ban on travel by US citizens to Libya was introduced in late 1981. However, the 1,000–1,500 Americans working in Libya still managed to get into the country on special papers. They were treated as honoured guests, and so they should have been. Americans were also the consultants and engineers behind many of Qaddafi's prestige development projects, notably the $3 billion man-made river designed to bring water from well-stocked aquifers in the south of the country to the parched, populated Mediterranean coast. This connection guaranteed a sizeable export market for US goods. Not surprisingly in late 1981 the US Senate voted narrowly against applying additional sanctions against Libya. It opted instead for a six-month study of 'concrete steps' to confront Qaddafi.

Advocates of a further embargo focused on oil as the most obvious symbol of the US/Libyan economic relationship. In 1981 the United States was still buying 40 per cent of Libyan oil production, though this represented only 7.7 per cent of its total oil imports. Lobbying led to a progressive rundown of Libyan imports. By early 1982 only 3 per cent of US oil came from Libya. Finally in March 1982 an official boycott of Libyan crude oil imports into America was implemented. Licences were required for all US exports to Libya except agricultural supplies and medical products. The stated intention was to prevent the export to Libya of oil and gas technology and of equipment affecting national security.

However, Libyan-refined products still managed to get into the United States. In April 1985 Albert Bustamente, a Texas Congressman, told a House of Representatives sub-committee that exports of Libyan-refined products – principally low-sulphur fuel oil and naphtha from Libya's newly commissioned refinery at Ras Lanuf – were threatening the economic survival of refiners on the (US) Gulf coast. The authoritative *Middle East Economic Survey* reported that 244,521 barrels of Libyan naphtha entered the United States in April 1985 and 298,338 barrels of fuel oil in July.

Although the State Department then favoured a further embargo, a heavyweight coalition of the Office of Management and Budget, the Treasury and the Departments of Commerce and Energy reportedly opposed it, fearing this might be interpreted as protectionism in disguise. Congressman Bustamente kept up his campaign and in November 1985 President Reagan signed an executive order banning the import of Libyan-refined products. However, Libyan oil products (in the form of Libyan crude, refined in third countries, and therefore outside the scope of existing orders) continued to find their way on to the American market.

In January 1986, as Reagan sought to convince his European allies to join his economic boycott of Libya, he felt compelled to close the door on US/Libyan economic relations still further. He again ordered all Americans to cease working in Libya – this time under pain of prosecution and with a deadline of 31 January. All US companies in Libya were given similar deadlines, though the five US oil companies there – Occidental (the only operator), Conoco, Marathon, Amerada Hess and W. R. Grace, collectively lifting about 300,000 barrels of oil a day – were allowed until the end of June to wind up their affairs.

Reagan also threatened to freeze all Libyan assets in the United States, estimated at $2.5 billion. These included Libyan deposits in American banks, including the New York branch of the Arab Banking Corporation (ABC), and additional properties and holdings from a $5 million building in New York to a Texas-based oilfield equipment purchasing company.

Although one or two countries such as Italy had introduced an embargo on arms sales to Libya earlier in the year, and the European Community had voted in a ban on butter exports, it was not until the US raid on Tripoli and Benghazi in April 1986 that Europe began seriously to consider economic sanction against Libya.

In the circumstances Libya's network of foreign investments came increasingly under scrutiny. With a LAFICO employee charged with terrorist activities in Rome, the whole company was widely suspected of providing important assistance to Qaddafi's campaign of international subversion. If the US Defence Department could halt its dealings with Fiat because of LAFICO's shareholding in the latter, what about the other companies and financial institutions in which Libya had a holding? They certainly looked vulnerable.

Apart from a few individuals who act on its behalf, Libya's foreign investments are all now held by the Libyan Arab Foreign Bank (LAFB) and LAFICO.

LAFB, which had assets of $3 billion in 1985, looks after Libya's investments in banks and financial institutions. Its main interest is the successful Bahrain-based consortium, ABC, headed by Abdullah Saudi, the man who negotiated Libya's purchase of Fiat in 1976. Libya owns one-third of ABC's $750 million paid up capital. In 1984, with income from loan syndications falling, ABC became acquisitive, snapping up Richard Daus, a prestigious Frankfurt merchant bank, Banco Atlantico, a large Spanish retail bank involved in trade finance between Spain and Latin America (formerly part of the bankrupt Rumasa empire) and (in March 1985) a 75 per cent stake in Sun Hung

Bank, Hong Kong's largest deposit-taking institution.

LAFB's other main holdings are in Arab Financial Services, a successful Bahrain-based Arab travellers' cheque company also headed by Abdullah Saudi, Banco Arabe Español (chairman: Abdullah Saudi), the Arab Latin American Bank (chairman: Abdullah Saudi), Union des Banques Arabes et Françaises (UBAF) in London, Arab International Bank in Cairo, and a variety of lesser-known institutions such as the Banque Arabe Libyenne Mauritanienne pour le Commerce Extérieur et Développement and the Libyan Arab Uganda Bank for Foreign Trade and Development.

In July 1986 UBAF was one of six defendants sued by the British airline British Caledonian for breach of contract following Libya's cheeky purchase of two of its surplus Airbuses, in breach of a US embargo. UBAF allegedly helped fund a deal whereby the Airbuses, powered by General Electric engines, were sold initially to a Hong Kong company and later, via a London broker, unbeknown to British Caledonian, sold on to Libya. Only a few months previously the US Department of Commerce had vetoed the purchase of Airbuses by the Libyans on the open market.

In addition, Libya's state-owned National Commercial Bank has a stake in European Arab Bank in Brussels, while another public sector institution, Wahda Bank, had a holding in Banque Arabe et Internationale d'Investissement (BAII), which in 1985 became the first Arab Bank to participate in the City of London's Big Bang, taking up 29 per cent of stockbrokers Sheppard and Chase.

LAFICO, with offices in Rome, Athens and Malta, is charged with 'managing Libya's foreign non-bank investments'. Its total assets are around $6 billion, mostly ($3.5 billion) in cash and due from banks. Other assets are put at $1.69 billion. In January 1985 LAFICO's Rome chief, Mohammed Naas, revealed that the company had investments in ninety-four companies world-wide – thirty-four in Africa, twenty-seven in Europe, twenty-five in the Middle East, four in Asia and four in Latin America. Assets included companies involved in shipping, mining, agriculture and manufacturing, as well as holding companies in countries such as Pakistan, Uganda and Malta.

With Libya's windfall from Fiat toward the end of 1986, there were again signs that LAFICO was in the market for acquisitions. Libyan companies have been active in the market-place in Europe securing vital supplies for Qaddafi's economy, particularly the oil sector. The geographical diversity and overall sophistication of Libya's financial and business network has been vital in ensuring the continued viability of Qaddafi's regime.

15   *Still on Top*

On the 1st of September 1986 Qaddafi put on one of his less ornate military uniforms and his dark glasses to celebrate the seventeenth anniversary of the Libyan revolution. He took the salute on Omar Mukhtar Street, two blocks from Green Square, from more than 10,000 Libyan troops. An impressive array of his Soviet-built tanks, armoured cars and missiles rumbled past the parade stand. After the American raid in April that year Qaddafi had virtually disappeared from the public view. He had retired, as he often does at times of crisis, to a government villa in Benghazi and then to an oasis in the desert, leaving the more visible functions of government to his deputy, Major Jalloud, the head of the popular militias, Colonel Khweldi Hameidi, the security chief, Mustafa Kharroubi, and the army chief of staff, Abu Bakr Younis. There were indications that this gang of four were, in the wake of the US raid and the military humiliation of Libya, moving the country on a more moderate course. Some private sector food shops that had been previously closed were allowed to reopen and small farmers allowed to sell their produce on the open market. The murder, in Mafia style, in August 1986 of a senior member of the revolutionary committees, Ahmed Wafali, as he attended the wedding of his brother, seemed to some outside the country to represent another attempt by the traditional leadership in the army to rid themselves of the revolutionary zealots who were, they feared, poised to remove them from power. There was, as usual, no official comment on or an explanation for the murder.

Once again – and this is a theme of the reporting and analysis of modern Libya – speculation, based on meagre evidence, flourished. There was a flurry of press reports that Qaddafi had been deposed in a palace coup and that this grip on power had been loosened and perhaps broken. The London *Sunday Times* suggested that Qaddafi was under the influence of 'mood control drugs', although their names were not given. There was speculation when Qaddafi appeared on Libyan television looking worse for wear with his face strangely bloated that drug abuse had caused his condition. Other newspaper reports, based on 'Western intelligence sources', said that he was suffering from 'chronic depression'.

Edward Schumacher, a *New York Times* correspondent in Libya in September, was surprised to find the normally tight-lipped citizens of Tripoli willing, and in some cases eager, to give their views of the Qaddafi regime. Occasionally they were critical. Libyans in shops and cafés, Shumacher said, would criticize Qaddafi's foreign policy, saying that his eagerness to confront the US had led to the punishing raid and that at home conditions were hard. They complained that they no longer had any cash, they were starved of foreign currency, the shops were largely bare and there were restrictions on their travel abroad. In a closed society like Libya, such criticisms to a foreigner are astonishing. Qaddafi evidently had a problem.

In the early summer of 1986 the British Foreign Office received a spate of US intelligence reports which attempted to show that, after a brief lull, the Libyan terror machine was in action again. The reports were classified, but, according to officials who saw them, they contained information about the movement of Libyan terrorists or their surrogates in the Mediterranean and Europe. There were suggestions that Libyans planned to hit US targets in Malta and Crete and evidence of Libyan activity in Europe. The US government gave some British diplomats the impression that it intended to take further military action against Libya. The Foreign Office was not impressed by this 'evidence'. 'The Americans were getting incredibly excited,' said a British official. 'Their intelligence data, and there were volumes of it, was accompanied by wild assertions. It was evidence of the movement of Libyans or their surrogates around Europe and the Mediterranean with these wild interpretations. Our impression when we read the material was "so what?" '

The British were exasperated and, according to some officials, angry. They felt that the US did not have enough firm evidence even to contemplate further military action against Libya.

In fact, the US intended to do no such thing. On 2 October Bob Woodward, a reporter on the *Washington Post* and a member of the reporting team that exposed Watergate, wrote that the US National Security Advisor, Admiral John Poindexter, had sent President Reagan a secret memorandum which outlined a 'disinformation' programme aimed at destabilizing Qaddafi by generating false reports that the US and Libya were once again on a collision course. The Poindexter memo outlined a plan which was adopted at a White

House meeting on 14 August. It recommended 'a series of closely co-ordinated events involving covert, diplomatic, military and public actions'. It was the latest phase of the US administration's policy to topple Qaddafi. The *Wall Street Journal* and other newspapers reported much of the false information generated by the plan: they described renewed Libyan backing for terrorism in the wake of the US raid and a looming US/Libyan confrontation.

It was deliberate deception. The reality, according to the genuine US intelligence reports, was that Qaddafi was marking time. The Poindexter memo said that, 'although the current intelligence community assessment is that Qaddafi is temporarily quiescent in his support of terrorism, he may soon move to a more active role'. There was no evidence at the time to suggest that Qaddafi intended to launch a new terror campaign.

The 'disinformation campaign' hurt the US administrations's credibility with its own media and led to the resignation in October of the Assistant Secretary of State for Public Affairs, Bernard Kalb.

It is convenient to talk of 'the policy of the US administration'. There is often no such thing. US policy towards Libya, perhaps a little less than its policy over nuclear arms limitations, is a battle-ground of conflicting views between different agencies and between departments of the same agency. The CIA, for example, contained at least two schools of thought, according to a Middle East analyst with special responsibility for Libya, who worked for it. The mainstream CIA analysts on the Libya desk saw all the information about Libyan terror but, like the members of the British Foreign Office, they were not impressed. They did not deny that Qaddafi funded, assisted and often instigated terror. They simply thought that among the players in Middle East terror he was not as significant as their masters in the White House believed. Their strong recommendation in dozens of memoranda was that the best policy towards Qaddafi was to ignore him unless he seriously increased his involvement in terrorism. They noted that Qaddafi had been cautious about hitting US targets and had only on rare occasions exported terrorism to the mainland United States. Their analysis of the majority of raw intelligence material about the movement of personnel and materials was that it really did not amount to much.

The clandestine services of the CIA, which are concerned more with covert operations than analysis and have gained in funds and influence under CIA director William Casey, thought differently. They argued, in this war of memoranda, that the best way of dealing with Qaddafi was to confront him. They believed that from the raw intelligence a real threat to the US could be pieced together. Their counsel held sway with the President when he decided to launch the raid against Libya, and the clandestine services urged that action should be taken after the raid to topple Qaddafi.

From this welter of contradictory advice two US aims emerged in the early summer of 1986. The administration felt that Europe was still soft on Libya, and that while the US officially banned all trade, for Europe it was very much business as usual. Throughout the summer of 1986 the State Department urged Europe to impose further trade sanctions on Libya and to expel the Libyan 'diplomats' and officials, especially members of the staff of Libyan Arab Airlines who worked directly for the Libyan Bureau of External Security. The British attitude perplexed the Americans. Mrs Thatcher was the only foreign leader wholeheartedly to support and give practical assistance to the US raid; Britain had been a prime target for Libyan terror and, sluggishly, the Home Office had begun to weed out suspect Libyans and to deport them. But, where business was concerned, the British were reluctant to take action. One striking anomaly was the position of the British company Plessey, which continued to do business with the Libyan government in one of the most sensitive areas of all, its air defence. Plessey has refused to discuss with the authors any details of its activities in Libya.

Plessey continued to work in Libya despite the US raid and despite the fact that one of its employees, James Abra, a fifty-seven-year-old radar engineer, had been arrested in Libya in June 1985 and sentenced to life imprisonment in April 1986 for 'endangering revolutionary security by passing information to agents of a foreign power'. Abra was picked up at Tripoli airport carrying a briefcase which contained details of a Libyan missile/radar system of Soviet design which Plessey, and Abra, had worked on six years before. Abra admits that he had the documents. They were out of date and the information they contained was so well known that, as Abra's defence lawyer revealed in the Tripoli court, it was all contained in *Jane's Weapons Systems*. According to British diplomats, Foreign Office officials and members of British intelligence, Abra is not a spy, nor was he about to hand these documents to any foreign agent.

On 12 April 1986 Abra appeared in court in Tripoli. The proceedings were in Arabic and, at first, Abra thought he had been condemned to die. However, a court official explained to him in English that the court had shown mercy and that he would be permitted to spend the rest of his life in jail.

At the time of writing, Abra had been moved to the Qwessia prison in Benghazi. Despite repeated requests for access by the British counsul in Tripoli, Hugh Dunnachie, Abra had been allowed no visits since his conviction in April. His case has received little public attention. Neither the British government nor his company, Plessey, have made any kind of public outcry. Plessey has continued to make radar systems for the Libyan government, while Abra languishes in Qwessia.

When the authors approached the Foreign Office about Abra's plight they were told: 'We are doing all we can but there is not much we can do. His company, Plessey, is taking the lead in this.'

Plessey directed our enquiries to its public relations company, Charles Barker Lyons. There are not very many. Paul Calderwood, an associate director of Charles Barker Lyons, told the authors: 'I don't know what the current situation is. I haven't had to find out. There hasn't been much media interest. The Plessey company is doing all that it can in conjunction with the Foreign and Common-wealth Office. I am afraid I cannot tell you what they are doing. That is all I can say.'

The Abra/Plessey case was a poignant example of the attitude that most angered the US government. The view of a senior US official, and an expert on counter-terrorism, was that European governments were prepared to give lip service to the battle against terrorism until it clashed with their own financial interests.

It was a persuasive argument until, in November 1986, the scandal of the secret US/Iran operation, and the revelation that for eighteen months the United States had opened a secret back channel and had been selling arms to Iran, at least in part for the release of US hostages in Lebanon, was revealed in a pro-Syrian newspaper in Beirut. Its effect on President Reagan's political reputation was damaging; its impact on US counter-terrorism policy was disastrous. 'What is our policy?' asked a Republican senator. 'We send arms to Iran, yet we bomb Qaddafi.'

Qaddafi himself seemed to have recovered quickly enough from his depression of earlier in the summer. After his appearance in Omar Mukhtar Street on 1 September, he went on to Harare in Zimbabwe for the Non-Aligned Summit, where he was in fine rhetorical, and sartorial, form. He wore a red, high-necked shirt and flowing black-and-white robes. He was accompanied by four female bodyguards who waved their fists and chanted in unison. He looked like an ageing star taking the stage at a Las Vegas night-club. There was nothing rusty about his performance, however. He spoke, without notes, for more than an hour, lashing out at the Nonaligned Movement: 'I want to say good-bye, farewell to this funny movement, farewell to this fallacy, farewell to this international falsehood.' Qaddafi was expressing the secret thoughts of some of the members and there was a ripple of applause. There were smirks of derision from many others. Qaddafi said he would form an international army of tens of thousands: 'I shall spread the troops of these forces all over the continents of the world to put fire under the feet of the United States.'

This was the iconoclastic spirit he showed at the Cairo conference in 1970 when he called for the execution of King Hussein, and at Arab conferences in the 1970s when he berated the Palestinians for their lack of mettle in the fight against the Zionist enemy. It was classic Qaddafi. But few can take it seriously any more.

When the Libyan leader came to take the salute at the eighteenth anniversary of his accession to power, he simply looked rather silly. He sat back in his chair playing with a baton, which he held delicately between his fingers. His face had a soft, rather thoughtful expression. His posture was limp and awkward as he watched the usual display of military hardware, most of it acquired from the Soviet Union, rumble past. Observers counted 4,000 Libyan soldiers and as many as 2,000 tanks, leaving the small number of Western diplomats present to conclude that the tanks had made two circuits of the Green Square. Two battalions of troops carried flippers and snorkel equipment. The official explanation was that they were ready to transform themselves into 'explosive fish-men'.

One major difference between this display and the previous couple of years was the lack of Western interest. Qaddafi's foreign policy was in disarray. Far from creating unity in the Arab, African or Islamic world, his allies could be counted on the fingers of one hand. His links with Sudan, South Yemen and Ethiopia were fragile. His forays into Chad had been a disaster. His tenuous 'unity agreement' with Morocco had collapsed after King Hassan had invited representatives of the two great Satans in Libyan demonology – William Casey, head of the CIA, and Shimon Peres, Prime Minister of Israel – to Rabat for talks.

Qaddafi's only real friend in the Arab world was Syria, and his firmest ally remained the Soviet Union, which agreed to replenish his military stocks after the Libyan army's abysmal performance during the American raid. According to Eastern European diplomats in Tripoli, however, relations between Libya and Russia, although publicly warm, were privately more strained than ever as the Soviet Union began to regain its influence in the Middle East and to improve its relations with the moderate Arab states and with Israel.

241

Qaddafi's erratic behaviour had become an embarrassment, and a senior diplomat from the Eastern bloc talked openly to journalists about the deep Soviet desire to find a replacement for him. According to this diplomat the Russians had looked closely at Major Jalloud, the most able of the ruling elite, but suspected that he was, beneath the veneer of revolutionary ideology, too pro-Western.

In Africa the only country that moved willingly into the Libyan camp was the tiny, central African nation of Burkina Faso ruled since 1983 by Thomas Sankara, a young army officer who lived behind a wall of bodyguards in his palace in Quagadougou in daily fear of a coup or assassination. 'Everyone is plotting against me, inside and outside the country,' a worried Sankara told the authors. The Burkina Faso leader was right to register his concern, for in October 1987 he was assassinated in a coup which overthrew his government.

During 1987, in the face of these reverses, Qaddafi began seriously to rethink his role in the world. In a cabinet reshuffle in February he replaced his ineffectual Foreign Minister Hassan Kamal al Maqhur with the more pragmatic Jadallah al Talhi. A year earlier he had ordered Maqhur, whose name means vanquished in Arabic, to call himself Mansour, meaning victorious. But even this piece of revolutionary sympathetic magic, so in keeping with Qaddafi's earlier arrogance, had failed to halt Libya's decline.

In the same cabinet reshuffle Qaddafi also appointed a new Prime Minister, Omar Muntasser, a patrician who was educated at the Arab world's leading public school, Victoria College in Alexandria in Egypt, and had good connections in the oil industry and with Western businessmen.

Qaddafi followed up his appointment of Muntasser with a speech on Libyan television in March 1987 when he openly talked of the need for private enterprise in the Libyan economy. Some of the old rhetoric was still nominally there. 'Does this contradict the theory of partners, not wage slaves?' asked Qaddafi. 'Never', he cried, though the true answer was clearly 'Yes'.

Such is the unpredictable nature of Libyan politics that, towards the end of 1987, there were reports that certain opposition leaders were so encouraged by Libya's continuing moderation that they were prepared to seek accommodation with Qaddafi himself. Algeria and the PLO emerged as important power-brokers in this process. They appeared to convince Qaddafi that, if he took a less bombastic line, he could have an important role to play in any future peace negotiations in the Middle East. The Libyan leader was so flattered that he even talked about setting up a political party again – with himself at its head, of course.

There was still the odd display of Libyan revolutionary fervour. The activity of revolutionary committee members in the South Pacific in early 1987 caused Australian Prime Minister Bob Hawke to warn Qaddafi to keep out of the region. There were also reports of Libya lending support to the IRA and to black gang leaders in Chicago. 'Libyan terrorists have not disappeared,' said a State Department official.'We get reports on them all the time, like background radio chatter.'

But the will of Libyan revolutionaries to lay down their lives for Qaddafi appeared to have gone. They were in the South Pacific because it was the only place they knew they could operate with impunity for a while.

If, in late 1987, Qaddafi were presented with a report card chronicling his time as ruler of Libya, it would show only one solid achievement: he had remained in power for over eighteen years.

It is a remarkable feat, none the less. In the 1980s alone he has survived an army mutiny at the military base in Tobruk, an army attack organized by Libyan dissidents on his barracks in Tripoli, a US air strike and a number of assassination attempts, including one early in 1986 in which the chauffeur of his car was killed. He faces opposition from his army and from within his own tribe.

Although Qaddafi has condemned and attempted to abolish tribal loyalties, members of his tribe, the Qaddaffa, still hold many of the most important positions in Libya. His cousin, Khalifa Khanish, has been head of his personal security since the late 1970s. Another kinsman, Mohammed Maghgoub, leads the revolutionary committees. Sayed and Ahmed Qaddafadam play a key role in foreign affairs; Colonel Messaoud Abdul Hafez, the military commander of the Fezzan, continues to play an important part in Qaddafi's regime. Others are entrusted with such crucial jobs as guarding the ammunition dumps. When weapons were needed in the 1980s a Qaddadfa was likely to have the key. But this reliance on his tribal roots created its own tensions.

The Qaddadfa are an elite and are resented, especially by the revolutionary committees, who had become an important force by the early 1980s. These 'shock troops of the revolution' were tribally much more broadly based than the other centres of power, and much of Major Jalloud's influence in the regime was centred in the committees where members of his Mega'ha tribe, such as Abdullah Senussi and Sayed Rashid, held top posts. The committees also contained important representatives of the Wafala from the Fezzan and the Obeidat from Cyrenaica. As oil prices slumped during the 1980s Qaddafi leaned heavily on the ideological fervour of the committees to keep the revolution intact and the people in line.

The Qaddadfa, who had seen how the committees ruthlessly toppled the merchants and senior army officers in 1979, began to fear for their own positions and privileges. Sections of Qaddafi's tribe were also genuinely embarrassed by the excesses of the revolutionary committees and their brutal behaviour both at home and abroad. They felt that as the most visible beneficiaries of Qaddafi's regime, they were seen by the average Libyan as the instigators of its policies.

The tribe found willing allies in many top army officers who were tired of Qaddafi's attempts to 'revolutionize' the regular army by forcing the officers to take orders from young, inexperienced committee members and even by banning them from their barracks outside working hours. They rightly saw these ploys as a way of limiting their authority and power. By 1985 it became clear where Qaddafi's sympathies really lay. The government-controlled press began to churn out invective against the army officers who, it said, abused their positions; the press demanded that 'bourgeois symbols' should be eradicated. The revolutionary committees knew a bourgeois symbol when they saw one and promptly set fire to brand new BMW saloons parked outside the officers' club by the harbour, next to the Italian embassy.

There were rumblings of discontent in the army and rumours of another coup attempt. In August 1985 army and air force units stationed at Al Watiyah in north-west Libya refused to budge when Qaddafi ordered them to move, on full alert, to the border with Tunisia. On 1 September 1985 Qaddafi cancelled the military parade through Tripoli because he caught the whiff of the coup and began to suspect the Qaddadfa of encouraging the army against him.

In October Qaddafi enlisted the support of the official *Jamahiriya* newspaper, the voice of the revolutionary committees, to launch a virulent and unprecedented attack on the 'impostor princes' and 'ignorant, greedy and nepotistic bigots' among his kinsmen. An editorial in the paper thundered: 'Muammar [Qaddafi] does not belong only to the Qaddadfa tribe but is the son, father, cousin and uncle of all revolutionaries.' It threatened 'to eliminate the Qaddadfa clique who are in no way in step with revolutionary ideas . . . if necessary in broad daylight in order to protect the revolution and its leader.'

After an incident in November 1985, when revolutionary committee members burst into land registry offices, tipped all the files relating to land tenure into the street and burned them, Qaddafi's own tribal elders, and senior army officers, thought they should do something to quench the fires of a revolution which was getting dangerously out of control. The only man, they thought, who would be able to confront and perhaps convince Qaddafi of the benefits of a little moderation was Hassan Ishkal. He had all the right credentials. He was a Qaddadfa, a cousin of Qaddafi and a soldier with a distinguished career as a commander in Chad in the mid-1970s and then, in 1979, as the commander of the Central Region based in Sirte. This was one of the most important jobs in Libya. Sirte is the heartland of the Qaddadfa and Ishkal had the delicate task of keeping watch on the tribesmen whose loyalty was vital to Qaddafi's survival. The town is also seen by military strategists as the pivot from which Libya's two largest provinces, Cyrenaica and Tripolitania, can be controlled.

Ishkal was a cultured man and wrote poems. He was not modest about his minor skill and used to read a selection from his works out loud to his guests after dinner. He kept their attention with outspoken attacks on the regime. He was rich from his many business interests and, unusually for a Libyan, would invite foreigners to his villas in Sirte and Tripoli. Ishkal was not afraid to tell his cousin what was on his mind. He had already broached a delicate subject, telling him that the army wanted an end to what it believed to be an unwinnable war in Chad. Qaddafi had not taken the news well. He suspected Ishkal of plotting against him and there was gossip in Tripoli that Ishkal would be Qaddafi's successor.

In November 1985 there was a brief official announcement in Tripoli: Colonel Hassan Ishkal, the commander of the region, had died in a car crash. It was followed, strangely, by another official statement that the Colonel had committed suicide. Neither official version quite fitted the medical facts. Ishkal's body had been examined by an Egyptian doctor at a Tripoli hospital and it contained six bullet holes.

The unofficial version of Ishkal's death has been pieced together from Libyan and Western diplomatic sources. On Sunday 24 November Ishkal opened the front door of his villa in Tripoli to find an armoured car and five soldiers in his driveway. The leader of the group saluted and told him he was required at the Aziziya barracks for a crisis meeting. One report says the meeting was about the Egyptian passenger plane which had been hijacked to Malta. Ishkal was delighted because he had been excluded from the centre of power in recent months and had feared for his own life. This summons might mean he was back in Qaddafi's favour. But to be on the safe side he carried a small pistol inside his shirt.

At the barracks Ishkal was taken into an ante-chamber and told that he was under arrest. It is reported that he then lost his temper, demanded to see Qaddafi and, when the soldiers refused, pulled his gun and shot two of the guards. Ishkal was overpowered and, according to one account, a guard phoned Qaddafi in his office to ask what they should do with him. 'What are you waiting for?' Qaddafi is reported to have said, and the guard promptly pumped six bullets into his prisoner.

Ishkal's death, and the transparent official cover-up, did not solve the problem of internal dissent, although Libyans may not be brave or foolhardy enough to express it so blatantly in future. The struggle between the army and the revolutionary committees, the moderates and the zealots, Qaddafi and his own tribe continue. There are signs that the four remaining members of the Revolutionary Command Council, the young officers who carried out the coup seventeen years previously, believe that Qaddafi's revolution may have gone too far, although none of them has the inclination or the popular support to depose him.

Qaddafi does have nightmares. He confessed to an old friend, a Syrian ambassador based in Europe, that he woke up sweating one night in September 1986. He had been dreaming of Iranian rocket attacks on the Iraqi capital Baghdad. He told the ambassador that he saw one of the Scud ground-to-ground missiles that Libya sold to the Iranians landing on his Arab brothers.

He must also fear for his own mortality. But it is almost certainly not Vice-Admiral Kelso on the bridge of the USS *Coronado* as he leads the Sixth Fleet across the Line of Death who floats into Qaddafi's nightmares. His real dread is of something far closer to home. It is a vision of a young Libyan sitting in a secondary school, reading Nasser's *Philosophy of the Revolution*, or, these days, more likely, a copy of the Koran, and harbouring the ambition to be the next leader of his country.

Index

Kreisky, 37; strangely inflated view of Libya's role in world, 38; abolishes police in Libya, 41; financial problems of, 44; launches grandiose schemes, 44; introduces austerity measures, 44; asceticism apparent in, 44; birth of, 45; as youngest child, 47; exact date of birth unknown, 47; his boyhood hero, 50; enrolled at primary school, Sirte, 52; enrolled at Sebha secondary school, 52; speech-making by, 55, 56; his ambitions, 55; organizes demonstrations against Syria and in favour of Egypt, 55; expelled from school, 56; at secondary school in Misurata, 56–7; famed for invective against English language-inspector, 57; plans revolution, 57; enrolled in academy, 58; a most backward cadet, 58–9, 60; frequently reported for insubordination and rudeness, 60; plans sedition, 60; suspected of involvement in assassination, 62; joins army's signals unit, 62; attends four-month's training course in Britain, 63; his hatred of British, 63; turmoil in Libya as starting-point for coup, 67–9; many theories concerning American role in coup, 67–8; plans to go to Britain for six-month training session, 70; plans for and the execution of coup, 70–2; success of coup, 73; attempts to secure support of army, 78; continued use of word 'people' in speech, 79; nationalizes shares of companies in Sarir oilfield, 83; lectures regarding Arab unity at conference, 84–5; wooing and flattering of by Arab world and West, 85; supports Palestinians, 88; states King Hussein should be hanged, 88; attempts to purchase nuclear bombs, 89; seeming incongruity in foreign policy, 90; hopes of creating merger with Sudan and Egypt, 91; a disastrous trip to Cairo, 91; ignominious end to unity agreement with Tunisia, 91; persuades thirty African countries to sever relations with Israel, 91; offers help to anti-Western revolutionaries, 92–3; funds Palestinian groups, 93; frees terrorists, 94; plans to blow up QE2, 99; announces resignation, 101; reverses resignation decision 101; as President of Arab Socialist Union, 108; hands in and withdraws resignation, 108; defines political philosophy, 109; a good listener, 109; attempts to impose idealistic political system, 113; basic concept of economic theory, 115; refers to increase in crime in Libya, 131; plans for women soldiers, 132; announces purge of army, 137; suspects coup planned against him, 137; identifies main source of opposition, 138; calls for intensification of revolutionary activity in universities, 139; orders execution of army officers, 140; his attitude to orthodox religion, 141–2; orders destruction of mosques, 143; his association with Children of God cult, 144–6; worries regarding continued dissension in army, 147; runs special camps, 147; high-lights corruption in armed forces, 148; despatches hit squads to kill key dissidents, 155; seeks to eliminate opponents, 155; boasts regarding murderous activities, 159; orders assassination of King Hussein of Jordan, 167, 241; asks Aziz Shenib to arrange destruction of Israel, 168; denies action defined as 'terror', 170; varying figures regarding amounts financing of terrorist organizations, 170–1; attempts to disrupt Egyptian/US relations, 174; plans to assassinate Herman Eilts, 174–5; attempts intervention in Sudan, 175; US report on particular hostility shown towards Israel and US by, 177; his most recent terrorist link, 180; arrest of 5,000 opponents of, 202; annoyance with nations refusing assistance with nuclear technology, 204; involved in arms deals with Soviet Union, 206; wooing of by Russians, 206–7; anti-Zionism of, 206–7; accused by many countries of funding opposition groups in their countries, 207; supports Eritrean rebels, 208; meddles in Chad, 208; supports Chad's northern rebels, 209; plan to oust General Felix Malloum, 211–12; denies presence of troops in Chad, 213; tries 'people to people' approach with Americans, 215–16; expels Italian farmers and small businessmen, 225; makes acquisitions in Italy, 228; his substantial

255